Poor Relief

Poor Relief

Why Giving People Money Is Not the Answer to Global Poverty

HEATH HENDERSON

Harvard University Press

CAMBRIDGE, MASSACHUSETTS • LONDON, ENGLAND • 2025

Copyright © 2025 by the President and Fellows of Harvard College
All rights reserved
Printed in the United States of America

First printing

EU GPSR authorized representative:
Logos Europe
9 rue Nicolas Poussin
17000 La Rochelle, France
contact@logoseurope.eu

LIBRARY OF CONGRESS CATALOGING-IN-PUBLICATION DATA

Names: Henderson, Heath, author.
Title: Poor relief: why giving people money is not the answer to global poverty / Heath Henderson.
Description: Cambridge: Harvard University Press, 2025. | Includes bibliographical references and index.
Identifiers: LCCN 2025002199 (print) | LCCN 2025002200 (ebook) |
ISBN 9780674296138 (cloth) | ISBN 9780674301931 (epub) |
ISBN 9780674301948 (pdf)
Subjects: LCSH: Poverty. | Transfer payments. | Basic income. |
Economic development. | Paternalism—Economic aspects. | Deliberative democracy.
Classification: LCC HC79.P6 H447 2025 (print) | LCC HC79.P6 (ebook) |
DDC 362.5/82—dc23/eng/20250417

LC record available at https://lccn.loc.gov/2025002199
LC ebook record available at https://lccn.loc.gov/2025002200

To Rick

Contents

1 The Rise of Cash Transfers 1

2 Defining Poverty 19

3 What the Evidence Shows 38

4 The Targeting Problem 58

5 Inequality within Households 78

6 When Markets Fail 99

7 The Diversity of Need 118

8 Transformative Change 137

9 Paternalism Revisited 157

10 Deliberative Democracy 177

Conclusion 197

Notes 203

Acknowledgments 229

Index 233

Poor Relief

CHAPTER 1

The Rise of Cash Transfers

CASH TRANSFER PROGRAMS—also known as guaranteed or basic income programs—have become increasingly popular tools for fighting poverty over the past few decades. Growth in the sheer number of such programs around the globe has been accompanied by similar expansions of academic research, public discourse, and media coverage emphasizing the benefits of assisting the needy with direct grants of cash. Leading international organizations like the World Bank and United Nations have increasingly funded cash transfer programs, and charities like GiveDirectly have been established for the sole purpose of soliciting donations and relaying funds to poor households. GiveDirectly alone, across the decade from 2014 to 2024, saw its cash transfers increase from $3 million to $543 million,[1]

Various influential people have expressed support for cash transfers. British politician Rory Stewart (who served a year as president of GiveDirectly) has asserted that cash programs reliably produce "extraordinary positive impact" and that a well-funded US program could "lift millions from extreme poverty."[2] Nancy Birdsall, cofounder of the Washington-based Center for Global Development, provocatively claimed the approach was "as close as you can come to a magic bullet in development."[3] In 2020, entrepreneur Andrew Yang famously centered his bid for the US Democratic Party's presidential nomination on the promise of a "Freedom Dividend"—a $1,000 monthly check sent to every American citizen aged eighteen or older. Many other entrepreneurs—including Bill Gates, Elon Musk, and Mark Zuckerberg—have similarly advocated for a universal basic income. In short, there's a growing consensus that a straightforward distribution of cash is the best solution to the poverty problem.

A closer look nevertheless reveals that cash transfer programs have some unsettling limitations. A useful starting point for understanding these limitations is in the experience of the Indian state of Jharkhand. In February of 2018, over a thousand people there amassed to protest the Direct Benefit Transfer for Food Subsidy (DBT), a trial program that did away with their ability to buy a quantity of rice each month at a dramatically discounted price, and instead gave them a financially equivalent benefit in the form of cash deposited to their bank accounts. The protesters gathered at a junction near the town of Nagri and marched eight kilometers to the governor's residence in the capital city of Ranchi. Upon arrival, they submitted a memorandum to the governor that read: "We demand the immediate withdrawal of the DBT pilot in Nagri in favor of the one rupee per kilogram rice at the ration shop. All households who were unable to purchase rice due to this pilot . . . should be compensated as per the provisions of the National Food Security Act."[4]

The context behind the DBT experiment was that the National Food Security Act of 2013 had mandated that central and state governments provide low-income households across all of India with adequate amounts of quality foodgrains at affordable prices. To accomplish this, the act expanded on an existing food aid system in Nagri, whereby eligible beneficiaries were able to purchase a certain quantity of rice from specific local shops for just one rupee per kilogram. It was in October of 2017 that the Jharkhand government began its experiment of instead transferring money into people's bank accounts. Again, importantly, DBT didn't change the value of the subsidy to anyone simply using the cash to make the same grain purchases. Paid for at the market rate, but with transferred cash, a kilogram of rice still cost them one rupee.[5]

In the eyes of many, this shift to direct cash payments could only leave people better off, as the option to spend on items other than rice gave them greater control over their household budgets. Yet, many residents of Nagri were clearly upset by the change. Part of the problem was the payment system, which created confusion about where and when the funds would be sent. Some people found themselves making multiple trips to the bank each month to see if the money had arrived.[6] In one case, a woman named Jamna Sanga paid 32 rupees each for four rides to the town of Nagri, where she twice paid 20 rupees to a "banking correspondent" middleman to check the balance in her account. In the process, she missed five days of work at a hotel that paid her 150 rupees per day, and her daughter had to take time away from school to collect water in her absence.[7]

The issues with cash programs like DBT go well beyond the payment systems. In April of 2018, Jharkhand's state government conducted an audit in which they surveyed over eight thousand beneficiaries about their experiences with DBT. The audit confirmed that collecting benefits was onerous and showed that many people failed to withdraw their money. Specifically, of the six installments to which recipients were entitled since the program began, the average beneficiary had claimed only 3.6.[8] Making the situation even worse was that, according to economist Jean Drèze, "the elderly, the disabled, the ailing and the most vulnerable" were the least likely to claim their benefits.[9] The people most in need of assistance were thus the most likely to be left behind.

Cash programs like DBT underserve such vulnerable populations in other ways, too. To the extent that people in these groups do manage to claim their benefits, they tend to take less advantage of them. In a detailed survey of people's views on cash transfers across nine Indian states including Jharkhand, a team led by economist Reetika Khera conducted interviews in roughly twelve hundred poor, rural households. Over two-thirds preferred in-kind transfers to cash. One prominent concern was with the constrained mobility of the elderly, the disabled, and many women, which made it difficult to "convert" cash into goods in markets that were often farther away than ration shops. In the words of one respondent, a sixty-year-old tribal widow named Aetwaribhai, "It is very difficult to get rice in the market. I am too old to go and search for rice."[10]

Other studies of cash transfers in India have raised different concerns. Most notably, a government's decision to disburse cash to individuals may mean that investments in certain public goods, such as schools, clinics, and infrastructure, are displaced. In this case, the cash transfers can undercut investments that the poor themselves believe are more critical for poverty alleviation. A 2018 poll conducted in Bihar, India, asked people about their social spending priorities and found strong preferences for investments in public goods over cash transfers. Out of approximately thirty-eight hundred respondents, 86 percent preferred investments in public health over receiving cash transfers, and 65 percent preferred investments in improved roads over cash.[11]

A further shortcoming of cash programs is that they don't address the systemic or structural barriers to poverty alleviation. Sometimes, in fact, they reinforce them. One program in India, because of the conditions it attached to cash transfers, actually increased the number of first pregnancies subjected to sex-selective abortions by somewhere between 1.0 and 2.3 percent. Introduced in 2002, the Devi Rupak program had intended the opposite: to combat persistent gender discrimination in household family planning by creating a financial incentive to have daughters. But because the program's designers also wanted to rein in population growth, they specified that cash would be distributed only to households with just one child—or two, if both were girls. Many families, however, maintained a strong preference to have at least one son, so to get benefits they took measures to make sure that their first (and only) child was a boy. Devi Rupak not only failed to address gender discrimination, but actually made the problem worse.[12]

Problems with cash transfers aren't unique to India and there aren't any easy solutions. Banking apps on handheld devices can be used to make benefits more accessible, but this requires a level of mobile technology penetration—which in India was far from complete when DBT was implemented. A 2015 report found that only about 36 percent of India's 1.3 billion people owned mobile phones, with devices in the hands of just 28 percent of women, versus 43 percent of men.[13] Bypassing banks to transfer the cash would in any case be only a partial solution, as many people would still struggle with limited market access, inadequate public goods, and structural barriers to overcoming their poverty. As we'll see, there are other problems with cash transfers that similarly resist simple fixes.

Nearly 97 percent of Nagri residents opposed DBT and the government eventually responded to the pressure by returning to the old system in August of 2018.[14] Unfortunately, this was by no means a satisfying resolution, in part because the old system had a history of severe corruption. It is an often-cited statistic from an audit of 2004–2005 distributions that 85 percent of food grains were siphoned off by corrupt middlemen. While the system has improved in recent years, important issues remain. Many households report that some members aren't listed on their ration cards, ration dealers routinely give people less than their entitlement, and the biometric authentication system is often out of order.[15] The case of Nagri is hardly a ringing endorsement of in-kind benefits.

The concept is simple and seductive: give people cash, lift them out of poverty. Simplicity can be misleading, however, and when it comes to fighting extreme poverty, cash transfers have important limitations—which show up in all different types of cash programs across all country settings. The goal of this book is not only to document these limitations but ultimately to propose an alternative that is more responsive to the needs of people living in poverty. Rather than a one-size-fits-all approach to poverty alleviation, the fight against economic injustice requires a more radical, democratic form of intervention. Making the case for this alternative begins with this chapter, which takes stock of the different types of cash programs, outlines a brief history of cash transfers, and discusses how the argument will unfold across the remaining chapters.

Cash Transfers, Explained

Cash transfer is a broad term applied to many different types of programs, including universal basic incomes, guaranteed minimum incomes, and negative income taxes, among others. To avoid any confusion about the scope of arguments made here, it's important to put a finer point on the definition and what kinds of programs meet it. While there's no universally accepted list of ingredients, most cash transfer programs share some basic ingredients: they are *noncontributory* programs that provide *direct cash assistance* to individuals or households to *reduce their poverty and vulnerability*. The three parts of this definition are worth discussing in more detail.

First, cash transfers are noncontributory in the sense that people don't make monetary contributions to the program. This contrasts with social insurance programs (such as old-age or disability pensions) where people pay premiums to be eligible for coverage or contribute a portion of their earnings to receive benefits. Second, while some forms of social assistance provide benefits in kind (for example, food rations or vouchers), cash-based programs involve monetary transfers, which are given directly to individuals or households rather than to their employers, local governments, or community organizations. Finally, the primary objective of cash transfers is to reduce poverty and vulnerability, meaning that assistance is generally given according to need rather than merit or some other criterion.

The range of programs that meet our definition of cash transfers is wide. This includes universal basic income schemes like Alaska's Permanent Fund Dividend. It includes job guarantee programs like India's National Rural

	Unconditional	Conditional
Universal	Universal basic income	Job guarantee programs
Targeted	Unconditional cash transfers Age-based allowances Guaranteed minimum income Negative income tax	Conditional cash transfers Temporary public works Earned income tax credit

FIGURE 1.1. Typology of cash transfer programs

Employment Guarantee Scheme. It further includes well-known conditional cash transfer programs like Brazil's Bolsa Família and Mexico's Progresa. We can also consider tax-based programs like the United States' Earned Income Tax Credit as a form of cash transfer. This list is far from exhaustive. To give a greater sense of the scope of the definition and key differences among program types, Figure 1.1 provides a typology of cash-based programs.

One dimension of the typology distinguishes between *universal* and *targeted* cash transfer programs. While a truly universal program makes everybody in a population eligible for its benefits, a targeted program distributes them only to people with particular attributes. Sometimes the universal label is applied a bit more loosely to describe a program that targets a specific age group, but within that cohort makes everybody eligible. Child allowances, for example, and social pensions are often classified as universal when they cover all children or elderly people. According to the definition used here, however, such programs belong in the targeted category because eligibility is actually restricted in an important way: by age.[16]

The second dimension of the typology distinguishes between *conditional* and *unconditional* programs. A conditional program requires beneficiaries to undertake some action to receive their benefits, while unconditional programs require no actions whatsoever. A job guarantee program, for example, is conditional in that it requires people to work if they want to receive benefits. While any cash transfer program that imposes conditions could technically be called a conditional cash transfer, the standard practice is to reserve the phrase for a particular type of program—namely, a targeted program implemented in a developing country that requires beneficiaries to make investments in the human capital of their children (such as having them attend school). Likewise, the phrase *unconditional cash transfer* tends to be reserved for targeted programs in developing countries where transfers are made without conditions.

Conditions can be viewed as existing along a continuum. At one end are *hard* conditions—ones that are formal, routinely monitored, and strictly enforced with penalties for noncompliance. Programs using hard conditions generally remove participants in the event of noncompliance, although often only after a series of warnings. At the other end are conditional programs that are *labeled*, meaning that certain behaviors are prescribed but there is no explicit requirement, monitoring, or enforcement of them—effectively making these conditions no more than suggestions. Between these two extremes are *soft* conditions, with the terms of compliance formally communicated but only gently enforced, and only light (if any) penalties for noncompliance.[17]

Figure 1.1 places several different types of cash transfers where they belong in the typology. In the upper-left quadrant, for programs that are universal and unconditional, a single type appears: the *universal basic income*. Stated simply, a universal basic income program provides cash payments to everybody in the relevant population (perhaps a country), without conditions or qualifications. Note that universal basic incomes, at least in their purest form, are viewed as individual entitlements, with payments made to individuals rather than just "heads of households." Further note that the term *basic* does not imply an amount of cash sufficient to cover a person's basic needs, but only a common floor of income on which all will stand.[18]

In the upper-right quadrant of Figure 1.1 are *job guarantee programs*, the only universal and conditional programs currently in existence. Job guarantee programs are essentially a promise that anybody who wants but is unable to find employment on their own will be provided with work and be fairly compensated for it with cash payments. While the type of work offered can vary, job guarantee programs commonly provide employment in the construction and maintenance of public infrastructure (such as building roads, irrigation systems, and sanitation facilities). India's National Rural Employment Guarantee Scheme is often held up as the world's sole job guarantee program, although in reality even it only approximates that. Eligibility is limited to rural residents, employment days are capped at a certain amount, and there is significant rationing of jobs in the program.[19]

In the lower-left quadrant of the typology are programs that are targeted and unconditional, including unconditional cash transfers, age-based allowances, guaranteed minimum income schemes, and negative income taxes. Regarding the first of these, the discussion here follows the common usage described above, using the term *unconditional cash transfer* to mean a cash-based program that is in some way targeted and implemented in a developing country. *Age-based allowances* are simply unconditional cash transfers that target a specific age group, such as children or the elderly. Child grants and social pensions are both classified as age-based allowances.

A *guaranteed minimum income* scheme targets all of those with incomes below some threshold, and provides payments just large enough to bring each up to that level. A key feature of this program type is that, in effect, it entails a 100 percent marginal tax rate on beneficiaries: any income they earn up to that threshold translates to an equal cut in the benefit they receive. A *negative income tax,* by contrast, aims to avoid the work disincentives created by such high marginal tax rates. This type of scheme also makes direct cash transfers to people based on how far they fall short of a specified income threshold, but any recipients growing their own earnings see their benefits shrink less dramatically than they would under a guaranteed minimum income program. For example, Milton Friedman's famous proposal was to guarantee $3,600 per year (in 1978 dollars) to households with no earnings, with each dollar of income reducing that benefit by fifty cents (equating to a marginal tax rate of 50 percent).[20]

In the lower-right quadrant, which is made up of programs that are targeted and conditional, there are conditional cash transfer programs, temporary public works, and earned income tax credits. *Conditional cash transfer,* again, is a label generally applied to targeted programs implemented in developing countries that impose conditions on human capital investments. *Temporary public works* are, like job guarantee programs, conditioned on work, but the work is performed in the context of time-bound projects with limited budgets. Finally, the *earned income tax credit* is similar to a negative income tax, but its benefits are specifically tied to labor income and vary from taxpayer to taxpayer according to earnings and other factors such as filing status and numbers of dependents. (People without labor income receive no support.)[21]

Before moving forward, it's important to note that the above typology differentiates among cash transfer programs along just two key dimensions—their degrees of universality and conditionality—but programs also differ in other ways. There are important variations in payment amounts, the frequency of payments, and whether payments are made to individuals or households. Programs can also be funded in a variety of ways, including through personal income taxes, natural resource revenues, or private donors. When personal income tax revenues are used, this can significantly change the effective distribution of benefits. Under certain circumstances, for example, a universal basic income financed through income taxes amounts to the same thing as a negative income tax.[22]

It must also be noted that cash transfers are not always implemented in isolation. "Cash-plus" programs, for example, have become increasingly popular in recent years. These aim to improve the effects of cash by complementing regular cash transfers with in-kind benefits such as nutritious foods, counseling to improve mental health, or greater access to insurance, microcredit loans, and other financial services.[23] While cash-plus programs are usually targeted, they can be conditional or unconditional depending on whether the receipt of cash is conditioned on participation in other components of the program. Therefore, where a cash-plus program is located in our typology depends on the details of the program.

A Quiet Revolution

Cash transfer programs have only recently become widespread, but as a tool for fighting poverty they are not new. One of the first well-documented programs with a cash component was a system of poor relief for England and Wales that formally began with the 1601 Act for the Relief of the Poor. The system, now known as the Old Poor Laws, designated the parish as the administrative unit of poor relief and gave parishes the power to levy taxes on local property owners through "poor rates." Poor people were placed into three broad groups: those who would work but could not find adequate employment; those who could work but chose not to work; and those unable to work because of age, disability, or illness. The first and third groups were deemed the "deserving" poor, whose poverty was not considered any fault of their own.[24]

The Old Poor Laws let parishes determine the mix of policies appropriate for local conditions, but assistance generally entailed *indoor* or *outdoor* relief. Those receiving indoor relief were people living in parish poorhouses. Outdoor relief consisted of food subsidies, direct cash transfers, wage subsidies, and public employment.[25] The Speenhamland System of 1795 was a particularly influential form of outdoor relief that was eventually used throughout southern England. This system guaranteed a minimum income to laborers by providing payments equal to the difference between a household's wages and its basic needs—with those needs calculated as the price of a "gallon-loaf" of bread times the number of loaves necessary to sustain the household. The costs of the system were covered by the revenues collected through poor-rate taxation of local landowners.[26]

In the late eighteenth and early nineteenth centuries, spending on poor relief grew substantially and the Old Poor Laws were increasingly criticized. The 1834 Poor Law Amendment Act, known as the New Poor Law, overhauled the system with the goal of reducing costs. The greatest impact of this new legislation came when the Poor Law Commission it established to administer poor relief decided that, barring exceptional circumstances, no outdoor relief would be provided to any man or woman deemed able-bodied. The role of the New Poor Law continued to decline in the late nineteenth and early twentieth centuries due to both the increased stigma associated with poor relief and the rise of another form of assistance, social insurance. Following the influential Beveridge Report of 1942, the National Assistance Act of 1948 officially repealed the increasingly irrelevant Poor Laws.[27]

The rise of social insurance in the United Kingdom was part of a broader shift toward contributory schemes for insuring workers against economic risks. Led by Otto von Bismarck, Germany developed a pioneering model in the 1880s, which included national compulsory social insurance for sickness, accidents, old age, and disability. The introduction of the German model was followed by similar legislation in other European countries, including Austria, Sweden, Norway, and France.[28] While social insurance quickly became the primary tool for poverty alleviation in many European countries, noncontributory schemes like cash transfers weren't entirely absent. In particular, Denmark, the United Kingdom, the Netherlands, and other countries introduced social pensions during this time.[29]

In the years following the creation of the International Labour Organization in 1919, the social insurance movement became a truly global phenomenon. By the middle of the twentieth century, many countries in the Americas, Asia, and Africa had implemented some form of social insurance. Much as in Europe, the global rise of social insurance was accompanied by the emergence of several noncontributory programs, most notably the age-based allowances introduced in Canada, South Africa, and the United States. Social insurance continued to expand in the postwar years in a trend largely unchecked until the 1980s, when concerns emerged over mounting financial difficulties.[30]

The 1960s brought waves of support for negative income taxes in Canada and the United States. Prominent welfare rights activists (such as Martin Luther King Jr.), futurists (Robert Theobald, Buckminster Fuller), and economists (Milton Friedman, John Kenneth Galbraith, James Tobin) supported the idea, which was viewed as a way to simplify the welfare system while also making it more comprehensive. In 1972, both candidates in the US presidential election supported some form of guaranteed income, with Richard Nixon calling for a negative income tax and George McGovern advocating a universal payment he called a "demogrant." While Nixon won the election, his negative income tax concept failed to gain widespread support, partly because conservatives were concerned about work disincentives.[31]

Several less sweeping cash-based programs were implemented, however, in the 1960s and 1970s. Canada and the United States experimented with negative income taxes on a smaller scale in a handful of cities in Manitoba, New Jersey, North Carolina, and Pennsylvania. Under President Gerald Ford in 1975, the United States implemented the Earned Income Tax Credit, which provided tax credits to low-income households, with benefits conditional on work. And in 1976, using invested revenue from the lease of the Prudhoe Bay oil field, Governor Jay Hammond established the Alaska Permanent Fund to distribute annual cash dividends to residents of that state. Given that the fund pays the same amount to every current resident who has lived in Alaska at least a year, this represents a true universal basic income.[32]

The 1990s brought a rapid rise of cash transfer programs in the developing world. This "quiet revolution" emerged partly in response to several economic crises at the end of the twentieth century, which had led to widespread privatization, liberalization, and austerity.[33] Most notably in Latin America and the Caribbean, rising unemployment and deep reforms to social policies produced sharp reductions in social insurance coverage. For example, while Argentina had nearly achieved full coverage of the labor force in the 1970s, this number fell to less than 40 percent by 2006.[34] The European model of social protection thus proved inadequate for many developing countries.

Mexico's Progresa—later renamed Oportunidades and then Prospera—pioneered the use of conditional cash transfers as a tool for fighting poverty in developing countries. Launched in 1997 under President Ernesto Zedillo, Progresa initially provided cash grants to roughly three hundred thousand households across twelve states. The households were targeted through means testing and the average monthly payment was $35, amounting to about 25 percent of the average income of a poor rural household. The program imposed "hard" conditions on beneficiaries, requiring them to have regular health checkups, attend health and nutrition seminars, and keep up their children's school attendance. Following its initial success, the program was rapidly scaled up to cover approximately five million households by the year 2005.[35]

Brazil's Bolsa Família was another highly influential conditional cash transfer program. In 2003, President Luiz Inácio Lula da Silva merged four existing cash transfer programs to create it. Bolsa Família initially provided poor households with an average monthly benefit of roughly $35, with families selected based on geographic location and household income per capita. The recipients were subject to conditions quite similar to Progresa's—including regular health checkups and school attendance, among others—although the conditions for Bolsa Família were less stringent, "soft" conditions. Also like Progresa, Bolsa Família grew rapidly after its inception, as it covered about 3.8 million families in 2003 and then expanded to reach 11.1 million families by 2006.[36]

Progresa and Bolsa Família are only two of several notable programs that emerged around the turn of the millennium. Building on decades of experience with social pensions, South Africa introduced an unconditional child support grant in 1998, eventually reaching 55 percent of all children by 2009. India launched its National Rural Employment Guarantee Scheme in 2006 and the program rapidly expanded to cover all rural districts by 2009. China introduced an unconditional cash transfer program called the Minimum Livelihood Guarantee Scheme (Di Bao) in Shanghai in 1993 and then extended the program nationally in 1999. And Indonesia implemented two programs during this period: an unconditional program called Bantuan Langsung Tunai, and a conditional program called Program Keluarga Harpan.[37]

By the early 2010s, cash transfer programs had been implemented throughout the developing world. By 2013, an estimated 113 out of 148 developing countries (about 76 percent) had some form of cash program, and because many countries had more than one, the total number of programs had reached 282. Nearly all countries in Latin America (32 out of 33) and Asia (44 out of 48) had cash-based programs. More modest, but still substantial, was the coverage in Africa (31 out of 54 countries) and Oceania (6 out of 13). While virtually all of these programs featured some form of targeting, conditionality was less pervasive. About 29 percent of them imposed behavioral requirements, with Latin America showing the highest concentration of conditional programs.[38]

The growth in targeted cash programs was eventually complemented by increased interest in universal programs. Mongolia established its Human Development Fund in 2009 with the goal of using the country's growing mining revenues to provide a universal basic income to all citizens. The program started distributing money in 2010, but plummeting copper prices quickly compromised the program's sustainability and it was discontinued in 2012. Around the same time, Iran implemented a universal scheme, having just made sweeping reforms to energy and food subsidies. Starting in December of 2010, households began receiving roughly $45 per person each month—equivalent to about 29 percent of median income per capita. While the program has endured longer than the Mongolian scheme, inflation has substantially eroded the real value of the program's benefits over time.[39]

Beyond the implementation of full universal basic income schemes, several countries have begun piloting basic income programs in recent years. Well-known pilots in developing countries include Namibia's program in the Otjivero-Omitara region, India's program in Madhya Pradesh, and

GiveDirectly's long-term project in rural Kenya. Many developed countries have also conducted pilots, including Germany's Mein Grundeinkommen experiments, a program conducted by Finland's Social Insurance Institution, and a pilot in the Canadian province of Ontario. A group in the United States, Mayors for a Guaranteed Income, has also been instrumental in launching several pilots, most famously in Stockton, California.[40]

Overview of the Book

We've seen that cash transfer programs have experienced broad growth, in terms of both the variety of program types and their geographic coverage. As the goal of this book is to provide a comprehensive critique of cash transfers, its scope is similarly broad. The arguments made here apply to both targeted and universal programs, and to both conditional and unconditional programs. They also apply to countries of all levels of development, although the experience of less developed countries is emphasized, reflecting a primary concern with alleviating poverty in its most extreme forms.

Yet even as the scope of this book is broad in many ways, there are two important areas in which its arguments are limited. First, the focus here is on the use of cash to alleviate poverty that is chronic as opposed to transient or temporary. In humanitarian or emergency situations, such as natural disasters, conflicts, and pandemics, cash transfers are frequently used to assist people abruptly affected by unemployment or dislocation. For example, during the Covid-19 pandemic, many countries used cash transfers to help infected people get treatment, to compensate workers for lost income, and to respond to the broader economic effects of partial or total lockdowns.[41] While cash alone isn't a sufficient response in these situations, it can be an effective way to rapidly distribute help to people facing temporary poverty.

Second, the aim here is to present critiques that are either entirely new or frequently overlooked. The typical criticisms of cash programs—that they're too expensive, that they disincentivize work, or that the money is wasted by recipients—are well-known. Even when they are not disingenuous attempts to avoid helping poor people, these arguments are generally unsupported by published evidence. A variety of studies have shown, for example, that people use cash transfers for productive purposes, including starting new businesses, making investments in their health, and educating their children, among others.[42] While this book will describe some situations where the usual criticisms have relevance, revisiting and rebutting them is not the focus here.

To briefly preview the content to come, the next two chapters are devoted to dispelling some common misconceptions about cash programs. One misconception is that poverty is defined by a simple lack of income and therefore giving poor households cash is sufficient to alleviate poverty. This purely monetary view of poverty has been criticized for overlooking important dimensions of deprivation and ignoring the reality that people have different abilities to "convert" income into well-being. Chapter 2 argues for a broader definition that instead views poverty in terms of "capabilities," which relate to what people can do or be with the resources they have. By definition, this alternative approach shifts the focus to the aspects of well-being that people ultimately value, such as being healthy, well-nourished, and well-educated, to name just a few.

Another misconception is that the evidence clearly shows that cash transfers are an effective way to alleviate poverty. Chapter 3 argues that the evidence should be viewed with caution. While cash transfers have been shown to generate impacts in some areas (such as consumption and investment), the evidence is weaker in others (such as important health and education outcomes). Several recent studies also show that the impacts of cash programs tend to erode over time, meaning that the long-term effects are limited. A further concern is that the evidence focuses almost exclusively on the average effect of cash, and this may not be what is most relevant to policymakers with moral or political values that emphasize reducing inequality, helping the most vulnerable, or expanding people's capabilities.

Chapter 4 gets to the core of the book's critique and considers two important issues related to targeted programs. The first is the remarkable difficulty of identifying people living in poverty, which has caused many programs to exclude large numbers of poor people—and to include many of the non-poor. The second issue is that targeted programs can have significant harmful effects because they routinely divide communities into recipients and non-recipients. These divisions can produce conflict, erode trust in government, and adversely affect the economic well-being of non-recipients (for example, through price increases). There are no easy solutions to these problems. Changing a program to be universal, for example, is often too costly or would lead to limited funds being spread too thinly to have substantial impact.

Chapter 5 turns to the question of how resources are allocated within households, given how important this is in determining how individuals benefit from cash programs. As will become clear, household decision-making can undermine the objectives of cash programs, particularly with respect to the well-being of women and children. Cash transfers can cause harm to women by burdening their time, compromising their bargaining power, or even subjecting them to increased domestic violence. Moreover, children don't always benefit from living in households receiving cash because certain cultural forces, market failures, and characteristics of household decision-makers can distort how households allocate resources.

Even if cash programs could reliably reach the intended beneficiaries, it would still be true that money can't buy everything that matters to well-being. In particular, having cash to spend doesn't get an individual any closer to many of the things that are most critical to well-being, including a stable climate, clean air and water, and even quality education and healthcare. Chapter 6 exposes the limits of markets and provides several examples to illustrate the prevalence of missing or inefficient markets, especially in lesser-developed countries. It also addresses the argument that cash recipients can overcome market failures by pooling their resources, but ultimately contends that both theory and evidence suggest that this is unlikely.

Chapter 7 engages more deeply with our definition of poverty and argues that the most vulnerable groups of people face especially severe challenges converting income into well-being. A close look at three especially vulnerable groups—people with disabilities, children, and the elderly—will illustrate the challenges they face. As will be shown, "conversion failures" often mean that members of these groups are not only left behind by cash transfer programs but sometimes outright harmed. Research shows, for example, that cash programs can increase mortality rates among older people, in part because cash benefits induce lifestyle changes that increase the risk factors associated with some deadly chronic diseases.

A final concern with cash programs is that they don't combat the systemic or structural issues that play a critical role in causing and perpetuating poverty. Chapter 8 explores the two primary theories of the causes of poverty, with the *individualist* view locating the causes of poverty in the attributes of individuals and the *structuralist* view locating the causes in broader economic, political, or cultural structures. The argument here is that interventions addressing structural issues can have transformative effects on poverty, whereas individualist interventions tend to be more palliative by comparison. Given that cash transfers provide assistance at the individual or household level, they are deeply individualistic and thus unlikely to have transformative effects on people living in poverty.

It's commonly argued that "cash works because it does not require outsiders to guess what a community needs; they decide for themselves."[43] While empowering people to make their own decisions is important, it's not true that giving people cash leaves them with complete decision-making power. The unifying theme of the critiques presented here is that cash programs impose many decisions on people living in poverty and that these decisions are both wide-ranging and consequential. In particular, cash programs target some households while leaving others behind; they direct resources to some household *members* rather than others; they prioritize market goods over nonmarket goods; they neglect the unique needs of some of the most vulnerable people; and they privilege an individualist rather than a structuralist approach to poverty.

Chapter 9 argues for "radical decentralization" as a promising alternative to cash transfers, because it democratically delegates these decisions to people living in poverty. The chapter begins by arguing that cash transfers can and should be viewed as paternalistic due to the variety of decisions they impose on people. The chapter argues that this paternalism is morally wrong because it fails to respect people's status as equal and autonomous decision-makers. Radical decentralization avoids such paternalism, and additionally carries important benefits in terms of poverty alleviation. The limitations of radical decentralization are also shown here to be surmountable, at least with the use of democratic procedures that are designed to facilitate quality decision-making.

Finally, Chapter 10 considers several different ways to implement decentralized, democratic decision-making for poverty alleviation. Focusing on three basic democratic values—deliberation, equality, and participation—it notes that attempts to realize any two of these values will undermine the third. The most promising way to navigate this democratic trilemma is with *microcosmic deliberation,* a procedure that engages a representative sample of people to deliberate about the appropriate programs or policies for fighting poverty in their communities. While there are many different variants of microcosmic deliberation, one variant—known as deliberative polling—turns out to be especially well-suited to developing poverty-alleviation strategies.

In summary, this book provides a survey of the limitations of cash transfers and then proposes an alternative approach that genuinely empowers people to make decisions for themselves. The argument isn't that cash programs are necessarily bad, but rather that they have clear limitations and are not always the best way to fight poverty. Though cash transfers delegate some important decisions to people living in poverty, they should still be viewed as a top-down or technocratic approach to poverty alleviation because many of the most critical decisions are imposed from above. Cash transfers are just another example of paternalism in international development, and this critique can thus be viewed as part of a broader criticism of technocratic poverty-alleviation strategies.

The conventional wisdom in the global development community is that cash transfers are among the most flexible and powerful tools we have to combat extreme poverty. Challenging this conventional wisdom requires not only revisiting the vast literature on cash transfers, but also questioning some of our most basic assumptions about the nature and causes of poverty. The goal in the subsequent chapters isn't to assert an alternative perspective on these issues, but rather to *explain* why and how such an alternative perspective is critical for fighting extreme poverty. These explanations will often require engaging with somewhat complicated topics, but my hope is that the patient reader will find them both accessible and thought-provoking.

Finally, it's worth mentioning that the terms *developing* and *less developed* will occasionally be used in these pages to refer to countries that are less affluent or characterized by high levels of poverty. There is active debate about these terms, in part because they suggest a false dichotomy between developed and developing nations.[44] Various alternatives have been proposed, but unfortunately these also have limitations. The popular term *global south,* for example, is technically inaccurate because some southern countries, such as Australia and New Zealand, are quite affluent. With no clear alternative, the text will occasionally make reference to developing or less-developed nations, but with no intent to suggest any rigid hierarchy or definitive ranking of countries.

CHAPTER 2

Defining Poverty

AN INCREASINGLY COMMON argument for cash transfers is that "poverty is a policy choice." The idea is that reducing poverty is a basic math problem: pick a poverty line, find out how far people's incomes fall below that line, and then give them the money they need to reach the line. A government or other policymaking organization "can literally make the poverty rate whatever it likes. It could continue reducing poverty year after year. . . . It just needs to make that choice."[1] This argument rests on a critical assumption, which is that poverty is properly defined as a lack of *income*. Interestingly, a bold experiment conducted by a group of college students shows that this definition of poverty is actually quite problematic.

Four American college students traveled to the rural Guatemalan village of Peña Blanca in the summer of 2010 with the simple objective of living on a dollar a day for roughly two months. The experiment was devised by two economics students at Claremont McKenna College, Chris Temple and Zach Ingrasci, who wanted to supplement their studies in international development with firsthand experience living in extreme poverty. Chris and Zach set their income level to mimic the standard of living in rural Guatemala, where roughly 70 percent of the population lived below the dollar-a-day international poverty line. With the help of filmmakers Sean Leonard and Ryan Christoffersen, the experiment was documented in the film *Living on One Dollar*.

To replicate the standard of living in Peña Blanca as closely as they could, the group incorporated two important features into their experiment. First, because many residents of Peña Blanca worked as farmers or informal day laborers at the time of the experiment, their incomes varied from day to day. Instead of giving themselves exactly one dollar a day, the students thus made their incomes unpredictable by drawing a random amount out of a hat each day. Second, to experience starting a business and obtaining credit, the group took out a microloan of $125, and used it to pay for a small house and a plot of land to farm. In line with standard repayment schedules for microloans, every two weeks they had to make set payments on the loan.

Throughout the documentary, we see the four students experiencing severe hardships. In one scene, they calculate that their daily food intake amounts to roughly 900 calories per person, which is under half the calories required to maintain their ideal weights. As a result of this deprivation, they experience weight loss, lethargy, dizziness, and other problems. Zach collapses at one point because of the inadequacy of his diet. The quality of the water in Peña Blanca also becomes a major concern, especially when Chris simultaneously contracts two waterborne illnesses and requires medical attention. Under the strict rules of the experiment the prescribed medication is unaffordable (though, for the sake of continuing it, Chris takes pills brought from home in case of just such an emergency).

Despite not speaking the local language of Kaqchikel, the students eventually develop some meaningful relationships with their neighbors, giving us a glimpse into the lives of other residents of Peña Blanca. They become especially close with a twelve-year-old boy named Chino, who lives with his mother, father, and five siblings in a one-room house. Living below the poverty line presents serious challenges for Chino's family. Chino's father expresses concern that his kids' growth is stunted because they often eat only tortillas and salt. We learn that Chino doesn't go to school and instead works as a day laborer because his family can't afford the cost of books and supplies. We also learn that Chino's mother has a life-threatening illness and that the family must rely on neighbors to pay her medical bills.

The documentary makes it quite clear that living on a dollar a day is extremely difficult, but it also inadvertently raises deeper questions about the nature of poverty. Do we truly believe that these four American college students, during the months they are subsisting on incomes similar to Chino's family and other neighboring households, are experiencing the same level of deprivation? If poverty is properly defined by meagerness of income, the answer to this question must be *yes*. Yet for most if not all people, the answer is an unambiguous *no*. It's easy to think of many ways in which the college students are better off than their neighbors. In fact, the experiment conflicts with our intuitions about what it means to be poor in at least three ways.

First, we know that, despite their having a comparable level of income, the college students are experiencing temporary poverty, whereas families like Chino's are experiencing chronic poverty. After their experiment is over, the college students can exit poverty, but Chino's family doesn't have a similar opportunity. The college students even have the option to quit their experiment at any time rather than waiting the full two months to return to a more comfortable standard of living. Chris reminds us of this when he breaks with the experiment to use medications from an emergency stash. Generally speaking, being deprived by choice is very different from being deprived by circumstance.

Second, the college students can achieve greater well-being with a given level of income. While they have some disadvantages at the start of the experiment, their neighbors soon bring them up to speed by teaching them the basics of cooking, farming, and bargaining in local markets. Their advantages prove to be more durable. Their educational backgrounds not only directly contribute to their well-being but also help them keep detailed budgets that give them a decision-making advantage over their less literate and less numerate neighbors. Despite some setbacks, the students are also in relatively good mental and physical health, which again contributes to their well-being both directly and indirectly. An obvious indirect effect is that, unlike Chino's family, they aren't burdened with medical bills and can spend more money on other things that contribute to their well-being (such as food).

Third, we shouldn't ignore the fact that the students are United States citizens, which means they have greater political and civil liberties than Guatemalan citizens. In the same year as the experiment, Freedom House scored countries on a scale from one to seven with lower values associated with greater political and civil liberties.[2] While Guatemala received a score of four and was classified as "partly free," the United States received a score of one and was classified as "free." United States citizens enjoy greater liberties in terms of free and fair elections, freedom of expression and association, equal treatment under the law, and more. The college students are thus afforded many things that money simply can't buy.

Limited income is closely associated with many forms of deprivation, but an exclusive focus on income overlooks other critical dimensions of poverty. This is a point that economist and philosopher Amartya Sen has made. "In studying poverty, there is an excellent argument for *beginning* with whatever information we have on the distribution of incomes, particularly low real incomes," he wrote. "There is, however, an equally good case for not *ending* with income analysis."[3] This chapter will outline the case for going beyond income by revealing critical issues with the dollar-a-day approach to poverty. It will then consider a broader view of poverty proposed by Sen and see that his approach addresses many of the limitations of the monetary view. While taking seriously various criticisms of Sen's approach, the chapter will conclude that a broad view of poverty is crucial for understanding the limitations of cash transfers.

Poverty as a Lack of Income

In the broadest terms, poverty can be defined as a "pronounced deprivation in well-being."[4] While well-being can be specified in different ways, the most common interpretation focuses on poverty as a lack of income or consumption. The World Bank's main measure of poverty, for example, classifies as poor anybody with an income or consumption level below a specific monetary threshold. The bank set the international poverty line at $1 per day when it first assessed global poverty in 1990, and the line is periodically updated due to changing prices. At this writing, it is set at $2.15 per day. Using that amount, the bank estimates the number of people living in poverty at about 700 million people, or 9 percent of the global population.[5]

The World Bank's approach to measuring poverty builds on a long tradition in the social sciences that has viewed poverty in monetary terms. One of the earliest researchers to attempt a systematic survey of poverty was Charles Booth, who produced color-coded maps showing the living conditions of hundreds of neighborhoods in London between 1886 and 1903. As part of the notes describing the seven classes he was mapping, he described a "poor" street as one in which the "moderate family" lived on an income of 18 to 21 shillings per week. Inspired by Booth, Seebohm Rowntree conducted a similar analysis of York in 1899. Rowntree set his poverty line at 18 shillings and 10 pence for a family of four, having calculated the least income a family would require to maintain "mere physical efficiency"—that is, to procure sufficient food, clothing, fuel, and other basic necessities.[6]

Rowntree's method proved particularly influential and variants of it emerged across the globe in subsequent years. For example, after Lyndon Johnson declared a "War on Poverty" in the United States in the 1960s, his Office of Economic Opportunity adopted a monetary measure of poverty developed by economist Mollie Orshansky. Much as Rowntree had, Orshansky defined her poverty line as the minimum level of income required to meet a family's basic needs. Orshansky's line was calculated in a somewhat rudimentary way and set at three times the cost of a minimally adequate diet for a family of a given size and composition. The factor of three was derived from a 1955 survey showing that food expenditure accounted for approximately one-third of a typical family's budget. For a family of four, the resulting poverty line was $3,130 in 1963 dollars.[7]

By the 1980s, there were at least thirty-four countries with well-defined monetary poverty lines, which laid the foundation for the World Bank's measurement of poverty.[8] While the organization had historically prioritized economic growth over direct poverty alleviation, those priorities began to change when Robert McNamara became president in 1968. McNamara also oversaw an expansion of the World Bank's role as a "knowledge bank," with an increased emphasis on research, data collection, and data analysis. These changes eventually culminated in the 1990 World Development Report, which was the first official World Bank publication to lay out a comprehensive definition and measurement of global poverty.[9] The report set the international poverty line at a dollar a day, asserting that this line was typical of the low-income countries that already had poverty lines in place.

Response to the World Bank's poverty measure has been mixed. On the one hand, the measure has been extremely influential and viewed by some as "the most important poverty indicator in the world."[10] It's featured, for example, in Target 1.1 of the Sustainable Development Goals, the seventeen goals created by the United Nations to serve as a guiding framework for global development policy. On the other hand, the bank's measure has been heavily criticized. Poverty scholars Sanjay Reddy and Thomas Pogge, for instance, have argued that "the World Bank's approach to estimating the extent, distribution, and trend of global income poverty is neither meaningful nor reliable."[11] In what follows, we'll look at some of the measurement and conceptual problems with the World Bank's approach and see that they reveal significant flaws with the monetary view of poverty.

Regarding measurement issues, several critiques relate to how the World Bank sets and applies its international poverty line. Rowntree's and Orshansky's methods illustrate the standard approach to setting national poverty lines, basing it on the minimum amount of income necessary to meet the needs of the average household or person. By anchoring poverty lines to people's basic needs, the standard approach can claim it is directly interpreting human well-being. While the World Bank's poverty line intends to reflect "typical" national poverty lines, there's actually a fair amount of variation in the national lines, partly due to differences in how countries define basic needs. Because the bank's line doesn't correspond to any particular definition of basic needs, the resulting poverty measures have no direct interpretation in terms of basic needs. Not surprisingly, they frequently disagree with well-defined measurements by the nations in question.[12]

Another measurement issue is associated with how the dollar-denominated poverty line addresses price differences across countries. The World Bank uses purchasing power parity (PPP) conversion rates to translate income or consumption denominated in local currencies into US dollars. The idea behind PPP conversion is to translate an income or consumption amount expressed in one currency to the amount in another currency that would give consumers the same power to make equivalent purchases. Many people have argued that the existing PPP rates are unreliable for poverty measurement, in part because the prices faced by the poor often differ systematically from the national averages used to calculate the conversion factors. Reddy and Pogge, for example, have shown that using PPP rates that better reflect the consumption of the poor produces substantially different (and higher) estimates of global poverty.[13]

A related problem with the World Bank's determination of the global poverty line is that it doesn't adequately account for cost-of-living differences *within* countries. Generally speaking, the bank calculates the poverty of a given country by comparing its people's incomes or consumption expenses to the global poverty line. If price differences within countries aren't accounted for, however, this results in overestimated poverty in low-cost areas and underestimated poverty in high-cost areas. For some countries, the bank recognizes this problem; for example, separate rural and urban poverty estimates are produced for China, India, and Indonesia.[14] Such adjustments are, however, imperfect and the estimates for many countries are not refined in this way at all. Several studies show that adjusted and unadjusted poverty measures can be dramatically different.[15]

Other measurement problems emerge when we consider how the World Bank estimates people's living standards. For one, its estimates for some countries rely on income to measure people's living standards whereas estimates for other countries rely on consumption. Income and consumption are related but distinct: incomes are generally more variable than consumption because households "smooth" consumption through saving and dissaving. According to the bank, "given that incomes can be very low or negative, poverty rates are typically higher when income is used rather than consumption."[16] Consumption is nevertheless typically viewed as a more reliable gauge of people's living standards, which means that the bank tends to overestimate poverty in countries using the income standard.[17]

Another problem is that both income- and consumption-based measures are prone to error. Consider consumption. A complicating fact is that many households in developing countries consume goods they produce themselves, such as food grown or raised on a farm. Accurate measurements would factor this in, but attaching a value to this consumption is extremely difficult if the goods are not also sold locally or if they differ in quality from what is sold. People's consumption of housing and public services would require similar imputations, but these are routinely ignored because valuing such consumption is challenging.[18] No less important is that consumption estimates are affected by aspects of household survey design, such as the period of time over which respondents are asked to recall their consumption. A recent review of the literature on socioeconomic measurement issues concluded that the effects of survey design are "nothing short of staggering."[19]

Still another problem with how the World Bank estimates living standards is that income and consumption are observed at the *household* level whereas poverty is a condition of *individuals*. To estimate the income or consumption of an individual, the bank takes the total income or consumption of that person's household and divides it by the number of people in the household. In other words, a household's income or consumption is assumed to be distributed equally across all its members. It is well established, however, that women and children typically receive less than equal shares of household resources, so that averaging in this way understates poverty among them. Using data from Bangladesh, Caitlin Brown and her coauthors found that taking a more fine-grained approach and recognizing inequality within households yielded poverty rates that were greater by 17 to 27 percent.[20]

Even if the bank's measurements were perfectly accurate, several conceptual problems with the monetary approach would remain. Recall the observation made above, reflecting on the *Living on One Dollar* documentary, that deprivation by choice is quite different from deprivation by circumstance. This is a distinction that the monetary approach fails to make. Instead, it views any two people with the same income or consumption as equally well off, even if their opportunities are very different. There are many reasons why people might forego opportunities for better living standards: they may prefer leisure over work, taking care of their children over sending them to daycare, or having fulfilling occupations over well-paid jobs. The point here isn't to deny that people are often poor because of circumstances beyond their control, but rather to highlight a significant conceptual limitation of the monetary view.

Another conceptual problem relates to the fact that humans are diverse and have different needs. People with disabilities, for example, regularly incur extra costs due to their greater needs for healthcare, transportation, and assistive products, among other things. As a result, they typically require higher incomes to approximate the well-being of people without disabilities. In a study drawing on UK data, Asghar Zaidi and Tania Burchardt looked at the incomes and living standards of people with varying levels of disability using a well-established, twenty-two-point scale of disability severity. According to their analysis, every additional point of severity is associated with a 1.1 to 7.7 percent increase in income required to maintain a given standard of living.[21] Put another way, the research shows that people with the same income can have very different abilities to satisfy their basic needs—and this limits the usefulness of income (or consumption) as a gauge of human well-being.[22]

Finally, money can't buy everything that matters to well-being. Income or consumption is helpful only for those dimensions of well-being that can be advanced through markets. But markets routinely fail to deliver many goods that are vital to well-being, including clean air, clean water, or even quality education. For example, roughly two billion people don't have access to safely managed drinking water, with nearly five hundred million people relying on unprotected or open-access sources (such as springs, rivers, and lakes) that are frequently contaminated.[23] There have been attempts to incorporate people's use of such nonmarket goods into consumption estimates, but it's remarkably challenging to measure the quantity and quality of people's consumption.[24] Further, assigning a value to some "goods" (like political and civil liberties) is almost certainly infeasible.

No measure of poverty is perfect, so it's unsurprising that the World Bank's measure has limitations—and in fact, the bank has responded to some of these limitations with refinements and creations of new measures. The broader point, however, is that the problems with the bank's measure largely stem from a basic flaw with the monetary view of poverty. Specifically, income and well-being are distinct concepts, and complications arise when well-being is viewed "within the space" of income. This problem is obvious with regard to conceptual issues, but it also applies to measurement issues. For example, recognizing that the World Bank's poverty line isn't based on a clear conception of well-being means accepting that income and well-being are distinct. The monetary approach thus views poverty only indirectly, through the filter of income, when what is needed is a more direct view.

Poverty as a Lack of Capabilities

At Stanford University in 1979, Amartya Sen initiated a fundamental rethinking of poverty, development, and justice when he delivered his lecture "Equality of What?"[25] In it, he outlined a critique of the prevailing approaches to conceptualizing inequality and proposed an alternative view we now know as the *capability approach*. Along with other scholars across the social sciences and humanities—most notably, philosopher Martha

Nussbaum—Sen refined his ideas in subsequent writings and developed the capability approach into the leading alternative to the monetary view of poverty. This line of work has been vastly influential—especially as it inspired the United Nations' well-known Human Development Reports—and contributed to Sen's winning the Nobel Memorial Prize in Economic Sciences in 1998.

The capability approach is human-oriented: it claims that to understand people's well-being we must focus not on the resources (such as income) they have but rather on the kinds of lives they are leading.[26] The approach conceptualizes a life in terms of a person's *functionings,* which include both states (a person's beings) and actions (a person's doings). Examples of beings include being well-nourished, being well-sheltered, being educated, and being healthy. Examples of doings include working, resting, spending time with family, and participating in political life. The concept is somewhat abstract, but in simple terms functionings are nothing more than a description of a person's life.

The concept of functionings is an extremely flexible one, starting with the fact that functionings can be viewed as generally or as specifically as one chooses. Consider the general functioning of being healthy, which could, of course, be made more specific by focusing on being physically or mentally healthy. The specificity could go further into particular aspects of physical or mental health, like being free of chronic pain or being free of depression. Consider another abstract functioning like participating in social life. We could parse this functioning more specifically into spending time with friends, attending church, or helping other people. Martha Nussbaum referred to this feature of functionings as "multiple realizability," meaning that functionings could be specified in more or less specific ways depending on the context of the application.[27]

Functionings are also value-neutral in the sense that they can be beneficial, harmful, or altogether irrelevant to a person's well-being. The functionings noted so far have generally been beneficial or positively valued ones. Examples of harmful or negatively valued functionings might include being hungry, being sick, or committing a crime. Functionings that are irrelevant to a person's well-being might include being ticklish, whistling, or finger-snapping. The idea here is not that all functionings can be unambiguously classified as beneficial, harmful, or irrelevant. The value of a functioning can be a matter of dispute and the value judgment may depend on the context or application in question.

A final form of flexibility worth noting is that functionings can relate to a person's own narrow self-interest, the interests of others, or nobody's interests at all. I might vote in an election, for example, because I want to support a candidate who will advance my own interests. I might instead vote because I want to support a candidate whose policies will advance the interests of other people in my community, even if they involve some harm to me (by, for example, raising my taxes). Or I might vote out of a simple sense of duty to do so, independent of the impact I expect on my interests or the interests of others. Functionings reflect a wide range of motivations and are not necessarily aimed at narrowly promoting one's own interests.

The capability approach derives its name from a concept closely related to functionings—namely, *capabilities*. A person's capabilities are his or her real opportunities or freedoms to achieve functionings. To understand the concept of capabilities, imagine two people going without food, one of whom is starving while the other is fasting. The critical difference between these two is that the latter has the capability or opportunity to stop fasting and become more well-fed whereas the starving person does not. The fasting person arguably has a greater level of well-being, not due to different functionings but due to greater capabilities. The implication of this is that we need to look beyond functionings and also take capabilities into account when considering a person's well-being.[28]

Should we focus on functionings when assessing a person's well-being, or on capabilities—or on both? As its name suggests, the capability approach emphasizes capabilities. One reason for this is that the approach doesn't endorse any particular view of the good life and instead stresses that people should be able to choose from a range of possibilities. There are, however, some important situations where people (for example, infants or people with severe cognitive disabilities) don't have the capacity to make decisions for themselves, and in these cases a focus on functionings is typically acceptable.[29] Capabilities will often be emphasized in this book, but it should be understood that the choice between functionings and capabilities can depend on the setting or context.

Either way, any application of the capability approach faces an inescapable need to decide which dimensions are relevant to the application. When making these decisions, the capability approach tends to defer, at least to some extent, to the values of the people whose lives are at stake. While the approach itself doesn't commit to any specific method for determining what dimensions are valuable to people, there's some agreement that affected people should be encouraged to participate in the process. The capability approach thus claims that human well-being should be viewed in terms of those functionings and capabilities that people value. Similarly, poverty is viewed not as a lack of income, but rather as a lack of valuable functionings and capabilities.

Let's now consider three core features of the capability approach in more detail. The first characteristic worth mentioning is the *means-ends distinction*. The *ends* of well-being are those outcomes that are ultimately valuable to a person, whereas the *means* of well-being are intermediary and valuable only to the extent that they help a person achieve those desired ends. The capability approach argues that functionings and capabilities are the ultimate ends of well-being and that a person's resources (including income) are valuable only as tools or means to securing functionings and capabilities. If, for example, what I ultimately value is being well-fed, my income is only valuable to me to the extent that it helps me procure food.

Focusing on the means of well-being rather than the ends can be misleading, in part because people differ in their abilities to translate or convert the means of well-being into valuable functionings, or capabilities. While a nondisabled person can generally use their income to become well-educated, a disabled person may not be able to do the same if local schools can't accommodate their special needs. There are also some important ends that can't be obtained by anyone with material means. For example, no amount of income can guarantee a life free from discrimination, persecution, or social exclusion. To understand what's really important, we thus need to consider the ends of well-being.

An individual's ability to translate resources into capabilities is determined by a variety of factors, which we can call *conversion factors,* and they can be categorized into several types. Personal conversion factors are associated with the features of a person and are influenced by traits such as age, sex, race, and physical abilities. Social conversion factors relate to the society in which a person lives and are determined by laws, public policies, beliefs, and social norms, to name a few. Environmental conversion factors refer to the physical environment of a person and include the climate, the quality of water, the presence of roads, and the availability of communication technologies, among others.[30] The point here is that the means-ends distinction is more than a theoretical curiosity. There are numerous real-world examples of things that mediate the link between the means and ends of well-being.

The second core characteristic of the capability approach is *value pluralism*, meaning that the approach endorses multiple objects of ultimate value. Value pluralism is most immediately evident in the concept of functionings, which are a multidimensional description of a person's life. The capability approach emphasizes that to reduce human life to any single dimension would be misleading. Some might argue, for example, that happiness is the only thing that is ultimately valuable. The capability approach counters this by pointing out that subjective states are deceptive: people in dire situations often adapt to their situations and find happiness in the little that they have.[31] To understand well-being, we must additionally look to the objective situations of people, which are irreducibly multidimensional.

Relatedly, the capability approach holds that both functionings and capabilities are ultimately valuable. There are good reasons for looking beyond functionings to also consider capabilities. As already mentioned, where people have different views of the good life, shifting the focus to capabilities avoids imposing any particular view on them. Beyond this, the capability approach holds that having the ability to choose one's own functionings is valuable in itself. Rather than viewing people as passive "patients," the approach thus views people as "agents" who can realize their goals through their own actions.[32] Agency is central to the capability approach and, in fact, can be viewed as a type of capability itself.

Philosopher Rutger Claassen defined an *agent* as a person who is able to deliberate autonomously when forming or revising their goals, and able to act freely when trying to realize their goals. Notice the repetition of the words "able to" in that definition. Deliberating and acting can be viewed as two highly abstract functionings, and to be an agent—to have agency—entails having the capabilities to perform these two abstract functionings. "The concept of agency should not be set apart from the concepts of capabilities

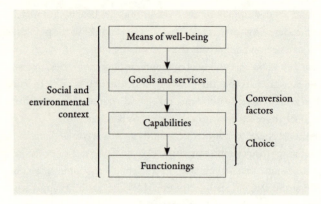

FIGURE 2.1. A graphical summary of the capability approach

and functionings," Claassen elaborated. "Agency can be fully captured in the language of capabilities. It is itself a (complex) capability, and can be specified in terms of a set of capabilities that form the components of agency."[33]

A final core characteristic that deserves mentioning is *the principle of each person as an end*. The basic idea is that each person counts as a moral equal and we therefore must be concerned with how the well-being of each and every person is served or protected.[34] The most immediate implication of this principle is that it cautions against evaluating programs or policies in terms of their total or average effects. Instead, we should give consideration to the impacts on every person to make sure that nobody is treated merely as a means to somebody else's ends. The capability approach therefore stresses that all people are worthy of dignity and respect.

Figure 2.1 summarizes the capability approach by depicting the various steps required to translate the means of well-being into functionings.[35] The means of well-being—including income, nonmarket production, and any cash or in-kind transfers—determines the goods and services a person can buy. A person's goods and services together with their conversion factors then influences their capabilities. Finally, a person must choose their functionings from the capabilities available to them. This entire process is embedded in the broader social and environmental context, which influences everything from how people produce their means of well-being (for example, through the prevailing economic institutions) to how they choose their functionings (for example, through the social norms that influence their decisions).

Controversies and Criticisms

"The opposite of poverty is not wealth; the opposite of poverty is justice," wrote Bryan Stevenson, an American lawyer and founder of the Equal Justice Initiative.[36] Stevenson's words convey the basic message of this chapter: poverty isn't simply a lack of income or wealth, but rather an experience of injustice that's most visibly expressed as a lack of income or wealth. The monetary view of poverty thus defines poverty in terms of its symptoms, often leading to policy solutions that fail to address deeper injustices. The capability approach, by contrast, explicitly views poverty as injustice and describes the appropriate metric or standard for identifying and assessing injustice. In this view, capabilities are the "currency" of justice.

The capability approach provides a rich framework for poverty assessments, but it's not immune to controversy or criticism. One of the most controversial questions relates to selecting the life dimensions to prioritize for a given application. While there's broad agreement that the people affected by the application should participate in some way, there's no consensus on how extensive that participation should be. At one extreme, Amartya Sen advocated for a highly decentralized process that relies on public discussion to select the relevant dimensions. Sen provided little guidance on what this process might look like in practice, but argued that it would ensure that the chosen dimensions are in line with the purpose of the application, the prevailing social conditions, and people's beliefs about the significance of different dimensions.[37]

Martha Nussbaum has been especially critical of Sen's approach to this issue. She argued that public discussion may lead to either the inclusion of objectionable dimensions or the exclusion of important dimensions. In response to this issue, Nussbaum took a position on the opposite extreme from Sen's and argued for a centralized approach to selecting functioning dimensions. Specifically, she put forward a list of ten "central" capabilities that she believed should apply to all applications of the capability approach. Her list included dimensions like being able to live a life of a normal length, being able to have good health, and being able to move freely from place to place. Though Nussbaum's list was quite comprehensive, she viewed it as subject to ongoing revision and believed that the dimensions could be tailored to local circumstances through public discussion.[38]

Many people have criticized Nussbaum's list, with one major concern being that some items on the list could be problematic for certain groups. For example, because some religions consider certain medical treatments to be sinful, they may object to government support of these procedures to promote the capability of good health. In response to these criticisms, Rutger Claassen offered an intermediate route between Sen and Nussbaum that focused on the simple idea that the capability approach is strongly agency-oriented. He then proposed a list of three "basic" capabilities required for someone to be an agent—capabilities related to economic and physical security, civil liberties, and political liberties.[39] Claassen's approach occupies an intermediate ground between Sen and Nussbaum because it's structured, but avoids many of the controversial value commitments of Nussbaum's list.

The "list" debate is by no means resolved, but Claassen's list highlights many of the capabilities commonly referenced by scholars and practitioners. His economic and physical security capability refers to people's ability to be well-nourished, sheltered, and healthy. His civil liberties capability includes freedom of assembly and association, the right to privacy and private property, and the ability to be educated. And his political liberties capability covers the right to vote, the right to stand for office, and the right to a fair trial. Given that some focus is helpful as we investigate cash transfers, Claassen's list at the very least emphasizes several capabilities that are intuitive and unlikely to be controversial.

While the capability approach gives us a broader view of poverty, there are several other concerns worth mentioning. As capabilities represent certain choices available to a person, one criticism of the capability approach is that choice isn't always a good thing. For example, a person shopping at the grocery store might find it overwhelming to be confronted with a dizzying array of variations on bread, butter, or toothpaste. This critique is nevertheless based on a misunderstanding, as expanding a person's capabilities doesn't mean expanding all kinds of choices; rather, it means expanding a person's choices over things that ultimately constitute their well-being (that is, functionings).

Being presented with a wider selection of hair care options is quite different from having a greater set of choices to be well-fed, well-educated, or healthy.[40]

Another critique of the capability approach is that it's too individualistic and doesn't pay enough attention to social phenomena (that is, social relations, groups, or structures). Here it's important to distinguish between ethical individualism and methodological individualism.[41] Ethical individualism states that individuals are the units of ultimate moral concern in evaluating a state of affairs. In contrast, methodological individualism—also referred to as explanatory individualism—claims that all social phenomena can be explained in terms of individuals and their properties. The critical difference between these two concepts is that ethical individualism emphasizes individuals when *judging* a state of affairs whereas methodological individualism emphasizes individuals when *explaining* a state of affairs.

The capability approach is committed to ethical individualism, but doesn't rely on methodological individualism. A commitment to ethical individualism isn't a limitation of the capability approach, but rather a desirable feature. If we accept that all people have equal moral worth, we must be interested in how each and every person is served or protected by a given state of affairs. A framework that uses groups as the fundamental unit of moral concern risks overlooking inequalities within groups. For example, using households as the unit of concern neglects the fact that women and children are often disadvantaged by the intra-household allocation of resources.

As Figure 2.1 makes clear, social phenomena are integrated into the capability approach in a variety of ways. The means-ends distinction, for example, highlights the fact that people have different abilities to convert the means of well-being into valued ends. That is, people have different conversion factors and we've seen that social factors play an important role in the conversion process. Social phenomena may also play a role in how people choose their functionings from the capabilities available to them, possibly through social norms that influence their decision-making processes. In no case does the capability approach claim that these social phenomena must be explained in terms of individuals or their properties.

A further critique worth mentioning is that the capability approach is too difficult to "operationalize." This critique most often refers to the difficulty of translating the abstract concept of capabilities into well-defined measures that can be used for empirical analyses of human well-being. Bengt-Christer Ysander summarized the issue, writing that "capabilities are often rather elusive things to catch.... it is difficult to measure directly the counterfactual part which has to do with what a person might be or do—or might have been or have done."[42] The core problem is then that measuring capabilities requires understanding the alternative functionings a person could have chosen, which presents a challenge because these functionings aren't actually realized or observed.

Despite these challenges, there have been many interesting empirical applications of the capability approach.[43] For example, the Human Development Index and the Multidimensional Poverty Index have become widely used alternatives to monetary measures of living standards, such as gross national income or the poverty headcount ratio. While most of the empirical applications have avoided the problem of measuring capabilities by simply focusing on measuring observed functionings, these efforts have nevertheless shown that the capability approach can be applied in meaningful and policy-relevant ways. Moreover, some recent studies have developed innovative ways to measure capabilities using statistical methods and have demonstrated that the measurement challenge isn't insurmountable.[44]

A final point of concern is that the capability approach is often referred to as a "liberal" theory and people frequently misunderstand the meaning of this label. In everyday language, the term *liberal* is generally associated with certain political meanings, which can refer to the political left or right depending on the country. The term is also used to refer to (neo)liberal economic policies, which are market-oriented policies that emphasize the deregulation of markets, the lowering of barriers to international trade, and the privatization of state enterprises, among other things. In contrast to this everyday usage, the term can also refer to a philosophical tradition that values individual autonomy and freedom. Such philosophical liberalism entails no prior commitment to any social or economic policies, and isn't necessarily aligned with the political left or right.

The capability approach is generally viewed as liberal in the philosophical sense, albeit to differing degrees depending on the specific application. The approach itself, however, doesn't say much about which policies are most appropriate for expanding people's capabilities. While it might be tempting to believe that "free markets" are best-suited to advance human freedoms or capabilities, this isn't necessarily the case. In particular, in subsequent chapters we'll see that markets often don't function properly and that such market failures can constrain people's capabilities in important ways. As the capability approach can lend itself to more active policy solutions that intervene into markets for the sake of promoting capabilities, the approach is thus not liberal in the sense that it advocates for economic liberalization.

The capability approach isn't without limitations, but it's often regarded as providing a richer perspective on poverty that remedies many of the shortcomings of the monetary view. Most importantly, the capability approach shifts our focus from the resources people have to the people themselves. One immediate implication of viewing poverty in this way is that giving people money no longer automatically reduces poverty, as people can fail to translate resources into capabilities. The idea that "poverty is a policy choice" is then mistaken given that poverty alleviation can't be reduced to a basic math problem. While none of the arguments in this book require accepting the capability approach in its entirety, there are a few concepts that are crucial for understanding the limitations of cash transfers.

One of the most important points is that taking a broad view of poverty entails considering people's agency, or whether they can realize their goals through their own actions. Chapter 9 will examine, for example, whether cash transfers truly treat people as agents rather than patients. Another important concept is the means-ends distinction. The capability approach encourages us to acknowledge that cash transfers expand only the *means* of well-being, which requires us to ask additional questions about how people convert the means of well-being into valued *ends*. This means-ends distinction will be revisited in subsequent chapters, including in Chapter 3, where we'll see that the evidence on cash transfers, once we look beyond the means of well-being, is surprisingly weak.

CHAPTER 3

What the Evidence Shows

THE BABY'S FIRST YEARS STUDY was the first randomized controlled trial designed to examine whether income poverty affects the brain development of children.[1] The researchers started by visiting maternity wards in four American metropolitan areas—New York City, New Orleans, Omaha, and the Twin Cities—and recruited roughly a thousand low-income women who had recently given birth. They randomly assigned each of the mothers to one of two groups: 40 percent were selected to receive a large cash transfer of $333 per month while the remaining 60 percent were given a small cash transfer of $20 per month. For the typical recipient of the large cash transfer, the payment was substantial. On average, it increased the woman's annual income by roughly 20 percent.

After one year of the mothers receiving regular cash payments, the researchers measured each child's brain activity using electroencephalography (EEG). The technology painlessly detects the electrical signals produced by the brain through a special cap wired with electrodes. The study measured the "power" of each infant's brain activity at four different frequency bands: alpha, beta, gamma, and theta. Greater power in the alpha, beta, and gamma bands has been linked to better language, cognitive, and socio-emotional outcomes, and greater power in the theta band has been linked to behavioral, attention, and learning problems. The researchers hypothesized that the cash transfers, by influencing the infants' environments—for example, reducing parental stress levels—would lead to beneficial changes in their brains.

And this is what they claimed to find. The infants in the large cash transfer group exhibited no differences in the theta band relative to the small cash transfer group, but in the alpha, beta, and gamma bands, the researchers' baseline analysis showed differences that were statistically greater than zero. Reporting the results, they declared that "the weight of the evidence supports the conclusion that monthly unconditional cash transfers given to the mothers in our study affected brain activity in their infants. This is notable because the patterns of neural activity we observe in the high-cash gift group have been correlated with higher language, cognitive, and social-emotional scores later in childhood and adolescence."[2]

The study received considerable media attention, with the *New York Times, Forbes, Vox,* the *Los Angeles Times,* and others citing its findings. Several think tanks—such as the Brookings Institution, the Universal Basic Income Center, and the Niskanen Center—posted favorable commentary on their websites. Policymakers also took note. For example, Representative Suzan DelBene, a Democrat from Washington, said the study strengthened the case for child tax credits by showing that "investing in our children has incredible long-term benefits."[3] The study seemed poised to have widespread influence. But then several people took a closer look at the analysis and found that the conclusions weren't actually well-supported by the data.[4]

One issue was that the researchers were able to gather EEG data for only 435 infants, or just over 40 percent of the infants originally enrolled in the study. The whole point of randomization is to ensure that the treatment and control groups are similar in every way except for the treatment; this is what enables valid causal statements. When so many participants drop out of a study, there's a real risk that the two groups become dissimilar, which in this case means that the differences in brain activity could have been caused by dissimilarities between the groups rather than the treatment. Unsurprisingly, after a reweighting of the data to adjust for such differences (including racial and ethnic differences), the effects of the cash transfers became less pronounced.

There were other important statistical issues. The researchers tested multiple hypotheses by looking at the effect of cash transfers on different frequency bands. When testing multiple hypotheses, it's necessary to make certain adjustments for the increased possibility of false-positive results. After making these adjustments, the researchers found that, for nearly all of their tests, the impact of cash was no longer statistically different from zero. Beyond the discovery that their results were sensitive to adjusting for multiple hypotheses, they also found that the statistical significance of several of their estimates changed when effects were expressed in percentage rather than absolute terms. In short, even according to the researcher's own analyses, the results were remarkably fragile.

There's one more issue worth mentioning. Recall that the researchers appealed to previous studies when linking increased activity in the alpha, beta, and gamma bands to better developmental outcomes such as improved language, cognitive, and socio-emotional skills. The problem is that this previous research established only, at best, the existence of *correlations* between brain activity and developmental outcomes. Even if the results of the study were conclusive, the claim that cash transfers lead to better developmental outcomes through increased brain activity was largely speculative. The results thus don't tell us much about whether cash has any impact on the actual psychological development of children.

The study was flawed and several media outlets responded by either updating their articles or removing them altogether. For example, *Vox* updated its article to reflect the criticisms, the Niskanen Center added a disclaimer to its commentary, and the Universal Basic Income Center removed all of its posts about the experiment.[5] The lesson here, however, is not about the flaws of this specific study or even the media's response, but rather that so many people just really wanted to believe that the results were true. In the *Atlantic*, Stuart Ritchie wrote: "Plenty of people desperately want results like these to be real and meaningful, because they (understandably) want to use science to help poor mothers and their children. This study is just asking to be deployed by advocates for cash transfers or a universal basic income."[6]

Social policy is polarizing and poverty-alleviation policy can be especially divisive. The problem is that people are often insufficiently critical of evidence that supports their arguments, and are too quick to dismiss evidence that helps the other side. While this bias is hardly unique to cash transfers, there's something seductive about cash that captivates advocates and makes the line between science and advocacy especially blurry. As the "Baby's First Years" study shows, this can distort public discourse and result in bold claims about the effects of cash transfer programs—such as the declaration by former GiveDirectly president Rory Stewart that "more than three hundred academic papers have demonstrated the extraordinary positive impact of cash."[7]

This chapter takes a closer look at what the evidence actually says about cash transfers and shows that it's weaker than many believe. Although *condi-*

tional cash programs will be discussed, the main goal is to tease out what the evidence says about *unconditional* cash transfers, largely to gain clarity about what cash itself can accomplish. We'll first examine the short-term effects of cash programs and note that the evidence shows limited impacts on education, health, and other crucial outcomes. Then we will review the evidence on the long-term effects of cash transfers, which shows that cash doesn't have lasting impacts on poor households. Finally, the chapter concludes by highlighting additional concerns related to how informative the evidence base is for poverty-alleviation policy.

The Short-Term Effects of Cash

The literature on cash transfers is extremely large and it's often hard to know which studies are credible. Systematic reviews can be a helpful guide because they carefully screen studies for reliability and then synthesize the evidence on a given topic. Perhaps the most well-known systematic review of cash transfers was conducted by the Overseas Development Institute (ODI) and published in 2019.[8] Focusing on findings from low- and middle-income countries, the ODI review screened thirty-eight thousand studies—including both published and unpublished papers—from the years 2000 to 2015. The researchers ultimately selected 165 studies that both met their quality assessment criteria and reported on certain outcomes of interest.

The selected studies provide evidence on fifty-two different cash transfer programs from across all regions of the developing world, including Latin America and the Caribbean, sub-Saharan Africa, the Middle East and North Africa, Europe and Central Asia, South Asia, and East Asia and the Pacific. While most of the fifty-two interventions are conditional cash transfer programs (55 percent), the review also covers several unconditional cash transfer programs, social pension programs, and enterprise grants. It's important to note that the vast majority of these studies focus on the short-term effects of cash transfers, typically following up with beneficiaries after about two years of receiving benefits. The review thus focuses almost exclusively on the short-run evidence.

The ODI review looked at the impact of cash transfers on monetary poverty, education, health and nutrition, savings and investment, employment, and women's empowerment. For each of these outcome types, the researchers considered several specific indicators and then counted the number of studies reporting statistically significant results for each indicator. Importantly, when a study reports a statistically significant estimate that means the true effect is unlikely to be zero. The researchers then counted the number of significant estimates for each indicator showing positive and negative effects. While this approach doesn't tell us whether the effects are large or practically meaningful, it does tell us how often studies find non-zero effects and gives us an understanding of the direction of those effects.

Let's first consider the short-term effects of cash transfers on work. On the one hand, a common concern of policymakers is that giving cash to poor people will make them work less by reducing their need to earn income through labor. On the other hand, receiving cash support might actually permit poor people to work more by giving them the resources to start new businesses, grow existing businesses, or even migrate. The ODI review considered findings from fourteen studies examining the effect of cash on whether or not adults worked, and found that only five of the studies reported statistically significant effects. Of the five significant results, three reported an increased propensity to work and two reported a decreased propensity to work.

We need to take a closer look, however, at the two studies showing decreases in work. One of the negative work effects relates to a Mexican old-age pension that induced pensioners to reduce paid work in favor of doing unpaid work in family businesses.[9] That is, the results showed that the pensioners merely engaged in different forms of work rather than reducing work altogether. The second study focused on working-age adults living in households receiving a South African old-age pension.[10] The authors found that the program appeared to have an adverse effect on labor supply only because households receiving pensions attracted new nonworking household members. Neither of these studies then actually show that receiving cash transfers reduces the propensity to work.

While there's limited evidence that cash can have a positive effect on work, this result is far from universal and many studies show insignificant effects. We further find very little evidence that cash transfers have an adverse effect on labor supply.[11] There is, however, one notable study that was excluded from the ODI review of employment outcomes because its estimates weren't strictly comparable to the other studies considered. This study looked at the labor-supply effects of Albania's Ndihma Ekonomike, which was a somewhat unorthodox program because people's cash benefits were reduced one-for-one with additional labor income. The researchers found that Ndihma Ekonomike was associated with a strong negative labor-supply effect among working-age adults, most likely because the program's unorthodox design disincentivized work.[12]

The more compelling results of the ODI review pertain to the other indicators, particularly those related to monetary poverty. One of the most intensively researched aspects of cash transfers relates to their effect on household expenditures, and the ODI review looked at thirty-five studies that explored this relationship. Of these thirty-five studies, twenty-six showed statistically significant effects, twenty-five of which pointed to increased expenditures. The one study that found a significant negative effect on expenditures was the Albanian evaluation mentioned previously. Importantly, the authors argued that its negative expenditure result was driven by the adverse labor-supply effect of Ndihma Ekonomike, meaning that the expenditure result can also be traced back to the unusual design of the program.

The positive impact of cash transfers on household expenditures is among the clearest effects we'll encounter, though even in this case there are plenty of instances of insignificant results. The immediate concern with these results is that they don't tell us much about *how* households spent their cash. Policymakers commonly worry that people waste the money (for example, on alcohol or tobacco). As buying food is often considered a reasonable use of additional income, let's consider what the ODI review found about impacts on food expenditures. Here the review found that twenty-five out of thirty-one studies reported significant changes in food expenditures, twenty-three of which showed increased expenditures.

Much like the overall expenditure results, the food-expenditure results show reasonably consistent positive impacts. There are, however, two studies reporting significantly negative effects. One of these studies is the Ndihma Ekonomike evaluation already discussed. The other study was an impact evaluation of Paraguay's Tekoporã program, which found that beneficiaries witnessed a 12 percent reduction in food expenditure per capita on average.[13] An important component of the Tekoporã program was that beneficiaries were assigned "family guides," who helped households with budgeting and often recommended additional saving. The authors of the study argued that it was this "savings message" that induced households to reduce consumption and save more.

The Tekoporã evaluation is not the only study to find that cash transfers increased savings. The ODI review found that five out of the ten studies that examined impacts on savings showed positive and significant results, with no evidence of negative effects. The magnitude of these savings effects varies across studies, ranging from 7 to 24 percentage point increases in the share of households reporting saving. Similarly, out of seventeen studies that examined the accumulation of livestock assets, twelve reported significant increases and no study found significant decreases. Taking these results together with the expenditure-related results, we then see that there's a body of evidence showing that cash transfers tend to be used in the intended ways, both through increased consumption and savings.

While it's tempting to conclude that the evidence for cash transfers is convincing, recall from Chapter 2 that we need to carefully distinguish between the means and the ends of well-being. Both consumption and savings pertain to the means of well-being and are thus tools that people use to achieve what's ultimately valuable to them (their ends). Accordingly, we need to further ask whether cash transfers also impact the ends of well-being. There are, of course, many life dimensions we might consider to answer this question, but let's focus on two especially critical dimensions with a sufficiently large evidence base: education and health.

Regarding education, the ODI review looked at twenty-five different estimates of the effect of cash transfers on school attendance and found that fourteen were statistically significant. Of the significant estimates, thirteen pointed to a positive effect on school attendance and one showed a negative effect. Attendance isn't the only outcome relevant to education and the review also considered the impact of cash transfers on test scores and cognitive development scores. Across thirteen estimates related to test scores and cognitive development scores, the review found that only four showed positive and significant effects. While even here we begin to see more modest effects of cash programs, note that these results pertain to a mix of program types and we know that conditional programs often place explicit conditions on education.

In much of the recent discourse around cash-based programs—especially around universal basic incomes—the concern is about the pure effect of cash with no conditions placed on beneficiaries. What then is the effect of unconditional transfers on education? While the ODI review doesn't systematically explore the different effects of conditional and unconditional programs on educational outcomes, another review conducted by Sarah Baird and her coauthors does.[14] Baird's research team screened 4,167 relevant studies from low- and middle-income countries across the years 1997 to 2013. After removing those studies that didn't meet their review criteria, they were left with seventy-five studies that covered thirty-five programs across twenty-five countries.

Baird and her team looked at three indicators of educational outcomes: enrollment, attendance, and test scores. For enrollment, they identified thirty-five studies that estimated the effect of cash transfers on the probability that children enrolled in school. Of these studies, they classified six as unconditional and found that, while all showed positive effects, none were statistically significant. The authors then estimated a combined effect across all six studies, which showed that unconditional programs increased enrollment rates by about 2.9 percentage points on average.[15] These results contrast starkly with the studies of explicitly conditioned programs, where twelve of fifteen showed significant results and the combined effect was about twice that of unconditional programs.

The results on attendance and test scores tell a story that is similar to the enrollment results. For attendance, Baird's team looked at the impacts of five unconditional programs and found that four showed statistically insignificant results. The lone program showing significant effects was an HIV / STD prevention program conducted in Manicaland, Zimbabwe. For test scores, there were only three studies classified as unconditional and none of them showed any statistical significance. Overall, the review then considered fourteen different estimates of the impact of unconditional cash transfers on various educational outcomes and found only one instance of statistical significance. At least with respect to education, we thus find that the pure effect of cash on the ends of well-being is quite limited.

What about health? One outcome considered by the ODI review is the use of health services, and ten of fifteen studies covered by it found significant effects, with nine reporting increased health service usage. The review also considered the impact of cash transfers on three important outcomes related to child anthropometrics: stunting, wasting, and being underweight. Across twenty-seven different estimates related to these outcomes, the review found that seven showed significant effects in the direction of improved anthropometric indicators. Much like the case of education, the ODI review then shows somewhat modest impacts on health, though once again we need to be mindful of the fact that these results pertain to both conditional and unconditional programs.

To understand the health impacts of unconditional transfers, we need to turn to a different review of the evidence conducted by a research team led by Frank Pega.[16] Pega's team identified thirty-four studies of unconditional programs from low- and middle-income countries that met their review criteria. The studies included in the review span the years 2007 to 2020 and cover several developing regions, such as East Asia and the Pacific, Latin America and the Caribbean, South Asia, and sub-Saharan Africa. Further, the researchers considered several different health-related outcomes, including the use of health services, child anthropometric outcomes, the incidence of disease or illness, and food security, among several others.

Regarding the use of health services, the results contrast starkly with those from the ODI review: across seven different estimates of the impact of unconditional transfers on health service usage, none showed any statistical significance. The study's authors also estimated a combined effect which implied that unconditional programs increased the use of health services by about 2 percentage points on average.[17] With respect to child anthropometric indicators, Pega's team looked at the outcomes of children being stunted or underweight. Out of six different estimates that were eligible for their final analysis, once again, none displayed any statistical significance. For both indicators, the combined effects were at or near zero.

Several of the other indicators considered by the researchers also showed overwhelmingly null results, including whether children had recent growth checks, up-to-date vaccinations, or symptoms of depression. Not all outcomes, however, showed such modest effects. For example, three of six estimates showed significantly negative impacts on the incidence of illness in treated households, with a combined effect indicating about an eight percentage point reduction in the incidence of illness. Further, across two different measures of food security, five of nine estimates showed significantly positive impacts. The effects of unconditional programs on health are then a bit more promising than those on education, though it's still difficult to conclude that the impacts are anything more than mixed.

The Long-Term Effects of Cash

Northern Uganda has historically lagged behind the rest of the country in terms of economic development, largely due to long distances from trade routes, low levels of public investment, and persistent conflict and instability. In an attempt to promote development in the northern parts of the country, the government introduced the Youth Opportunities Program (YOP) in 2006. YOP invited groups of young adults, roughly between the ages of sixteen and thirty-five, to apply for one-time cash grants to support their work in skilled trades, such as metal fabrication, carpentry, and tailoring. The program received more applications then it could fund, so administrators decided to randomly select beneficiaries from the list of screened and eligible grant proposals.

The list of proposals consisted of 535 groups averaging about twenty-two members per group. The program randomly selected 265 groups to receive the one-time cash grants and left the remaining 270 groups to serve as controls for an evaluation of the program. The grants were disbursed in 2008 and the selected groups received about $7,500 on average (in 2008 dollars), which amounted to just under $400 per person. The grants were sizable and roughly equivalent to the average annual income of the recipients. Further, and perhaps more importantly, the grants were unconditional in that there was no government monitoring after the money was disbursed. While YOP is distinct from other cash programs that provide recurring payments, we'll see that it holds lessons with broader implications.

A research team led by Christopher Blattman collected data on the treatment and control groups in the years 2010-2011, 2012, and 2017 (that is, two, four, and nine years after the grants were disbursed).[18] An especially interesting feature of the evaluation was its extended duration: many programs have a limited window for evaluation because the control group is eventually given benefits, but this wasn't the case for YOP. As the control group was preserved, Blattman's team was able to continue evaluating the program well beyond conventional time horizons. Moreover, unlike the Baby's First Years study, the researchers were able to follow up with most of the participants, and they reported interviewing 74 percent of them after nine years.

So, what did they find? The economic impacts after four years were pronounced and the treatment group saw 17 percent greater work hours, 38 percent greater earnings, and 11 percent greater consumption than the control group. All these effects were statistically significant. The nine-year evaluation nevertheless told a different story, as Blattman's team reported that the program's impacts on work hours, earnings, and consumption were insignificant in the long run. The only two economic indicators that showed persistent effects were durable assets and the fraction of people working full-time in a skilled trade. The researchers noted, however, that the asset effects were sensitive to adjusting for initial differences between the treated and control groups.

Regarding the nine-year effects on health and education, Blattman's team found that the program had insignificant effects on the physical and mental health of the beneficiaries. They found similarly insignificant effects on school enrollment and educational attainment of children living in treated households. One possible exception to these underwhelming results is that treated children saw a 0.08 standard deviation increase in an index of their health, which included a measure of physical functioning, a subjective assessment of the child's health, and reported malaria cases in the previous year. While this result was statistically significant, it was only so at a more relaxed standard and, much like the assets result, proved to be fragile.

The results of the YOP program give us rare insight into the long-term effects of cash transfers. Overall, the results show that the program had some notable short-term impacts, particularly on the means of well-being, but that these effects faded out almost completely in the longer term. The basic explanation for the results is that YOP helped underemployed young Ugandans get into skilled trades more quickly, either through finding steady wage work or starting new businesses. Without YOP, however, people in the control group were eventually able to find similarly lucrative work or to save enough to also start their own businesses. In short, the control group eventually caught up to the treated group, so the program had limited long-term effects.

While the YOP evaluation is an especially clear illustration of the long-term effects of cash transfers, fortunately it's not the only study. A systematic survey was conducted by a group of researchers led by Adrien Bouguen.[19] Focusing on experimental evidence (gained from randomized controlled trials), they identified only four studies, including the YOP study, that looked at the longer-term impacts of unconditional programs. The studies included one from South America (Ecuador) and three from sub-Saharan Africa (Ethiopia, Malawi, and Uganda). Technically speaking, two of the studies (Ethiopia and Malawi) don't meet the research team's criterion of long-term, which they formally define as reporting impacts after roughly ten years. The review nevertheless discusses these studies and this chapter will as well.

The other truly long-term study was conducted by Caridad Araujo and a group of coauthors.[20] Araujo's team looked at the impacts of Ecuador's Bono de Desarrollo Humano (Human Development Bonus), which was a large-scale cash transfer program created in 2003. At its peak, this program gave recurring cash transfers to about 40 percent of households in Ecuador. The transfers were also generous and by 2010 amounted to about 20 percent of household income on average. At the start of the program, eligible households were randomly assigned to one of two groups: an early treatment group that began receiving cash in 2004 and a late treatment group that began receiving cash in 2007. While there were no conditions placed on the transfers, households were encouraged to spend the money on their children.

As part of the impact evaluation, data was periodically collected on the early- and late-treatment groups until 2014, or about ten years after the program began. The researchers were especially interested in understanding the ten-year differences between the two groups in terms of the educational outcomes of children. Specifically, they looked at the impact of the cash transfers on learning through several standardized test scores, including language and math test scores, among others. Despite the early treatment group's receiving about twice as much in cumulative transfers, the researchers found no positive and significant impacts on any type of test score. Much like the YOP study, the Ecuadorian program's evaluation thus shows no long-term positive impacts of cash transfers on educational outcomes.[21]

In yet another longer-term evaluation, Sarah Baird led a group of researchers that looked at Malawi's Schooling, Income, and Health Risk program.[22] Beginning in 2007, it provided recurring cash support to young women between the ages of thirteen and twenty-two. While the transfers lasted for only two years, Baird's team followed up with a sample of these women in 2012, roughly five years after the program began. The study was somewhat complicated by a design that first grouped the women according to their school enrollment status and then granted different types of cash transfers (conditional or unconditional) to them depending on their status. Nevertheless, by focusing on just the findings pertaining to the impact of unconditional transfers, we can make progress in teasing out the pure effect of cash in the longer term.

Women who were still in school at the start of the Malawi study were randomly assigned to one of three groups: an unconditional cash group, a conditional cash group, and a control group. Despite some positive impacts after two years of the program, the researchers found virtually no statistically significant impacts of unconditional transfers after five years. This was true across a wide range of indicators, including measures of education, marriage and fertility, health, labor-market participation, and women's empowerment.[23] The researchers did find that children born while their families were receiving unconditional support had grown taller than their control-group counterparts, but because of some methodological challenges, they could describe this result only as "suggestive."

The final study from Ethiopia tells a story consistent with the others. Also led by Christopher Blattman, this study randomly assigned nearly a thousand young adults to one of three groups: one group was offered a job in an industrial firm, one group was given a one-time cash grant to help recipients start businesses, and one group was used as a control.[24] The cash-grant group was told that the support was unconditional, although it was framed as a business start-up grant and was accompanied by a few days of training. Further, much like the YOP study, the one-time grants were large and roughly equivalent to the annual income of the recipients. The treatments began in 2012 and Blattman's team followed up with all groups one and five years later.

Looking at the impacts on the cash-grant group, the research team found that after one year they had income and consumption levels that were about

0.15 standard deviations above the control group. This effect was statistically significant. However, after five years, the program showed negative and insignificant impacts on consumption and income. The authors also looked at the impact of the grants on employment and health, and similarly found statistically insignificant effects after five years. The explanation for the long-term convergence between the two groups was that the grants initially gave the recipients a boost by helping them start their own businesses, but after five years many had closed their businesses while some control-group members were able to start their own businesses without the grant.

These four experimental studies show fairly clearly that the long-term impacts of unconditional cash transfers are limited. But what about conditional cash transfers? In another systematic review, a group of researchers led by Teresa Molina Millán took an especially detailed look at this question.[25] Considering both experimental and nonexperimental studies, Molina Millán and her colleagues reviewed the evidence from ten conditional cash transfer programs that had been subject to longer-term evaluations. While the majority (seven out of ten) of these programs were in Latin America, the authors also considered evidence from three countries outside of Latin America (Cambodia, Malawi, and Pakistan).

Given that a major purpose of conditional cash transfers is to break intergenerational poverty traps, Molina Millán's team focused on the long-term impacts of conditional programs on children. Specifically, they focused on two groups of children: those exposed to conditional programs either in utero or during early childhood (before age six); and those exposed during school ages (six to eighteen years old). One important consideration is that not all the studies included in the review had been able to identify the absolute effects of the programs on children, because the control groups were often given cash after a period of time. As a result, the review considered a mix of studies, some examining absolute effects and others comparing early- and late-treatment groups.

Regarding the early childhood group, the researchers analyzed results across five different indicators of impact, including anthropometrics, cognitive development, socio-emotional development, schooling, and learning.[26] They found consistent impacts on schooling (such as differences in enrollment, attendance, and grade progression), with four out of the five available impact estimates being positive and statistically significant. This was an expected result, however, given that education-related conditions required that children attend school. The evidence on the other indicators was somewhat less clear. For example, one of two estimates related to learning showed positive and significant impacts while two of four estimates on anthropometric indicators showed positive effects.

For children exposed during school ages, the team looked at four indicators of impact, including schooling, learning, labor force participation, and income. Their results confirmed the expected impacts on schooling, as nearly all estimates indicated positive and significant effects. Once again, however, we see more limited impacts on the indicators that aren't directly influenced by conditions. With respect to learning, two of six estimates indicated clear positive effects, three indicated no effects, and one showed mixed effects.[27] Finally, across seventeen different estimates on labor force participation and income, the authors found that four were positive and significant, eleven showed no effect, and two indicated mixed effects.

In contrast to the evidence on unconditional cash programs, the literature on conditional programs shows at least some longer-term effects. Most clearly, we see that conditional programs almost universally improve schooling outcomes like enrollment or attendance, though this is unsurprising given education-related conditions. The long-term effects on other indicators—including important ends such as learning or anthropometrics—are more inconsistent and likely depend heavily on contextual factors such as the quality of schools. While increased schooling might be expected to translate into later increases in labor force participation and income, the evidence is underwhelming. One possible explanation for this lack of a clear effect could be that some children treated during their schooling years have yet to complete their educations.

The Evidence in Perspective

There are a few things missing from our discussion of the evidence. For one, it has omitted some important areas of research related to the gendered effects of cash, spillover effects on nonbeneficiaries, and evidence from developed countries, among others. Later chapters will discuss much of this research.

Perhaps more importantly, there are areas where the literature is altogether silent. Recalling Claassen's basic capabilities outlined in Chapter 2, we've seen that the evidence speaks most directly to the effects of cash on economic and physical security, but says very little about impacts on capabilities related to civil or political liberties. One reason for this relates to a key theme of this book: there are simply few compelling reasons to expect that cash influences these types of capabilities.

We've nevertheless covered several important topics, so let's review what we've found. Remember that the ultimate goal of this chapter is to understand what the evidence says about unconditional cash transfers and, with that in mind, Figure 3.1 summarizes the strength of the evidence across four different areas. Regarding short-term effects, cash transfers show fairly consistent impacts on the means of well-being (for example, consumption, savings, and investment), so we'll categorize this evidence as "strong." The strong effects on the means of well-being, however, don't necessarily translate into correspondingly strong effects on the ends of well-being (for example, education and health). While most indicators show only weak impacts on the ends of well-being, there are notable exceptions (such as food security), so we'll categorize the strength of this evidence as "moderate."

With respect to long-term effects, the evidence related to both the means and ends of well-being is clearly "weak." In particular, we discussed studies from several developing countries and found that they tell a remarkably con-

	Short-term	Long-term
Means	Strong	Weak
Ends	Moderate	Weak

FIGURE 3.1. A summary of evidence on unconditional cash programs

sistent story. The common narrative suggests that any short-term impacts of cash transfers tend to erode over time, with the treatment and control groups eventually converging to similar living standards. Moreover, it isn't necessarily the case that the treated and control groups converge at a heightened standard of living, as the Ethiopian study showed that the treated group actually regressed following the initial impacts of the program. If the goal of cash transfers is to make truly enduring progress against poverty, this evidence is concerning.

Is it possible that existing programs just don't give people enough money to produce lasting effects? Many of the programs discussed in this chapter provided transfers that were far from small relative to people's living standards. For example, we've discussed programs from Uganda and Ethiopia that gave people grants large enough to double their annual income. Giving people transfers much larger than these amounts would likely be prohibitively costly or require sacrificing resources from other programs. Perhaps more importantly, results from a variety of studies suggest that cash programs can face challenges when they scale. Inflation can undermine the impacts of cash, households may not have sufficient business or investment opportunities, and capacity constraints in local schools or clinics can limit the returns to education and healthcare spending.[28]

In short, it's unlikely that the impacts of cash programs are dramatically understated due to limited transfer sizes. The more likely possibility is that the evidence *overstates* the impacts of cash programs. One critical issue is site-selection bias, which arises when the likelihood of implementing or evaluating a program in a given location is correlated with its impacts. It's commonly argued that site-selection bias is positive, meaning that programs are more likely to be implemented or evaluated in sites with greater impacts. This may be due to organizations prioritizing sites where their limited resources are potentially most impactful, or because they select sites where local partners are especially capable of designing and implementing effective programs.

Evidence on site-selection bias is hard to find because it requires knowing impacts from sites that haven't been subject to evaluation. Hunt Allcott was able to gain insight into the issue by examining 111 different randomized controlled trials of an energy conservation program that provided households in the United States with conservation tips and information about the energy consumption of their neighbors.[29] Allcott found that the first cohort of sites that adopted the program showed consistently larger effects than the sites that adopted the program subsequently. This positive site-selection bias was driven by earlier programs targeting higher-usage households, more environmentalist consumer populations, and types of utility companies associated with greater impacts.

Another type of bias that can lead to overstated results is selective outcome reporting. Selective outcome reporting occurs when an individual study reports only certain results, typically favoring statistically significant results. For example, a given study might examine the impact of a program on a long list of indicators, but refrain from reporting some insignificant results. Similarly, a study might find insignificant effects on the entire sample, but continue examining subsamples (looking only at women, for example, or children, or rural households) until a favorable result can be reported. Selective outcome reporting is closely associated with what psychology researcher Norbert Kerr famously called HARKing—hypothesizing after the results are known—in which researchers check their results and then add or remove hypotheses based on those results.

There are two primary reasons why evaluators might selectively report outcomes: it's easier to publish significant results; and the organizations (often donors) commissioning evaluations often want favorable results. Researchers may respond to these incentives unconsciously or consciously, but either way they can distort evaluations. Arnaud Vaganay screened 233 evaluations spanning thirteen years of government-commissioned social research in the United Kingdom.[30] Of the 233 evaluations, Vaganay identified thirteen that found insignificant effects on their primary outcome and analyzed those studies for seven forms of selective reporting. Vaganay found that all of the studies resorted to at least one type of selective reporting and that the studies exhibited roughly three types on average.

Even in the context of a single hypothesis test, there are things researchers can do to produce favorable results. They have discretion over how, for example, they define the sample (perhaps by omitting outliers), how they measure or transform the outcome variable, what control variables to include or exclude, and how they calculate standard errors (including their choice of the level of "clustering"). These practices are often referred to as specification searching or p-hacking, and they lead to not only exaggerated levels of statistical significance but also inflated effect sizes. Again, it's not necessarily the case that researchers consciously manipulate their results, but when faced with ambiguous methodological decisions, it's well-known that researchers have a tendency to conclude that the "right" decisions are those that result in statistical significance.[31]

Further, data-related issues can produce spurious results even when researchers aren't engaging in specification searching. Consider food security, which is one of the indicators that showed positive short-term effects. A group of researchers from the International Food Policy Research Institute examined whether the estimated impacts of an Ethiopian asset-building program were affected by how food-security data were collected.[32] When comparing the standard method using self-reported measures to an indirect approach used to elicit more reliable responses, the authors found that the estimates based on self-reports were severely biased with inflated significance levels. Households thus misreported their food security in different ways depending on whether they were in the treated or control group.

None of these issues mean that we should ignore the evidence. Instead, we should approach the literature with due caution and avoid updating our beliefs on the basis of a single study. We also need to be clear that the evidence itself provides only certain facts, which may or may not be useful to policymakers. To see this, it's important to understand that the literature we've discussed summarizes the impact of a policy through the *average treatment effect,* which is calculated as the difference between the average outcomes in the treated and control groups. For example, if we're interested in a program's effect on food security, the average treatment effect is the difference between average food security in the treated group and average food security in the control group.

With that said, assume we have resources to improve food security in a given country and we need to choose between two different programs to implement across the whole country. Let's say we run a pilot of one of the programs, which we'll call program A, and find that the average treatment effect is zero. While evaluations can't generally estimate the full distributional effects of a policy, assume we know that this program improves the food security of the least well-off while correspondingly reducing the food security of the most well-off. Now say we run a pilot for a second program, call it program B, and find that the average treatment effect is positive. In this case, let's assume that the program reduces the food security of the least well-off, but that these losses are more than offset by improvements in food security among the most well-off. Which program should we choose?

If we are basing our decision exclusively on the average treatment effect, then we must choose to implement program B for the whole country. There are nevertheless reasons why this could be objectionable. A policymaker who believes we should promote equality or prioritize the well-being of the least well-off would undoubtedly favor program A. By contrast, a policymaker who respects "the principle of each person as an end" could object to both programs because, as noted in Chapter 2, each harms some people to secure benefits for others. Finally, a policymaker who wants to promote the expansion of freedoms or opportunities might claim that the available information is insufficient because it doesn't tell us how the programs affected people's capabilities.

The point of this is to emphasize that the available evidence focuses almost exclusively on the average treatment effect, which might not be the relevant statistic to policymakers with different moral or political values. Stated differently, the average treatment effect can't be linked to action in any logical way without making a debatable (ethical) claim that the mean effect is the sole criterion for judging the right policy.[33] The literature on cash transfers is thus characterized by three distinct issues: the evidence is mixed with respect to impacts on important outcomes, it likely overstates the impacts of cash because of certain biases in the research process, and it may have limited value to real-world policymaking. Contrary to popular belief, the evidence then shows that cash programs are unlikely to deliver deep and enduring progress against extreme poverty.

CHAPTER 4

The Targeting Problem

MÉVENTE IS A FRENCH WORD that literally means a slump in sales. It's an impersonal-sounding word, but can refer to very personal conflicts that take place within markets. Following the implementation of a cash transfer program in Chad, the term was frequently used to characterize certain practices used by nonbeneficiaries of the program to undo the economic benefit bestowed on the beneficiaries. Examples of mévente included abnormally high prices charged to beneficiaries, refusals to purchase goods and services from beneficiaries, and failures to pay for items purchased from beneficiaries on credit. These behaviors were direct consequences of the targeting procedure used by Chad's cash program, which raises deep questions about how targeted programs can stoke tension and conflict within communities.

In 2016, Chad's government initiated the program in the Bahr el Gazel and Logone Occidental regions, which are home to some of the highest levels of chronic poverty in the country. The program focused specifically on rural areas and sought to reach poor women with children under the age of twelve, including pregnant women. Beneficiaries were selected through a two-stage targeting procedure. First, the program selected the poorest fourteen rural cantons in the Bahr el Gazel and Logone Occidental regions, and then randomly selected 116 villages within those cantons. Second, the program identified 6,200 households within the selected villages through a proxy means test, which is a targeting method that ranks each eligible household according to a score based on their sociodemographic characteristics.

The details of the program were communicated widely through community assemblies, flyers, and radio. The community assemblies were viewed as an especially important communication channel because they didn't require literacy to read the flyers or access to a radio. One particularly important assembly took place after the program's targeting had been completed and the primary objective of the assembly was to publicly announce the list of beneficiaries in each village. People in the treated villages therefore knew exactly who had been selected. Following the assemblies, beneficiary households began receiving cash payments of 45,000 Central African Francs every three months for a period of two years. This amount was equivalent to about 23 percent of the international poverty line and the payments were typically made to women in the beneficiary households.

A group of researchers led by Anne Della Guardia conducted a series of qualitative interviews after the program's completion.[1] These interviews were of three different types. First, the researchers conducted twenty-eight key stakeholder interviews across seven villages in Logone Occidental, typically with people who had overseen the program's implementation (such as village chiefs, religious leaders, and women's representatives). Second, they convened fourteen focus groups across the same seven villages, with the focus groups consisting exclusively of program recipients. Finally, the researchers chose three of the seven villages to conduct deeper individual interviews of both beneficiaries and nonbeneficiaries. They completed a total of sixty such interviews across the three villages.

The issue of mévente emerged repeatedly in the researcher's interviews. As mentioned, one common instance of mévente occurred when a non-recipient would purchase something from a program recipient using credit, but then never pay the recipient back. One program recipient, Gilfa, summarized the issue as follows:

> What bothers me in my business is there are days when there is *mévente*, and people will buy on credit and then refuse to pay ... because they don't have money to pay, and some do it out of spite. They say that it's with my beneficiary money that I'm able to do my business, and since it's not with my own money, they don't pay.[2]

This quote highlights an important point, which is that non-recipients would refuse to pay back recipients precisely because beneficiaries had received cash transfers and were therefore seen as wealthy enough to be able to absorb this kind of loss.

Another form of mévente occurred through a double-standard pricing scheme wherein non-recipients would charge recipients higher prices for goods or services. Once again, the justification for this treatment was because program beneficiaries were viewed as being wealthy enough to afford the higher prices. Rose, a program recipient, recounted the issue as follows:

> The purchases at the market have become more expensive than before. The traders say that we transfer recipients have money so everything becomes expensive. We also have problems when we go to market, because the shopkeeper does not want to give us change. They say they have no change so we have to buy more than we planned.... It is meanness and jealousy that drives them to behave like this, because they haven't had the chance to be beneficiaries like us.[3]

This double-standard pricing issue was reported by several other beneficiaries, who similarly claimed that the nonbeneficiaries "augment the prices of their merchandise" or "tax us by making us pay higher prices."[4]

Conflicts in the treated villages were by no means confined to mévente and extended to other spheres of interaction as well. Some of these other conflicts were minor, including incidents where nonbeneficiaries refused to respond to the greetings of beneficiaries or refused to lend beneficiaries small household items like salt. There were nevertheless several reports of more severe issues where non-recipients accused the program of corruption, friendships ended because of jealousy, and recipients received insults or physical threats from non-recipients. Gilfa expressed these issues concisely: "They were so frustrated that they insult us, saying that we're all [the beneficiaries] going to die ... that we were selected due to affinity [favoritism]."[5]

At the heart of the grievances with Chad's cash transfer program is a seemingly technical problem: targeting. Targeted programs confine eligibility to some portion of the population, but beneficiary selection is often highly imperfect in practice. As some poor people are routinely excluded from targeted programs (exclusion errors) and some nonpoor people are commonly included (inclusion errors), targeted programs can create confusion and sometimes outright conflict. Further, even in the absence of significant targeting errors, targeted programs can divide communities and create scope for a variety of negative effects on nonbeneficiaries. One beneficiary, Priscilla, summarized the issue, saying "We are divided in two parts: beneficiaries and nonbeneficiaries. They [nonbeneficiaries] envy us, because we were identified by the project, and they weren't."[6]

The targeting problem is remarkably difficult to avoid. Universal basic income programs, for example, are quite rare and are mostly implemented in places with substantial natural resource revenues, such as Alaska. Most countries, especially in the developing world, are simply unable to mobilize the resources necessary for universal programs with non-negligible transfer amounts.[7] Within the context of existing budget limitations, even poorly targeted transfers can outperform universal programs in terms of welfare outcomes.[8] While geographic targeting, for example, can potentially mitigate intra-community tensions by providing benefits to everybody within certain regions, we'll see that this approach is less than ideal and commonly associated with substantial targeting errors.

This chapter begins with an overview of targeting, which includes a description of the different types of targeting procedures used in cash programs and some statistics on the relative popularity of the different procedures. We'll then discuss the "targeting problem" and see that the methods commonly used to target poverty-alleviation programs are remarkably inaccurate. Finally, we'll take a closer look at several different ways that targeted programs can produce negative spillover effects, such as through stoking conflict within communities, increasing local prices, and worsening inequality. While these issues apply to any targeted program, cash programs are especially prone to problems because the influence of cash inevitably extends beyond the household and into the local economy.

Targeting, Explained

The overall goal of any targeting method is to correctly and efficiently identify beneficiaries for poverty-alleviation programs. Various targeting methods have been proposed and they can be broadly classified into three types: individual / household assessment, categorical targeting, and self-targeting.[9] Individual / household assessment is a method in which program administrators directly assess each individual or household for program eligibility.

Categorical targeting refers to a method where all people within some pre-specified category (perhaps in a given age group or geographic region) are deemed eligible for a program. Finally, self-targeting occurs when a program has universal eligibility, but the program is designed in such a way that only the poorest people are encouraged to participate.

Let's first consider individual / household assessment in more detail. The "gold standard" for targeting is the full means test, which conducts targeting on the basis of comprehensive information on household income or wealth that has been verified against independent data sources (such as pay stubs or tax records). This method is most often found in high-income countries, whose predominantly formal economies and administrative data systems permit reliable verification. For example, as of 2020, the United States used a full means test to target seventy-nine different federal programs, including Medicaid, the Earned Income Tax Credit, and Temporary Assistance for Needy Families, among others. There are also (limited) examples of full means testing in middle-income countries, such as Brazil, China, and South Africa.

The full means test is difficult to implement in less-developed countries because economic activity is heavily concentrated in the informal sector, which consists of casual labor, undocumented firms, and small firms. Anders Jensen showed that countries with high degrees of informality tend to have correspondingly high tax exclusion thresholds, meaning that the share of people paying any taxes is quite low in less-developed countries.[10] Specifically, Jensen found that around 1–10 and 30–50 percent of the economically active population is taxed in low-income and middle-income countries, respectively. The prevalence of informal work in these countries means that the government doesn't observe any income information for many people, particularly the poor.

The proxy means test is a popular alternative when a full means test isn't feasible. As mentioned, the proxy means test conducts targeting according to a score assigned to households on the basis of their sociodemographic characteristics (such as demographics, dwelling quality, assets, and occupations). One common form of the proxy means test relies on statistical methods to generate the weights used in the final formula. The procedure can be summarized in two steps: first estimate, using household survey data, a statistical model that predicts household income per capita on the basis of household sociodemographic traits; and second, use the model to predict income per capita for all eligible households given their sociodemographic information. In short, rather than relying on observed and verified income information, the proxy means test conducts targeting based on predicted income levels.

The proxy means test was first implemented in Chile in 1979, and then adopted by several other Latin American countries in subsequent years. Leading early examples include Colombia, Mexico, and Costa Rica. The method has since been adopted by countries in other regions, such as Burkina Faso, Cambodia, India, Indonesia, Nigeria, Pakistan, and Turkey, to name a few. While the proxy means test is quite popular in low-income settings, it's also somewhat controversial. Some people view the proxy means test as a data-driven, objective approach to targeting, whereas others argue that it leads to considerable targeting errors and lacks transparency. As demonstrated by Chad's cash program, these limitations are not trivial and can severely compromise a program's success.

Community-based targeting is another method for conducting individual / household assessment when a full means test isn't viable. With community based targeting, community members or local leaders decide themselves which people should receive program benefits. One common method for implementing community-based targeting is through community assemblies wherein residents of a community meet to discuss and rank their neighbors on the basis of need. There are two primary advantages to this approach. First, communities can conduct targeting based on their own definitions of poverty, which may or may not coincide with the standard monetary definition. Second, it's often argued that community members possess local information about their neighbors that can be used to better target poverty-alleviation programs.

There are nevertheless some important drawbacks of community-based targeting. One issue is that community-based targeting can be costly to potential beneficiaries. The community assemblies can be time-consuming, which means that people have to forego devoting valuable time to productive activities. There can also be psychological costs whereby community members find it shameful or embarrassing to discuss private matters (such as their living standards) in a public setting. A further issue is that community-based targeting can be subject to elite capture, which occurs when local elites use their influence to privilege relatives or friends in the beneficiary selection process. Elite capture is not uncommon and has been documented in China, Ethiopia, India, Malawi, and Tanzania, among other places.

Turning to categorical targeting, there are two primary types that are commonly used: demographic and geographic targeting. Demographic targeting is when programs are targeted according to membership in well-defined demographic categories, such as age, gender, or ethnicity. Age-based allowances, including both child allowances and social pensions, are leading examples of programs that rely on demographic targeting and both are quite common in developing countries. Demographic targeting is generally easy to implement and arguably more transparent than many other methods. Further, demographic targeting may have certain political advantages, as children and the elderly are often considered deserving of public support independent of their poverty status.

The extent to which demographic targeting reaches poor households depends on the strength of the correlation between poverty and the chosen demographic category. Since children and the elderly often don't work, for example, we would expect households with greater shares of younger or older members to have lower per-capita incomes, all else equal. The strength of these correlations varies considerably depending on the demographic category and the country under consideration, but they are commonly found to be modest. The implication of this is that demographic targeting can give rise to substantial inclusion and exclusion errors. In fact, demographic targeting can be viewed as a simplified proxy means test that incorporates only a single sociodemographic trait, meaning that its targeting performance will generally be inferior to the proxy means test.

Geographic targeting is a categorical method that attempts to allocate resources to a country's neediest states, districts, or villages. There are several variations of geographic targeting. One entails selecting specific areas where a program will operate, and then either providing benefits to all households in those areas or using additional eligibility criteria to identify specific households within areas. Another permits all areas to receive program benefits, but allocates benefit quotas across the various areas on the basis of need. All variants of geographic targeting nevertheless rely on poverty maps, which characterize the spatial distribution of poverty within a given country. One important consideration with poverty maps is that they must be estimated using statistical methods, because sub-national poverty rates are not directly observed.

On the one hand, household surveys provide rich information on household incomes and expenditures, but cover only a sample of households in any country. On the other hand, censuses cover (nearly) all people in a country, but generally don't collect detailed information on incomes or expenditures. Poverty maps are estimated by "linking" these data sources using a procedure like the following: (1) using household survey data, estimate a statistical model that predicts household income per capita on the basis of household sociodemographic characteristics, (2) using census data, predict income per capita for the entire population given their sociodemographic traits, and (3) use these predictions to estimate poverty rates for different areas of a country.[11] There are many different ways to estimate poverty maps, but they all generally rely on some version of this basic procedure.

Especially when only some areas are selected for program operation, geographic targeting can lead to substantial targeting errors because of inequality within areas. That is, nonpoor households often live in selected regions and poor households often live in unselected regions. This issue is compounded by the fact that, like the proxy means test, poverty maps are prone to statistical errors. A further complicating factor is that censuses are conducted infrequently because of their expense and complexity, meaning that poverty maps frequently have to rely on information that is several years out of date. There have been some recent attempts to instead use nontraditional data sources (such as satellite imagery and mobile phone data) for poverty mapping, but this research is still in its early stages.[12]

The final method for targeting poverty-alleviation programs is self-targeting. As mentioned, this method places no restrictions on eligibility, but rather relies on program design elements to encourage only the poorest to participate. This is accomplished by influencing incentives, either by increasing the cost of accessing benefits or by manipulating benefits such that they're not attractive to nonpoor households. For example, subsidized food schemes commonly make benefits available to everybody, but the subsidies are often placed on less desirable foods (for example, yellow rather than white maize) so that wealthier people are less likely to purchase the subsidized products. Using similar strategies for cash transfers is challenging because it requires either making the transfer amounts limited or making program participation arduous in some way.

Job guarantee programs, such as India's National Rural Employment Guarantee Scheme, use self-targeted cash transfers by providing payments in exchange for some form of work. To confine participation to the poor, the work performed as part of these programs is usually low-paid, low-skilled, and physically strenuous. The nature of the work can lead to the exclusion of many vulnerable people, including the elderly, disabled, or women whose work is limited by caregiving responsibilities. Targeting errors can arise for other reasons as well: nonpoor people routinely apply if wages are set too high, local elites may get preferential treatment in the event that participation needs to be rationed, and failures in labor, land, or capital markets can distort incentives for participation in complicated ways.[13]

How frequently are the various targeting methods used for cash programs? Marina Dodlova led a research effort that compiled a comprehensive database on noncontributory social transfer programs in developing countries.[14] The database covers 186 programs from 101 developing countries, with the most recent information corresponding to the year 2015. Several different types of programs are included in the database, such as unconditional cash transfers, conditional cash transfers, social pensions, and job guarantee programs. While the vast majority of the programs in the database provide cash assistance, it's important to note that some provide food aid and other services.

The 2015 data show that many programs used more than one targeting method: 40 percent used a single method, 48 percent used two methods, and 12 percent used three or more methods. Chad's cash program is a good example of how methods can be used in combination, as the program used geographic targeting to select villages and then a proxy means test to select households within villages. In terms of the relative use of the different methods, 66 percent used demographic targeting, 29 percent used geographic targeting, 26 percent used full means tests, 26 percent used proxy means tests, 19 percent used community-based targeting, and 8 percent used self-targeting. These percentages don't add up to 100 because programs frequently use multiple methods.

The relative use of the methods varies considerably across regions. In more developed countries, there is a greater reliance on full means tests, largely because these economies tend to have smaller informal sectors. For example, in Europe and Central Asia, full means tests are the leading targeting method and used in about 65 percent of programs. Lesser-developed countries, as expected, rely on methods that are more appropriate for economies with greater degrees of informality. In sub-Saharan Africa, for example, geographic and community-based targeting are more common, with approximately 42 and 46 percent of programs using these methods, respectively. Demographic targeting nevertheless remains the most popular method in sub-Saharan Africa.

The Targeting Problem

There are no perfect solutions for distinguishing the poor from the nonpoor when targeting poverty-alleviation programs, particularly in lesser-developed countries. Each targeting method has its limitations and each will give rise to exclusion and inclusion errors. This is often referred to as the "targeting problem." A useful starting point for understanding the magnitude of this problem is to simulate the performance of different targeting methods when applied to the same country. Margaret Grosh, along with several colleagues from the World Bank, conducted simulations along these lines using data from an unnamed middle-income country with representative levels of inequality and poverty.[15] The country's poverty rate is 30 percent when using an income poverty line commonly applied to middle-income countries ($3.20 per day).

Grosh's simulations considered a hypothetical policymaker that has a budget of 0.5 percent of gross domestic product and wants to distribute cash transfers to poor households in the country. With a poverty rate of 30 percent, this implies that the policymaker could give each person below the poverty line a transfer equivalent to about 14 percent of the poverty line. The simulations focused on several basic targeting methods: a proxy means test, geographic targeting, and three versions of demographic targeting (households with young children, households with elderly members, and households with widows). The authors also considered some more complicated approaches, including combinations of methods, but it's sufficient for our purposes to concentrate on the basic methods.

How well do the various targeting procedures reach poor households? One way to answer this question is to look at the exclusion error rates of the different methods, which tell us the share of poor households that fail to receive program benefits.[16] The proxy means test achieved the lowest exclusion error rate at 37 percent, which means that 37 percent of poor households were excluded from the hypothetical program. The next-best methods were demographic targeting of households with children (48 percent) and geographic targeting (54 percent). The remaining two demographic targeting methods performed the worst, with the targeting of households with elderly members and households with widows achieving exclusion error rates of 79 and 90 percent, respectively.

We can also look at how much poverty was reduced after hypothetical transfers were made to the households selected by the different targeting procedures. Grosh's team took a simple approach to allocating benefits and distributed the program's budget equally across all people living in households selected by a given targeting method. As the coverage of the population differs across the targeting methods, this means that the budget is spread more thinly for the methods that select more households.[17] The proxy means test led to the largest reduction of poverty at around 3.6 percentage points. This is unsurprising given that the proxy means test had the lowest exclusion error rate. Interestingly, the geographic and demographic targeting methods all performed similarly, with poverty reductions at just over 2.5 percentage points.

These simulations illustrate the limits of our ability to reach poor households with cash assistance: the best targeting method (the proxy means test) still misses over one-third of poor households and leads to only modest poverty reductions. Other researchers have found comparable results using data from other countries. For example, Caitlin Brown and her colleagues conducted similar simulations using data from nine African countries.[18] Averaging their results across the countries, they found that the proxy means test achieves exclusion error rates of roughly 30 and 44 percent when using two alternative poverty rates.[19] They further found that the proxy means test reduced poverty rates only to about 16 percent on average (from a starting point of 20 percent), despite using a budget sufficient to completely eradicate poverty if perfectly targeted.

Simulation results like the above can be optimistic because they don't capture targeting errors that arise because of implementation issues. In particular, households may fail to take up the program, people can strategically misreport their information to gain access to the program, or the "formula" used for statistical targeting procedures can become outdated. Consider the real-world performance of the proxy means test. Stephen Kidd and Diloá Athias of Development Pathways estimated the exclusion error rates for nineteen programs that used the proxy means test and found sobering results.[20] The average error rate across the programs was approximately 60 percent, with the lowest value at 29 percent (Uruguay) and the highest value at 96 percent (Guatemala).

What about the performance of community-based targeting, self-targeting, or the full means test? Let's first take a closer look at community-based targeting. Along with several coauthors, Vivi Alatas of the World Bank conducted an influential experiment that directly compared the effectiveness of community-based targeting and proxy means testing in the context of an Indonesian cash transfer program.[21] The researchers randomly assigned 640 eligible villages to one of three different targeting procedures: community-based targeting, proxy means test, or a hybrid method where a proxy means test was used to select beneficiaries from a longer list of households identified through community-based methods. After targeting was finished in each village, they then compared the results to expenditure data on the participating households.

The researchers found that the proxy means test was the best-performing method, though only by a narrow margin. For example, they found that the proxy means test had an exclusion error rate of 52 percent, with the hybrid method and community-based targeting only slightly higher at 53 and 54 percent, respectively. Similar experiments have been run in other countries—such as Burkina Faso, Kenya, and Niger—and have also found that the proxy means test outperforms community-based targeting.[22] In addition to elite capture, a reason for the seemingly high error rates in community-based targeting is that communities may not select beneficiaries according to income poverty. Error rates can be misleadingly high in this case, because they're not calculated based on the local definition of poverty.[23]

While the performance of self-targeting is less well understood than the other methods, some insights can be gained from India's National Rural

Employment Guarantee Scheme. This is a job guarantee program that provides rural Indian households with up to a hundred days of work each year on demand. The program is self-targeted in the sense that any rural household can apply for the program and the government is obligated to provide work for any applicants within fifteen days. Stephen Kidd and Diloá Athias, mentioned previously, looked at the targeting performance of the program and found it associated with substantial exclusion errors.[24] Specifically, they found that 71 percent of the poorest rural Indian households were excluded from the program.

One obvious reason for the high exclusion error rate is that not all of the poorest households applied for the program, whether because they weren't aware of the program, didn't want to participate, or couldn't participate for some reason (perhaps because of poor health or disability). Another reason is that the program has historically faced implementation challenges and has frequently been unable to provide jobs for everybody that applies. Importantly, the evidence suggests that this unmet demand is higher in poorer Indian states because these states are less able to implement the scheme effectively.[25] The case of the National Rural Employment Guarantee Scheme thus shows that self-targeting has clear limitations when it comes to delivering benefits to the poorest households.

The final targeting method to discuss is the full means test. Recall that this method is unavailable to many developing countries because their high levels of informality mean that their governments don't observe any income information for much of the population. A few middle-income countries have nevertheless targeted programs using the full means test, with leading examples including Albania, Brazil, and South Africa. While the full means test is often considered the "gold standard" for targeting, in practice there can be substantial implementation issues. Most notably, the full means test is data-intensive and requires capable staff for collecting information and managing databases, the definition of income used for eligibility purposes may not capture all types of income, and some income information may be self-reported and thus unreliable.

These issues can lead to substantial targeting errors. Kidd and Athias examined eleven programs that used full means testing and found an average exclusion error rate of 56 percent across all programs, which is only slightly lower than that for the proxy means test.[26] Uzbekistan's Low-Income Allowance registered the highest exclusion error rate, at 93 percent, whereas South Africa's Old Age Grant registered the lowest rate, at 8 percent. South Africa's success is partly due to the fact that it used only the full means test to screen out the richest households from the program rather than directly targeting the most poor (so that program coverage was 84 percent of the relevant population). By covering a large share of the relevant population the program achieved a low exclusion error rate, but many households above the poverty line also received benefits.

While we shouldn't expect any targeting method to perform perfectly, we've now seen that all methods are *quite* far from perfect, particularly as they often lead to the exclusion of many income-poor households. The targeting problem clearly limits the ability of any poverty-alleviation program to achieve its goals, and this includes the vast majority of cash-based programs. And there are still some deeper issues to consider. For one, the discussion so far has focused on targeting *households* with the lowest income or expenditure levels, and has implicitly assumed that doing so will also reach the poorest *individuals*. The problem is that resources are frequently distributed unequally within households, which means that many poor individuals reside in nonpoor households (and vice versa).

Let's assume that we somehow had perfect information on household incomes or expenditures and could therefore reliably identify the poorest households. To what extent would we also be reaching the poorest individuals? This is a difficult question to answer because we don't generally observe the share of resources consumed by each household member. Using data from Bangladesh, Caitlin Brown and her coauthors nevertheless attempted to tackle this question by estimating the degree of consumption inequality within households.[27] Their estimates showed that 37 percent of the *individuals* with consumption levels below the poverty line would be misclassified as nonpoor based on *household* consumption. Importantly, 41 and 45 percent of poor girls and boys resided in households with consumption levels above the poverty line.

A final issue is that the focus here has been exclusively on targeting incomes or expenditures up to this point, yet this can be misleading. Recall the means-ends distinction from Chapter 2, which highlights the fact that people have different abilities to convert the means of well-being into valuable ends. Targeting on the basis of incomes or expenditures neglects this basic fact and is therefore insensitive to human diversity. Consider two people, call them A and B, and assume that both have the same income, but that B has limited market access because they live in a remote rural area. On the basis of income, these two people appear equally well-off, but B is arguably more disadvantaged when it comes to meeting their basic consumption needs. Let's call this issue *diversity neglect*.

Also recall from Chapter 2 the functionings-capabilities distinction, which argues that the real opportunities available to people must be considered when making well-being comparisons. Income- or expenditure-based targeting can be misleading because it focuses exclusively on achieved outcomes rather than opportunities. Consider a different situation where A and B also have the same income level, but A has a greater earning capacity than B. Here, A simply chooses an income level equivalent to B (perhaps because of a stronger preference for leisure) and therefore appears equally well-off to B in terms of income. Yet, once again, B is arguably more disadvantaged because of more limited opportunities. A useful term for this issue is *agency neglect*.

The issues of diversity and agency neglect suggest that targeting on the basis of capabilities is preferable. Though capabilities are challenging to measure, Lendie Follett and I attempted to estimate the extent to which traditional income- or expenditure-based targeting gives rise to errors due to diversity and agency neglect.[28] Using data from Indonesia, we found that somewhere between 37 and 44 percent of households that we estimated as capability poor would be misclassified as nonpoor based on expenditures. We further found that both diversity and agency neglect play a significant role in generating targeting errors, with errors due to agency neglect being slightly more prevalent. Taking these results together with everything else shows that the methods commonly used to target poverty-alleviation programs are remarkably inaccurate.

Negative Spillover Effects

Following the reduction of fuel subsidies in October of 2005, the price of kerosene in Indonesia increased over 185 percent. The price increases hit poor households disproportionately hard due to their heavy reliance on kerosene for cooking and lighting. As an attempt to compensate poor households for their increased cost of living, Indonesia's government introduced Bantuan Langsung Tunai, an unconditional cash transfer program. The program intended to provide Rp100,000 per month for six months to all "near poor" households with a monthly expenditure per capita below Rp175,000. These payments amounted to about 22 percent of monthly household expenditure on average and roughly one-third of Indonesian households were to receive the cash transfer.[29]

Because Indonesia had no national database on household incomes or expenditures, the government decided to use a proxy means test to target the program. To apply the proxy means test, village heads across nearly seventy thousand villages were asked to compile a list of all households that they believed would be eligible. Enumerators from Indonesia's statistical agency then interviewed these households to collect the data they needed to apply the formula for the proxy means test. Any household that received a score below a certain threshold was classified as poor and selected to receive the cash transfer. Unfortunately, the targeting procedure was quite error-prone: 47 percent of recipients reported per capita expenditures above the Rp175,000 threshold and 18 percent of households with expenditures below the threshold didn't receive payments.[30]

The program's mistargeting produced substantial social unrest, including protests, damage to government buildings, and situations where community leaders were the targets of threats and violence. Estimates show that protests took place in approximately 35 percent of program villages, with physical injuries and threats to local officials in 15 and 12 percent of villages, respectively. The unrest led to political turmoil in some cases. In one instance, a village head organized an informal redistribution scheme to appease some people who didn't receive benefits. The village head's political rival, however, urged the program's recipients to resist the scheme and reported the village head to the local police for extorting the recipients. The village head was charged and forced to temporarily vacate his position.[31]

Indonesia's unconditional cash transfer program even led to a surge in crime in the villages it targeted. Lisa Cameron and Manisha Shah found that people living in program villages experienced a 21 percent increase in the probability of being a victim of crime.[32] They further found that these crime effects were directly related to the program's targeting errors, as the probability of being a victim of a crime increased by roughly 4 percent with every additional 10 percent of nonpoor households receiving benefits. The reason for the crime increases was that the program weakened social cohesion, reduced participation in community groups, and made communities more susceptible to existing criminality.

We've now seen two examples—Chad and Indonesia—where poverty targeting has had unintended consequences for social relations. Unfortunately, these aren't the only two examples; similar situations have been documented in Kenya, Malawi, Yemen, Zimbabwe, and other nations.[33] While targeting doesn't always lead to social conflict, these examples show that the common practice of targeting cash benefits can be harmful in important ways. And social conflict isn't the only type of negative spillover effect that can occur when communities are divided into recipients and non-recipients. Another issue is that non-recipients can be harmed if the influx of cash increases prices in local markets and diminishes people's purchasing power.

A team of World Bank researchers led by Deon Filmer examined the price effects of a large-scale conditional cash transfer program in the Philippines called Pantawid.[34] In the pilot phase of Pantawid, 130 villages across eight municipalities were randomly assigned to treatment or control status, and then households were selected within villages based on a proxy means test. Filmer's team used a unique data source to examine the impacts of Pantawid, which included information on both eligible and ineligible households from both treatment and control villages. The data were gathered in 2011, roughly two-and-a-half years after the program began, and used by the researchers to look at the impact of cash transfers on *ineligible* households in the treatment villages.

The researchers hypothesized that the cash transfers would increase the price of protein-rich perishable foods (such as eggs and fresh fish) because these foods are less easily traded across villages due to high transport and storage costs. They found that Pantawid increased the prices of perishable foods by about 6 to 8 percent in program villages, and that these effects were most pronounced in remote villages where a large share of households received transfers. The increases in the prices of perishable foods decreased the real incomes of ineligible households and led them to consume less protein-rich diets. Importantly, as these types of food are critical to the growth and development of children, they documented that the price increases had adverse health impacts on young children, specifically in terms of increased stunting (or failing to reach average heights for their ages).

Their estimates showed that these adverse effects were sizable. Specifically, they found among young ineligible children in treatment villages a rate of stunting 12 percentage points higher than the 34 percent average in control villages. The same children also showed an increase in wasting (having weights below average for their heights). Furthermore, the researchers found that in eight of the sixty-five villages studied the increase in stunting among ineligible children was sufficiently strong that it offset any decreases in stunting among eligible children. When considering the overall effect of the program on both eligible and ineligible children, they therefore found that stunting actually increased in these villages.

Pantawid isn't the only cash program that has been associated with negative spillover effects on food security. Kathleen Beegle and her coauthors examined the spillover effects of Malawi's Social Action Fund.[35] This job guarantee program began in the 1990s, but was scaled up dramatically in 2012 to cover about five hundred thousand households per year. Eligible households could apply each year to work on public projects (such as road rehabilitation or construction) for two cycles of twenty-four days each. Households were paid three hundred Malawian kwacha for each day of work, or roughly one dollar per day. Beegle's team focused on 182 villages across Malawi, where 38 were randomly assigned to control status and the remaining villages were assigned to some variation of treatment.[36]

The researchers examined several waves of data collected during the early 2010s before and after the Malawi program expansion. Because a key objective of the program was to improve food security among poor households, the team considered the impacts of the program on several measures of food security for both eligible and ineligible households in the treated areas. The results showed little or no effect on the food security of eligible households in the treated villages, and frequently negative effects on the ineligible households—most notably in the northern region of the country, where per-capita caloric intake fell by about 400 calories per adult equivalent. The explanation for the consistently negative effects on food security was nevertheless unclear, though the researchers were able to rule out some possible explanations. (For example, unlike in the Philippines, food prices hadn't increased.)

Yet another channel through which negative spillovers can occur is through increasing "relative deprivation," where untreated households are harmed because they fall behind their treated peers in terms of income, consumption, or status. In an evaluation of a different Malawian cash transfer program, conducted by a team of researchers led by Sarah Baird, relative deprivation was found to increase psychological distress among untreated adolescent girls.[37] Starting in 2008 in the Zomba district, the program provided cash support to families with school-age girls, including girls that were in school and those that had dropped out. Eligible families were randomly assigned to control and treatment groups, with some of the treated receiving conditional transfers and some receiving unconditional transfers.

The treatments were assigned by "enumeration area" and only a fraction of eligible families received cash in each area. Both during the program and after it ended, the researchers thus followed up with three different groups: households in the control areas, households in the treated areas that received cash, and also households in the treated areas that didn't receive cash. The impacts on adolescent girls living in untreated households in the treatment areas were pronounced: after one year of the program, the incidence of psychological distress among these girls was roughly 10 percentage points higher than in the pure control areas. The researchers believed that this was due to relative deprivation, in part because the effect subsided shortly after the program ended.

While the point here is to highlight the possibility of negative spillovers in targeted cash transfers, it's worth mentioning that spillover effects can be positive as well. Perhaps the best-documented positive spillovers occur when cash transfers stimulate the local economy and increase the incomes of non-recipient households. This was demonstrated in rural Kenya where a GiveDirectly program increased the consumption expenditure of non-recipient households by 13 percent, largely via increases in earnings from wage labor.[38] Similar effects can occur through informal credit and insurance markets whereby non-recipient households receive gifts or loans from recipient households.[39] Finally, cash transfers have been found to improve social cohesion in some cases by reducing distributional inequalities and improving community participation.[40]

The fact nevertheless remains that there are important issues with targeted cash transfers that can't be ignored. This chapter has highlighted two distinct issues. First, the remarkable difficulty of targeting accurately means that the vast majority of cash programs erroneously exclude many poor people (and include many nonpoor people). Second, targeted cash transfers can be associated with significant negative spillover effects, which can adversely impact non-beneficiaries and compromise broader social relations. While any targeted program is potentially subject to these issues, the problem is especially acute for cash transfers, in part because the influence of cash extends well beyond the household and into the local economy.

But can't these problems be fixed by making cash programs universal? As mentioned, most countries are unable to mobilize enough resources to implement universal programs, especially in the developing world where the vast majority of extreme poverty is concentrated.[41] Even if universal programs were widely accessible, estimates suggest that targeted programs have stronger poverty-reducing effects, even if they're badly targeted.[42] One alternative is to rely more heavily on categorical approaches, as these methods are less divisive than, say, a proxy means test. Using categorical methods, however, typically comes at the cost of increased targeting errors relative to individual or household assessment. There are thus no easy answers to the targeting problem.

CHAPTER 5

Inequality within Households

SEX-SELECTIVE ABORTION, female infanticide, and inadequate investment in girls have led to excess female mortality in many parts of the developing world. Writing in the early 1990s, Amartya Sen estimated that roughly a hundred million women were missing from the world population as a result of gender discrimination, with China and India alone accounting for eighty-one million of the missing women.[1] While Sen's estimates have been revised by several scholars, the broad consensus is that these biases are substantial and persistent.[2] The missing-women problem vividly illustrates how household decisions can lead to deeply discriminatory outcomes, which highlights a central issue with cash transfers. Specifically, how women and children are affected by cash programs depends on decisions made within the "black box" of the household, and these decisions are often unjust and inefficient.

Male-biased sex ratios are driven by "son preference," whereby households exhibit a stronger demand for boys due to their perceived higher economic value.[3] Son preference is often expressed shortly after conception through sex-selective abortions, which are enabled by the diffusion of sex-screening technologies, such as ultrasound. For example, China began witnessing notable increases in sex imbalances at birth in the 1980s, which coincided with the introduction and diffusion of diagnostic ultrasounds. One estimate shows that approximately 40 to 50 percent of the increased sex ratio could be explained by increased access to ultrasound technologies, suggesting that sex-selective abortions are an important driver of China's missing-women problem.[4]

The issue of sex-selective abortion is compounded by the fact that, in many developing countries, women are having fewer children. As fertility declines, so does the probability that couples will produce their desired number of sons. Where son preference remains sufficiently strong, it follows that parents become more likely to resort to sex-selective abortion to realize their goals. Seema Jayachandran examined the case of India and found that the desired male-to-female sex ratio increases sharply as fertility declines, as parents continue to want at least one son despite having fewer children. Jayachandran further estimated that about 33 to 50 percent of India's increased sex ratio over the past thirty years can be explained by a shift toward smaller families.[5]

Another factor contributing to the missing-women problem is that families tend to invest less in the health of girls. Evidence from India shows that these discriminatory practices can begin in the womb, as women visit antenatal clinics and receive tetanus shots less frequently when they're pregnant with girls.[6] Inequality in health investments can also be quite pronounced in early childhood due to gender differences in vaccinations, nutrition, and treatment for illnesses. Emily Oster, for example, found that excess female mortality prior to the age of five is large enough to explain nearly the entire imbalance in India's population, and that discriminatory health investments account for about 50 percent of excess female mortality.[7]

The missing-women problem is a product of household decisions that result in the systematic mistreatment of women and girls. These decisions are nevertheless influenced by deeper cultural and economic issues that lower the perceived value of girls and produce son preference. Consider the practice of patrilocality, which is a norm whereby daughters live in extended or joint families with their husband's parents after marriage. Given that sons continue to live with their birth parents after marriage, having a son ensures that parents have a caregiver in their old age. Daughters don't provide a similar benefit, which gives parents a strong motive for both having a son and investing in their sons to make sure they survive into adulthood.

Patrilineality—where family assets are passed through the male line—produces similar motives. Patrilineal societies are commonly characterized by son preference because families desire to have at least one son who can inherit the family's property. The effects of patrilineality are clearly illustrated by the case of Operation Barga, a land reform program introduced in West Bengal in 1977 with the objective of granting property rights to sharecroppers. The evidence shows that Hindu families in districts with high program participation rates witnessed a 5.1 percentage point increase in the proportion of boys born in households with a first-born girl. The explanation for this finding is that families were manipulating sex ratios to increase the chances of having at least one son to inherit their new property.[8]

Another issue that diminishes the perceived value of girls is dowry, which is a social norm where parents of daughters transfer money and other assets to the daughter's husband and his family upon marriage. The magnitude of dowry payments can be large and, as a result, girls are commonly viewed as substantial economic liabilities in places that practice dowry. These costs produce a strong disincentive for parents to have daughters, which can lead to sex-selective abortions, female infanticide, and a lack of investment in girls. The practice has also been known to give rise to "dowry deaths" or "bride burnings," where married women are murdered over dowry-related disputes. Similar to patrilocality and patrilineality, dowry thus incentivizes discriminatory behavior that leads to male-biased sex ratios.

Finally, economic factors can also contribute to son preference. Ester Boserup famously argued that the physical nature of plow-based agricultural systems favors male labor, which limits the role of women in the economy. As women have a lower economic value where their opportunities are more limited, plow-based agricultural systems tend to be associated with son preference and therefore skewed sex ratios.[9] More broadly, economic development can lead to improvements in sex imbalances, particularly because development increases the labor force participation of women. Falling fertility rates, greater access to sex-screening technologies, and persistent gender norms can nevertheless counteract the improvements that accompany economic development.

Cash transfers have been proposed as a way to mitigate the missing-women problem by providing families with financial incentives to have daughters. As cash programs don't generally challenge the deeper institutional issues that produce son preference—particularly patrilocality, patrilineality, and dowry—they can give rise to unintended household responses. Research on the relationship between household wealth and sex ratios provides some useful insights in this regard. Most notably, increased wealth has been found to skew sex ratios through increasing the accessibility of sex-screening technologies, reducing fertility, and strengthening inheritance motives in patrilineal societies. Gender imbalances in marriage markets can also increase the possibility that girls from less wealthy families "marry up," which weakens their son preference relative to wealthier households.[10]

A conditional cash transfer program in India called Devi Rupak illustrates some of these issues. The program sought to encourage parents to have more girls, but to avoid increases in fertility it gave cash only to parents of either one child or two girls. This, however, ended up incentivizing sex selection because families with a strong son preference could only get benefits by ensuring that their first (and only) child was a boy. The result is that Devi Rupak *increased* the male-to-female sex ratio at first birth by somewhere between 1.0 and 2.3 percent. While excluding one-boy families from receiving benefits could reduce this issue, it would also lessen the program's impact on fertility because families with a strong son preference would no longer have an incentive to have only one child.[11]

Devi Rupak is a clear example of how household decisions can undermine the objectives of cash programs, especially those related to women and children. This chapter will first consider some economic theories of household decision-making, which will provide useful background information for understanding how households respond to cash programs. The theoretical discussion will also highlight a main theme of the chapter, which is that household behavior is complex, heterogeneous, and frequently inefficient or inequitable. We will then consider several channels through which complex household responses to cash programs can lead to unintended consequences for women and children. As with Devi Rupak, we will see these unintended consequences typically arising when household responses to cash incentives are mediated by deeper cultural or economic issues.

Theory of the Household

Before considering in more detail how households respond to cash programs, it's useful to understand some theory of household behavior. What theories are supported by the evidence and what do these theories tell us about how households allocate resources? Microeconomic theory, generally speaking, assumes that human behavior is driven by people's attempts to satisfy their preferences. Preferences are mathematically represented by a utility function, which captures the satisfaction a person achieves by consuming some bundle

82 | POOR RELIEF

of goods and services. Human behavior is then viewed as the result of people maximizing their utility function subject to a budget constraint that defines the alternative bundles of goods and services that are affordable.

Let's consider an example to make this more concrete. Assume that a person consumes only two goods, x and y, and must decide how much of each to buy. Figure 5.1 illustrates the problem graphically, where each point in the quadrant represents a possible consumption bundle. The straight line represents the consumer's budget constraint: only the consumption bundles under the budget constraint are feasible, because the consumer has a limited income. The location of the budget constraint is determined not only by the income of the consumer, but also by the prices of the two goods. The consumer must then decide which of the feasible consumption bundles is preferable.

The figure represents preferences by indifference curves, where each curve tells us which consumption bundles give the consumer equal amounts of utility. For example, all consumption bundles on indifference curve A give

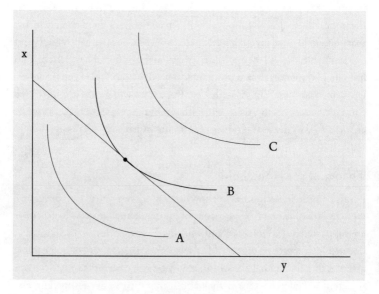

FIGURE 5.1. An illustrative example of consumer theory

the consumer the same amount of utility. Indifference curves that are further away from the origin give the consumer more utility, although some indifference curves aren't feasible given the budget constraint (for example, indifference curve C). To maximize utility subject to the budget constraint, the consumer then chooses the consumption bundle where the indifference curve is just tangent to the budget constraint. This consumption bundle is marked by a black point and corresponds to the highest feasible indifference curve (which is indifference curve B).

The traditional approach to modeling household behavior—known as the unitary model—assumes that households make decisions much like individuals. That is, households act as a single decision-making unit whose preferences can be represented by a unique utility function.[12] Roughly speaking, the assumption is that all household members either share the same preferences or that a single member makes decisions for the good of the entire household. A further assumption of the unitary model is that the non-labor incomes of household members (such as cash transfers, remittances, and gifts) influence household decisions only through the budget constraint, and even then only through their contribution to overall household income. Stated differently, household choices wouldn't be affected by a redistribution of non-labor income among household members.

The unitary model has been criticized in many ways. One important criticism is that preferences are a property of individuals rather than households. The model then requires some account of how individual preferences are aggregated into a household utility function and these accounts often require strong assumptions. Relatedly, the unitary model leaves little room for understanding the distribution of consumption and welfare within the household. It's often argued, for example, that household decisions are influenced by the relative bargaining power of different household members, with bargaining power in turn depending on several important variables (including individual incomes, wealth, human capital, and more). The unitary model doesn't provide a way to account for these factors.

The alternatives to the unitary model can be classified into two basic types: cooperative and noncooperative models. The two model types are primarily distinguished by whether they assume efficient household outcomes, where an efficient outcome is a situation where no household member can be made better off without making another worse off. Specifically, cooperative models assume that household members work together to make efficient decisions whereas noncooperative models allow for the possibility of inefficiencies through a lack of cooperation. While the unitary model also assumes that household outcomes are efficient, we'll see that cooperative models are distinct from the unitary model in the sense that they explicitly recognize that households consist of several individuals with distinct preferences.

The most popular (and general) cooperative model is known as the collective model. In the collective model, the efficiency assumption implies that households maximize the weighted sum of the utility functions of the individual members. The typical interpretation of the weights is that they represent the bargaining power of each household member. For example, if one household member receives all the weight in the household's maximization problem, then that means that they have complete control over household decisions. An especially critical feature of the collective model is that the weights generally depend on prices, incomes, or other factors that might affect a household member's bargaining power. Unlike the unitary model, this allows certain variables, such as the distribution of non-labor income, to affect household decisions.[13]

Noncooperative models, by contrast, don't assume that household members work together to achieve efficient outcomes. A household on the verge of a conflictual divorce would be a somewhat extreme example of a noncooperative household. To understand these models, it's important to understand the distinction between private and public goods. In brief, private goods can't be consumed by multiple household members at the same time (food and clothing are good examples), while public goods (such as housing or childcare) can be consumed by multiple people simultaneously. Noncooperative models then assume that each household member maximizes their own individual utility function, taking as given the choices by other household members, particularly everybody else's contribution to household public goods.

The fact that household members make decisions independently in these models implies the possibility of inefficiencies. Specifically, when household members make their decisions about how much to contribute to public goods, they don't fully account for the benefits the other members get from their choices. Public goods then tend to be underprovided. Another feature of these models is that changes in the distribution of income within the household can have interesting effects on household decisions. In the simple case of a two-person household, for example, there's a range of distributional outcomes where any (small) change in the distribution won't affect the household's decisions. This result is similar to the unitary model, although we must note that distributional changes can have complicated effects outside of this particular range.[14]

Now that we've covered the basic ideas of the various household models, let's consider which of these models (if any) are supported by the data. The unitary model makes one especially strong prediction, which is that household demand for any good is unaffected by the distribution of non-labor income across household members. This is called the "income-pooling hypothesis" and it can be tested statistically by looking at how households respond to distributional changes while controlling for total household income. The evidence is pretty clear on the income-pooling hypothesis, as many papers have tested and rejected it.[15] This suggests that the unitary model is probably not a good characterization of household behavior.

Recall that the noncooperative model makes a similar prediction, but only says that income pooling holds within some range of distributional outcomes. Rejecting the income-pooling hypothesis then doesn't necessarily mean that the noncooperative model should be rejected too. Testing between the remaining two models—the cooperative and noncooperative models—requires a different approach that centers on their efficiency predictions. One way to distinguish between the cooperative and noncooperative models is to test the "proportionality condition," which relates to how households should respond to changes in bargaining power if they're behaving efficiently. Several studies have tested this condition using household survey data and have failed to reject it, lending support to the idea that households are cooperative and efficient.[16]

There are nevertheless important examples of studies finding that households exhibit inefficient behavior. In an influential study conducted in Burkina Faso, for example, Christopher Udry found that households farm plots controlled by women much less intensively than plots controlled by men, suggesting an inefficient allocation of resources.[17] Moreover, some researchers have argued that the failure to reject the proportionality condition may be due to measurement error or statistical issues. Rather than testing efficiency using household survey data, an alternative approach is to use laboratory-type experiments where households make decisions in a controlled environment. The results from these experiments are quite clear: households routinely allocate resources in inefficient ways.[18]

To cite an example, Vegard Iversen and his coauthors conducted some simple experiments with married couples in two different districts of Uganda.[19] In these experiments, each partner was given an endowment of money and then asked to decide how much to keep for themselves and how much to put toward the couple's common pool. Any contributions to the common pool were multiplied by 1.5 and then distributed back to the couples for them to bring home. While efficiency requires that each partner allocates all of their endowment to the common pool—because this maximizes the total payout—the majority of couples failed to do so. Despite being similar in many respects, the two districts in the study also performed quite differently, which speaks to the complexity and heterogeneity of household behavior.

While the experimental evidence suggests that inefficiencies are widespread, this doesn't necessarily mean that the noncooperative model is the best characterization of all households. Some households may behave noncooperatively and others cooperatively. Still others may not behave according to economic theory at all—adhering to social norms, perhaps, rather than engaging in maximizing behavior. In short, household behavior is complex and heterogeneous, and it would be a mistake to assume any uniformity in household responses to cash transfers. Some may allocate their cash benefits inefficiently, and even efficient households can allocate their benefits inequitably when certain members have limited bargaining power. With this in mind, let's now consider the channels through which cash programs can have unintended consequences for women and children.

Mothers at the Service of the State

Peru's Juntos program, a conditional cash transfer, was created in 2005 with the primary goal of reducing the intergenerational transmission of poverty in Peru's poorest regions. The program gave $35 each month to households with young children or pregnant women, and prioritized mothers within the selected households to be the recipients of the transfers. In return, mothers were responsible for ensuring that their families complied with the program's conditions, which focused on the regular use of health and education services (requiring, for example, regular prenatal exams, health checkups for children, and school attendance). These conditions were "hard" in the sense that any failure to comply could result in reduced payments, temporary suspension, or complete removal from the program.[20]

In an especially rich qualitative study of Juntos, Tara Patricia Cookson documented the substantial costs incurred by participating women to get their money.[21] One type of cost arose because, given the lack of modern banking infrastructure in remote parts of Peru, people had to go to a certain location in their area to physically collect their regular cash payments. In areas underserved by public transportation, women commonly had far to walk, some of them leaving their homes in the middle of the night or the day prior. Even after arriving at the distribution point, the women often waited extended periods of time to collect their money, without access to toilets, seating, or shade.

The program's demands on women weren't confined to paydays. In addition to fulfilling the program's conditions, women also had to attend frequent meetings, retrieve documents from municipal offices (such as birth certificates), and make sure their "co-responsibility forms" were filled out correctly by local managers. Complicating the completion of these forms was the fact that local managers, responsible for monitoring hundreds of households, placed much of the burden on the women. In a typical example, managers streamlined the task of filling out the health-related parts of the forms by summoning many women at once to the local clinic that served them. The women were then told to retrieve their medical records from the clinic, wait in line to show them to the manager who would complete their form, and then return the records to the clinic. The result was even greater chaos than payday, with some women enduring the wait only to be sent back to the clinic staff to resolve issues with their records and then rejoin the line—in some cases multiple times.

Other costs were less mundane. Most strikingly, many mothers reported having to comply with "shadow conditions"—requirements imposed by local managers that weren't formally part of the program. It was communicated to some that cash benefits would depend on whether, for example, they had given birth at a clinic, were growing a garden, had a latrine, used the state daycare, or marched in political parades. The women complied with the shadow conditions because the local managers threatened them with suspension if they didn't. Indeed, most women didn't think to object to the threat because very few knew what the program actually required them to do. The local managers thus had considerable power over the women and frequently exercised their power in opportunistic ways.

An example will help to illustrate this last point. Juntos required that the managers get signatures from local authorities to prove that they had been working. In one case, a manager visited a school director to obtain a signature, but found that the school director was upset because the Juntos women were refusing to cook for a school lunch program. In return for the signature, the director asked that the manager announce to the women that cooking for the school lunch program was a condition of Juntos and that the women therefore needed to comply with the director's wishes. The manager agreed to make the announcement regardless of the fact that cooking in the lunch program wasn't actually a condition of Juntos.

While cooking school lunches isn't generally hazardous, other shadow conditions had harsher consequences. In particular, managers often required that expecting mothers give birth in a local health facility rather than at home. Women frequently opposed this (shadow) condition because they lived far away from the clinic and feared that if they made the trip, the clinic wouldn't be open or staffed by a qualified professional. Moreover, as indigenous women were commonly subject to discriminatory treatment by Peru's health and education systems, expecting mothers were concerned that the clinic's staff wouldn't treat them in a dignified or caring way. The shadow condition nevertheless persisted despite these concerns and, as a result, many women were obliged to make the arduous walk to the clinic while in labor.

The case of Juntos vividly illustrates that women disproportionately bear the costs of participating in cash programs, and similar studies conducted in Bolivia, Ecuador, and Mexico support this conclusion.[22] The reason for this is straightforward: many cash programs place a strong emphasis on benefiting children, and women are primarily viewed as a means to reaching the children. Rather than seeking to undermine traditional gender norms, these programs instead capitalize on them and often view the costs incurred by women as simply part of their mothering responsibilities.[23] While unconditional programs can mitigate some of the costs imposed on women, they're still typically targeted toward women for similar reasons and therefore not completely immune to these issues.

There are many other ways that cash transfers can be harmful to women. It's commonly believed, for example, that cash transfers given to women improve their bargaining power within the household due to their increased control over resources. Because the unitary model of the household predicts that households pool their incomes, this bargaining effect is most closely associated with non-unitary models. Specifically, recall that the collective model claims that households maximize the weighted sum of each person's utility function, where the weights are partly determined by the resources controlled by each member. The basic idea is then that a cash transfer to a woman improves her weight in the household maximization problem, meaning that household decisions become more closely aligned with her preferences.

Household behavior, however, can be a bit more complicated. First, a woman's bargaining power can be undermined by a cash transfer if the money is immediately diverted to her spouse or another family member. Second, a woman's spouse may control the income generated from any investments made by the woman, similarly undermining her bargaining power. Finally, a woman may make certain investments (in livestock, for example) that shift her location of work and require her to spend more time at home to maintain the investments. Less movement outside the home (including, for example, fewer trips to the market) can mean that a woman has less physical control over household resources, which can yet again compromise her bargaining power.

There are certainly studies showing that cash transfers improve women's bargaining power, as measured by whether they're able to influence certain household decisions.[24] But negative effects are more than a theoretical curiosity. In one especially detailed study, Shalini Roy and her coauthors looked at the decision-making impacts of an asset-transfer program in Bangladesh that provided women with cash, livestock, and other benefits.[25] While women retained immediate control over the assets given to them, the authors found that any new investments made by the treated households were predominantly controlled by men. This effect, coupled with the fact that the program shifted women's work inside the home, exacerbated power imbalances within households and led to women having less influence in household decision-making.[26]

Relatedly, consider the impact of cash transfers on intimate partner violence, including physical, sexual, and psychological violence. On the one hand, cash transfers can reduce violence by improving women's bargaining position within the household or by reducing the stresses associated with poverty. On the other hand, there are several ways that cash transfers can actually lead to increased intimate-partner violence. A woman's spouse, for example, might demand that she hand over the cash benefit given to her, and resort to force if she refuses. Or that spouse might resent how cash transfers tend to elevate the status of women in households, and use violence to assert dominance. The impact of cash on violence then depends on the relative strength of these opposing effects.

Though the balance of evidence suggests that cash transfers tend to lead to modest reductions in violence on average, some subgroups of women are highly vulnerable to increased violence after receiving cash transfers.[27] Manuela Angelucci, for example, looked at the effect of Mexico's Oportunidades program on domestic violence, paying special attention to how the effects varied across different sociodemographic groups.[28] Most concerningly, she found that women with less-educated husbands experienced *increased* domestic violence when they received a large transfer. She argued that this was because less educated men tend to have more traditional views of gender roles and are therefore more likely to view their wives' receipt of cash as a threat to their status.

Melissa Hidrobo and Lia Fernald reported a similar finding from Ecuador's Bono de Desarrollo Humano, an unconditional cash transfer program.[29] Using data collected roughly two years after the start of the program, Hidrobo and Fernald looked at its impact on physical and psychological violence within the treated households. Among women with more than a primary school education, they found a reduction in psychological violence within those households. For women with a primary education or less, however, the impact of the program depended on their husband's level of education. Specifically, women whose husbands had similarly low levels of education experienced a 9 percentage point increase in psychological violence.

Finally, cash transfers can affect the nature of women's work, particularly their ability to "graduate" from informal work into formal types of employment. The conventional argument is that formal employment is more desirable than informal employment because workers in the formal sector generally have higher incomes, more stable incomes, and access to other important benefits (such as health insurance and pensions). Cash transfers can facilitate women's transitions into formal work in various ways, as receiving cash transfers can empower them to work outside the home, give them resources to pay for childcare, or provide them with the capital necessary to grow their own businesses.

Cash transfers can also, however, disincentivize women to take formal jobs. First, because income from formal work is more visible to the government than income from informal work, women may avoid formal jobs so that they can remain below the income threshold necessary for receiving cash support. Second, cash benefits can act as a substitute for some of the benefits of formal work (such as pensions), meaning that women might have a decreased desire to get a job in the formal sector. Finally, if cash benefits are conditioned on children going to school, women may be less able to work outside the home because their children are no longer available to help with household chores. Much like the case of intimate partner violence, then, the effect of cash transfers on women's work is theoretically ambiguous.

Several studies have found that these disincentivizing effects are real and often pronounced. Marcelo Bergolo and Estefanía Galván examined a conditional cash transfer program in Uruguay, for example, and found that female recipients were 17 to 22 percentage points less likely to work in the formal sector relative to the control group.[30] Interestingly, this effect was less pronounced for men, despite the fact that the program's regular income testing applied to all household income derived from formal activities. The authors theorized that the program's differing effects on men and women were due to women's status as "secondary" earners. That is, in households deciding whether to maintain eligibility by giving up some formal-sector income, the woman's employment was more likely to be sacrificed. The program therefore appeared to reinforce women's secondary status.[31]

We've now seen several channels through which cash transfers can be harmful to women. These harmful effects are by no means universal, but some are quite alarming and can't be easily foreseen or prevented. The main point is that household responses to cash incentives interact with gender norms in complicated ways and our understanding of these processes is far from perfect. We've further seen cases, such as with Juntos, where cash programs reinforce traditional gender norms and make heavy demands on women to secure material benefits for their children. Ironically, this may have the effect of perpetuating women's secondary status, thus undermining the goal of reducing poverty for future generations.

Cash and Kids

Is it safe to assume that cash benefits reliably reach children? Chapter 3 presented evidence that children benefit from cash transfers, most notably through increased use of healthcare, improved attendance at school, and greater food security. While this might suggest that households reliably allocate benefits to children, a closer look at the situation reveals some important issues. In particular, the extent to which households allocate benefits to children depends on several factors, including cultural norms, the functioning of local markets, and the characteristics of household decision-makers.

Regarding cultural factors, Jacob Moscona and Awa Ambra Seck examined how different forms of social organization shape the impacts of public policies.[32] They specifically looked at the distinction between kin-based and age-based societies. While in kin-based societies the primary social unit is the extended family, in age-based societies the primary unit is the "age set." An age set is a group of people of similar age that are initiated into adulthood at the same time and, as a result, hold strong feelings of allegiance toward each other. Age-based social organization is rare in more developed countries, but not uncommon in other parts of the world. For example, roughly 200 million people in Africa live in age-based societies.

Moscona and Seck hypothesized that the impact of cash transfers on children would be stronger in kin-based societies due to greater resource sharing within families. To test their hypothesis, they looked at a couple of cash programs in East Africa, including a pension program in Uganda called the Senior Citizen Grant (SCG). An explicit goal of SCG was to improve the well-being of children, as the government believed that pension recipients would invest part of the transfer in their grandchildren. The government, however, was only partially correct. SCG produced large positive effects on several measures of child nutrition in kin-based areas, but no observable effects in age-based areas. Moscona and Seck reported similar findings for Kenya's Hunger Safety Net Program.

While some norms can weaken intergenerational ties and moderate the impacts of cash on children, other norms that incentivize investments in children can be "crowded out" by cash transfers. For example, in many developing countries parents rely heavily on their children to support them in their old age, which gives parents an additional incentive to invest in the health and education of their children. Cash transfers can diminish these incentives. Most notably, a pension program can reduce the need for parents to rely on their children in old age, which reduces their incentives to invest in children. And this effect may have implications for gender inequality, because parents have different incentives to invest in girls and boys depending on whether they practice matrilocality or patrilocality.

Natalie Bau reasoned that cash transfers given to families practicing matrilocality would more strongly disincentivize investments in girls because girls provide old-age support in these families.[33] (The same argument, of course, applies to boys in families practicing patrilocality.) To test this claim, she looked at an Indonesian pension program called Astek, which was implemented in 1977. Bau found that women from traditionally matrilocal ethnic groups who grew up in areas where Astek operated had significantly lower educational outcomes than similar women who weren't exposed to Astek. In line with her argument, she further found that the program didn't affect the educational outcomes of boys from traditionally matrilocal groups. Astek was then detrimental to matrilocal girls, but not boys.

The functioning of local markets also influences the impact of cash on children. For instance, it's commonly argued that cash transfers tend to reduce child labor, as households become less reliant on income generated by children and better able to cover the costs of schooling. But the effect can also go in the other direction. Receiving a cash transfer allows households to accumulate productive assets, which may trigger an increased demand for labor. Where imperfections in labor markets make it difficult for households to hire outside labor, they're likely to use household labor more intensively after receiving a cash transfer. And this can include the more intensive use of child labor.

Several studies have found that cash transfers decrease household reliance on child labor, but some have shown that the opposite effect is a real concern.[34] Consider Bolivia's Bolivida program, an unconditional cash transfer paid to Bolivians aged sixty-five and older. Alberto Chong and Monica Yáñez-Pagans examined whether Bolivida affected the prevalence of work among school-aged children living with an eligible elderly person.[35] While they found that the program didn't significantly affect the labor of girls, their results showed that the program led to an 8 to 13 percentage point increase in the prevalence of child labor among boys living in rural areas. The authors argued that, due to labor shortages in rural areas, households responded to the program by increasing their demand for child labor.

One possible reason why Chong and Yáñez-Pagans didn't find that Bolivida increased work among girls is that their definition of child labor didn't account for domestic work. In an evaluation of Malawi's Social Cash Transfer (SCT) scheme, Katia Covarrubias and her coauthors used more detailed data on different types of child labor, including domestic tasks like household chores and childcare.[36] Much like the case of Bolivida, they found that SCT increased household demand for child labor, particularly during the harvest season. In addition to households relying more on child labor to support their farm and nonfarm businesses, the authors found that children also engaged in more domestic work, likely because adults shifted their time to other activities. As domestic work is a traditionally female activity, we'd expect girls to be disproportionately burdened by these additional tasks.[37]

In addition to cultural factors and market imperfections, certain characteristics of household decision-makers can also lead to counterintuitive effects on children. Recall that the evidence suggests that noncooperative household behavior is quite common, meaning that household members don't necessarily work together to make efficient decisions. This lack of cooperation means that spouses may not have reliable information on each other's preferences, which can create uncertainty that affects household investments in children. For example, a woman may be less willing to use the resources at her disposal to invest in children if she's uncertain about her immediate private consumption or if she's concerned that her husband will seize any future returns from investments in her children.

Debosree Banerjee and Stephan Klasen conducted a unique experiment in Karnataka, South India, to test this hypothesis.[38] In their experiment, they asked women with children to allocate different hypothetical amounts of money between their children and themselves. The money given to the children could be allocated across food or health expenses, and the amounts could be different for boys and girls within these categories. The money women allocated to themselves was explicitly framed as a contribution to their own private savings. Interestingly, for each decision, the women were asked if they'd expect their spouse to make a different allocation or whether they were uncertain about their spouse's preferences for that decision.

Women who were uncertain about their spouse's preferences allocated significantly smaller amounts of money to children and more to their own private savings. For example, when given 10,000 rupees to allocate, women who were completely uncertain about their spouse's preferences chose to put about 3,000 rupees more into private savings on average. These results offer an explanation for why cash transfers can have mixed effects on children: a lack of cooperation within households means that decision-makers may not have reliable information on their spouse's preferences and the resulting uncertainty can lead to inefficient levels of investment in children. Banerjee and Klasen therefore concluded that "cash transfers to mothers may not result in an increase in child investment."[39]

Whether or not cash transfers to women benefit their children also depends on women's preferences. Recall that the idea behind giving cash benefits to women is that it improves their bargaining power, which in turn increases the share of household resources devoted to children. The basic assumption here is that women are more strongly inclined than their spouses to support their children. While some early empirical work supported this idea, more recent research has raised doubts.[40] For example, as part of an evaluation of Morocco's Tayssir program, researchers randomly varied the gender of the transfer recipient and found that the recipient's gender didn't significantly affect children's educational outcomes.[41]

A possible explanation for these inconsistent findings is that investments in children are understood as investments in the future. This means that women's time preferences relative to their spouses' play an important role in determining the share of resources devoted to children. That is, when a woman is more willing to forego present benefits to obtain future benefits, she is more likely to allocate a greater share of resources to her children (and vice versa). Note that this explanation suggests that it's not the gender of the recipient but rather the time preferences of the recipient that determines investments in children. This is a challenging idea to test, but Charlotte Ringdal and Ingrid Hoem Sjursen conducted an interesting experiment to shed some light on the issue.[42]

The experiment was conducted with 287 couples in Dar es Salaam, Tanzania. Everyone was first asked in private to complete a simple task intended to gauge their time preferences. Specifically, they were given 3,000 Tanzanian shillings and asked how much of that amount they wanted to receive immediately and how much they wanted to receive after three weeks. They were told that any amount they chose to receive after three weeks would be doubled and then sent to them later through a mobile money service. The share of money that someone chose to receive later thus served as a measure of that individual's patience: people opting to receive more money after three weeks were deemed more patient than people choosing to receive less at a later date.

After completing the time preference task, couples were then asked to allocate 15,000 shillings across the wife, the husband, and one of their children. This time, they were informed that while money allocated to the husband and wife would be paid out immediately in cash, money allocated to the child would be paid out as a certificate for tutoring. Importantly, any amount given to the child yielded a tutoring certificate worth more than three times that amount. When making their decisions, couples were randomly assigned to one of four treatments, as shown in Table 5.1. Notice that the four treatments give an increasing amount of control or bargaining power to the wife. In line with conventional wisdom, the authors hypothesized that more bargaining power to the wife would increase the share going to children.

The results contradicted their hypothesis. On average, the share going to children didn't increase as women were given more bargaining power. If anything, the contributions to children fell as women gained control over the decision-making process. Time preferences turned out to be key in explaining

Treatment	Definition
Husband dictator	The husband chooses the allocation.
Husband bargaining	The husband proposes an allocation to the wife, which she can accept or reject. If she rejects, the endowment is reduced by 500 shillings and she must make her own proposal to the husband. The process continues until a proposal is accepted.
Wife bargaining	This treatment is the same as the husband bargaining treatment, except that the wife makes the first proposal.
Wife dictator	The wife chooses the allocation.

TABLE 5.1. Experimental treatment groups

these results. For women who were more patient than their husbands, having increased bargaining power increased the average share going to children. Conversely, for women who were less patient than their husbands, increased bargaining power was associated with decreased contributions to the children. And the magnitude of this effect was fairly large: relative to more patient women, less patient women gave about 19 percentage points less to children when given full control.

These results suggest that time preferences are critical to understanding the impact of cash transfers on children. When cash is given to relatively less patient women, the effect can be to *decrease* the share of resources devoted to children. As Ringdal and Sjursen found that men tended to be more patient than women, one might argue that targeting cash transfers toward men would be more efficient, at least if the objective is to benefit children. This, however, would come at the expense of gender inequality, as the results showed that when men were in control they devoted substantially more to boys than girls. Women displayed no such favoritism, implying the possibility of a tradeoff between equity and efficiency when deciding whether to target men or women within the household.

This chapter has established that household decision-making can and often does undermine the objectives of cash transfer programs. Specifically, cash transfers can prove harmful to women by burdening their time, compromising their bargaining power, subjecting them to increased violence, and affirming their status as secondary earners. Children may not reliably benefit (and are sometimes harmed) by living in households receiving cash, largely because certain cultural forces, market imperfections, and characteristics of household decision-makers can distort how households allocate resources. Stated simply, cash transfers can have unintended consequences and these are frequently to the detriment of women and children.

CHAPTER 6

When Markets Fail

THE PHRASE "money can't buy everything" is all too common, but few understand it like the Munjiru family. Sheilla Munjiru was born on January 5, 2020, with severe jaundice and needed an immediate blood transfusion.[1] To make matters worse, doctors informed the family that Sheilla's blood type was O-negative, not only rare but incompatible with transfusions from other blood types. The rural Kenyan clinic where Sheilla was born had no blood to give her and neither did the county hospital. The infant was thus whisked to Kenya's largest referral hospital, Kenyatta National Hospital in Nairobi, but there was no blood there either. After three days of waiting and hoping for a transfusion, Sheilla's mother, Catherine Wangari, was told that type O-negative blood was unlikely to arrive soon and she should try to find it on her own.

In desperation, Sheilla's family turned to social media to find a donor. Soliciting direct donations of blood is risky if it means the blood isn't subjected to the same rigorous testing procedures it would be through a blood bank. There are factors, too, that make it especially challenging to find donors in Kenya, including a common concern people have about contracting diseases when donating blood. Many donors are also held back by superstitions, such as a belief that a person can't receive blood from somebody of a different ethnicity. Despite these obstacles, Sheilla's family persevered and succeeded in finding two donors after just a few days.

Unfortunately, the day after the donors came, more challenges arose. The doctors and nurses told Sheilla's family that her blood type was *not* actually O-negative—it was B-positive—and also did not clarify that their donors' blood would still do, because O-negative blood can be given to patients with any blood type. In addition to believing they needed to find a new donor, the family was told that the hospital couldn't perform transfusions because it had run out of catheters. While Sheilla's family was able to find money to pay for the $130 catheter, none of the pharmacies in Nairobi had any in stock. They eventually found a catheter at the fifth private hospital they visited, and a new donor shortly thereafter, but eleven days had elapsed by the time Sheilla received her transfusion. It was a moment of great relief to her family but also bittersweet, as the doctors warned that Sheilla might have suffered permanent brain damage.

Persistent blood shortages in Kenya mean that experiences like this family's are not uncommon. In the year before Sheilla was born, for example, Kenya's transfusion service collected just 164,000 units of blood, only a fraction of the roughly one million units needed. Part of the problem was that the US government had been supporting Kenya's blood safety and transfusion infrastructure, but that funding was gradually reduced and then ultimately discontinued in 2019. While US officials claimed they provided ample warning, the opinion of the Kenyan government was that support ended abruptly and prematurely. As a result, the government failed to provide for transfusion services in its 2020 budget. These budget issues led to difficulties funding blood drives and shortages of equipment such as blood bags.[2]

In a well-functioning market for any ordinary good, shortages don't occur because prices adjust to bring supply in line with demand. But blood is no ordinary good and the price mechanism is suppressed by the Kenyan government. The government chooses to do this because it wants to comply with the World Health Organization's recommendation "to work towards and maintain 100% voluntary non-remunerated blood donation to provide universal access to safe blood and blood products for all patients requiring transfusion therapy."[3] To achieve this, WHO guidelines call for providing blood transfusions free of charge using blood provided by unpaid donors. The lack of a price for blood is evident in Sheilla's situation: while Sheilla's family was able to buy the catheter needed for the transfusion, they couldn't buy blood they knew to be safe.[4]

What's so problematic about a market for blood? In addition to the widely held belief that access to safe blood is a basic human right, there are concerns that payments for blood would disproportionately attract poor donors who are more likely to carry transmissible diseases. A further concern is that payments would compromise the blood supply because people donating for altruistic reasons may be less willing to donate if they're paid.[5] A market for safe blood is then somewhat of an oxymoron, as the act of paying can compromise the safety and sustainability of the blood supply. This is not to say that Kenya's blood shortages are justified, but rather that the shortages stem from deep ethical issues associated with attaching a price to blood.

The market for blood is an example of a repugnant market, which refers to situations where allocating resources through markets is ethically objectionable. Morality, of course, varies across time and place, but there are nevertheless many examples of "goods" for which exchanges are generally seen as repugnant. Trade in human beings is a leading example, as slavery, indentured servitude, and human trafficking are widely viewed as objectionable. Markets for human remains or organs—including cadavers, kidneys, or livers—also tend to be unacceptable. Other well-known examples include markets related to reproduction and sex, drugs and alcohol, or even friendship and love.[6] Because of their repugnance, many countries have laws or policies in place that heavily regulate or outright ban the exchange of goods and services in these cases.

Importantly, markets for many basic liberties are also constrained by repugnance, in part due to the widespread belief that these liberties are essential for a well-functioning, democratic society. This includes civil liberties, such as freedom of assembly, freedom of speech, the right to privacy, and the right to private property. It also includes political liberties like the right to vote, the right to stand for office, the right to a fair trial, and freedom from arbitrary arrest. Generally speaking, rights tend to fall outside the scope of the market. To view something as a right implies some entitlement that's independent of a person's ability to pay. Many rights are therefore literally priceless.

In her book *Why Some Things Should Not Be For Sale,* Debra Satz outlines a compelling theory of what makes certain markets repugnant.[7] On the one hand, Satz argues that some markets are repugnant due to the characteristics of people entering the market, either because they're disadvantaged by limited information or because they're so vulnerable that they'll accept any terms of exchange. On the other hand, she argues that repugnance can result from the outcomes of markets—namely, when markets are harmful to some participants or when they cause harm on a social level by undermining people's ability to interact as equals. Satz claims that when markets raise issues in any of these areas, they're likely to be viewed as repugnant.

Cash transfers are a market-oriented approach to poverty alleviation: giving households money is only effective when people can buy what they need to make themselves better off. For those dimensions of well-being that can't be advanced through markets, cash transfers are powerless. Being in good health, for example, may depend critically on having access to safe blood, but having cash isn't that helpful when blood is priceless. Repugnance is, of course, one important reason for "missing markets," but there are many other reasons as well. In this chapter, we'll first discuss why markets are missing for some goods and see several examples where markets have failed to deliver goods that are vital to human well-being. The chapter concludes by considering whether cash transfers can in any way contribute to overcoming the problem of missing markets.

Missing Markets, Explained

A missing market is a particular type of market failure, which is any situation where a market fails to achieve an efficient outcome.[8] The unique issue with missing markets is not just that the market is inefficient, but that it doesn't exist at all. In addition to repugnance, there are many reasons why markets can be missing. For example, some types of goods don't have well-defined property rights, barriers to market entry can prevent producers from offering certain goods or services, and asymmetric information can cause markets to unravel. In all of these situations, the absence of a market means that the net benefits to society aren't maximized.

A market maximizes the net benefits to society when marginal social benefits equal marginal social costs. Marginal social costs represent the costs to society associated with the production of *one additional unit* of a good or service, whereas marginal social benefits represent the benefits associated with *one additional unit*. To fix ideas, consider a simple market for bread that consists of a single producer and a single consumer. Let's say that the producer can bake as many loaves of bread as they'd like, but that their marginal costs are increasing with production: $1 for the first loaf, $2 for the second loaf, and so on. Similarly, the consumer can buy as many loaves as they'd like, but their marginal benefits are decreasing with consumption: $5 for the first loaf, $4 for the second loaf, and so on.

Assuming that the price for bread is $3, we know that the producer will want to continue selling bread until their marginal cost exceeds the price because at that point they'll lose money. The consumer will likewise want to continue buying bread until the price exceeds their marginal benefit. It then follows that the two parties will exchange three loaves of bread and that neither party could be made better off by exchanging more or less bread. The market is efficient because the net benefits to the producer and consumer are maximized. Interestingly, the two parties exchange up to the point where marginal benefits equal marginal costs, as the gains from trade are completely exhausted at that point. Just like in well-functioning markets with many producers and consumers, the price acts as a coordinating mechanism that brings about the socially efficient outcome.

Missing markets, however, lack prices and one reason for this relates to the type of good being traded. The standard typology of goods used by economists organizes all goods along two basic dimensions. Along one dimension, we can classify goods as either rival or non-rival. A good is rival in consumption if the same unit of the good can't be consumed by more than one person at the same time. The second dimension classifies goods as either excludable or non-excludable, where excludability means that producers can prevent people that don't pay from consuming the good. Figure 6.1 presents the resulting fourfold typology of goods based on these dimensions and provides a few examples for each type of good.

Non-excludable goods are frequently priceless, much like blood but for different reasons. To understand this, let's first consider excludable goods in more detail. Producers of bread, for example, have well-defined property rights over what they produce, including exclusive ownership, the right to sell their bread to other people, and the right to punish anybody that doesn't pay (for example, through legal action). A producer consequently has the right and ability to charge a price for a quantity of bread. In contrast, consider a non-excludable good like an open-access water resource: nobody has well-defined property rights over the resource and therefore nobody has a clear right or ability to make people pay to use it. It's extremely difficult to attach a price to non-excludable goods as a result.

	Excludable	Non-excludable
Rival	*Private goods* ·Blood ·Bread ·Clothing	*Common-pool resources* ·Water resources ·Forest ·Grazing lands
Non-rival	*Club goods* ·Streaming services ·Computer software ·Museums	*Public goods* ·Stable Climate ·Clean air ·Public safety

FIGURE 6.1. Types of goods

The deeper problem is that inefficiencies arise when non-excludable goods lack prices. Common-pool resources are rivalrous, implying that one person's use imposes a cost on other people by diminishing their ability to use the resource. In fisheries, for example, one fisher's catch reduces the stock of fish, hindering the ability of others to catch fish. The marginal social cost of fishing is then the sum of the marginal private cost of fishing (the production cost of additional fishing) and the marginal external cost (the cost imposed on others from additional fishing). Because of the lack of prices, fishers won't fully take into account the marginal external costs of their actions and will commonly fish until their marginal benefits equal their marginal *private* costs. Marginal *social* costs will then exceed marginal social benefits, meaning that the common-pool resource is over-exploited.

Public goods suffer from a similar problem. The fact that public goods are non-rivalrous means that many people can benefit from the production of a public good. Let's say somebody builds an air filtration system that provides clean air for themselves and for others downwind.[9] In this case, the marginal social benefit of running the system is the sum of the marginal private benefit (that is, the benefit to the producer of additional filtration) and the marginal external benefit (the benefit to others). As people won't generally pay for the public good, the producer won't fully consider the marginal external benefits of filtration and will only run the system until their marginal *private* benefits equal the marginal social costs. This means that the public good will tend to be under-provided because marginal *social* benefits will exceed marginal social costs.

These issues are known, respectively, as the *tragedy of the commons* and *free-rider* problems. In the absence of any collective efforts to solve the underlying market failures, people typically lack reliable access to non-excludable goods. Common-pool resources are degraded and public goods are deficient. And the lack of prices means that giving people money won't get them better access. It's worth noting that the market failures associated with non-excludable goods are instances of the more general problem of "externalities." An externality occurs when somebody's economic activity produces a side effect, negative or positive, for which they don't pay or aren't paid. Externalities can affect excludable goods as well.

Consider cars, a private good. Driving a car produces an externality because burning gasoline contributes to air pollution that adversely affects other people. As drivers don't incur any direct costs when they create air pollution, they'll tend to ignore the externality when they make decisions about how much to drive. In economic terms, they'll drive to the point where their marginal benefits equal their marginal *private* costs, but the presence of the externality means that marginal *social* costs will exceed marginal social benefits at this point. The market is then inefficient and drivers will tend to produce too much pollution. This is essentially a missing-market problem, as there's no well-defined price for clean air and people can therefore "use" it without paying.

Excludable goods can be affected by market failures in many other ways. One important problem is barriers to entry, which can prevent producers from supplying goods or services to a market. For example, producers might not be able to access some resource or input that is essential for production, they may not have the technological capacity to produce some good, or high up-front costs may deter their entry. When barriers to entry are moderate, markets are typically characterized by monopoly or oligopoly (respectively, one or a few producers). In the case of monopoly, the producer has the ability to influence the market price, setting it above their marginal cost to reap additional profits. This results in an inefficiently low quantity of goods or services traded.

When barriers to entry are more extreme, producers don't have the ability or incentive to enter the market at all. This type of missing market is quite common in markets for basic services—such as piped water, sanitation, or electricity—because these services frequently require substantial up-front investments in infrastructure. Electricity services, for example, require up-front investments in land, the construction of power plants, the purchase of costly equipment, and the extension of power lines. These up-front costs are a major reason why many people in developing countries aren't connected to the electrical grid. Most notably, only 68 percent of Africans live in areas connected to the grid, with countries like Burkina Faso (31 percent), Ethiopia (32 percent), and Niger (35 percent) having extremely limited coverage.[10]

Asymmetric information is another issue that can lead to missing markets. Information is asymmetric when one party to a transaction knows something the other doesn't. Information asymmetries can result from the problem of hidden attributes, which arises when some feature of a person engaging in a trade or some aspect of the good being traded isn't known to the other parties. (For example, somebody selling a plot of land may have better information on its quality than a potential buyer.) Another source of asymmetric information is the problem of hidden actions, which arises when one party to a transaction can't know or verify some action undertaken by the other party. (For example, a creditor may not know what a debtor will actually do with a loan.)

To see how asymmetric information can lead to missing markets, consider a simple market for health insurance. Let's say an insurance company offers a standard policy where everybody pays the same premium, which corresponds to the average cost of medical expenses among the group. Healthy people will know that they're unlikely to incur substantial medical expenses and, as a result, they'll find that the premium is too costly. Healthier people are then more likely to opt out of the policy, leaving only less healthy people in the insurance pool. To cover their costs, the insurance company then has to raise the premium, which further pushes healthy people out of the market. This process would continue until the market collapses completely and nobody has health insurance.

The hidden attribute problem in this case leads to "adverse selection" where healthier people drop out of insurance markets. Even if the insurance company could remedy this issue—for example, by screening policyholders—the problem of hidden actions still remains. The problem of hidden actions leads to "moral hazard" wherein people with insurance face distorted incentives to manage their risks. For example, having health insurance can reduce a person's incentive to exercise or eat healthy because they know that the insurer will cover their healthcare costs. While the insurance company can respond by monitoring policyholders or having them pay a deductible, these costs can undermine the market by making the policy unattractive to the company or policyholders.

Information asymmetries are closely related to yet another issue, namely "transaction costs." Transaction costs are basically the costs associated with trading in a market. The costs of screening or monitoring insurance policyholders are good examples of transaction costs. Other types of transaction costs include the costs of bargaining and negotiating prices, the costs of drawing up contracts, the costs of complying with regulations, or the costs of physically transporting goods from one location to another. Transportation costs are especially relevant to developing countries because poor infrastructure (including roads and bridges) makes it extremely costly for people living in remote rural areas to access certain goods and services.

Limited market access due to transportation costs has important implications for agricultural productivity, as many farmers in developing countries don't have adequate access to productivity-enhancing inputs like fertilizer or high-yielding seeds. For example, a recent study of 1,180 villages in northern Tanzania examined how the remoteness of each village affected the rate at which farmers adopted chemical fertilizers. The authors measured remoteness as proximity to major hub towns where distributors are located and found that the most remote villages experienced adoption rates *at least* 35 percentage points lower than the least remote villages.[11] Though the fertilizer market may not be completely missing in remote villages, transaction costs make accessing it extremely costly for many farmers.

Missing Markets Everywhere

In March and April of 2022, India and Pakistan witnessed an unprecedented heatwave. New Delhi saw temperatures rise above 110 degrees Fahrenheit for several days and Nawabshah in Pakistan experienced temperatures above

120 degrees. March in India was the hottest in recorded history and the hottest in Pakistan since 1961.[12] Heatwaves have become increasingly common in South Asia and the consequences are dire. India, for example, has witnessed a 55 percent increase in heat-related deaths over the past twenty years. Beyond increased deaths, the heatwaves have also led to cardiovascular and respiratory complications, adverse pregnancy outcomes, worsened sleep patterns, and deteriorating mental health.[13]

Unsurprisingly, there's a well-established relationship between extreme heat events and climate change. Research shows that the heatwaves in India and Pakistan were somewhere between thirty and one hundred times more likely to have happened because of climate change.[14] The effects of climate change extend well beyond heatwaves and include a heightened risk of many other extreme weather events, such as hurricanes, floods, droughts, and wildfires. Importantly, these extreme weather events disproportionately affect the least well-off given their dependence on natural resources, precarious housing conditions, and political marginalization, among other things. Some estimates show that climate change will push between 32 and 132 million additional people into poverty by 2030.[15]

Climate change is arguably the result of one of the biggest market failures ever experienced. In particular, the climate is a non-excludable good that suffers from a missing-market problem. Because the climate lacks a well-defined price, people don't bear the full costs of their actions when they burn fossil fuels for electricity, heat, or transportation. The result is that humans tend to produce inefficiently high levels of greenhouse gases and these emissions disrupt the climate. People with higher incomes, of course, have a greater ability to cope with the consequences of global warming by moving to safer locations, buying better housing, or paying for air conditioning. However, few would argue that extra cash is a perfect substitute for the harms caused by rising temperatures.

The issue of climate change clearly illustrates that missing markets are not just an obscure problem with limited relevance outside academic economics. In reality, missing markets are everywhere and present critical threats to the well-being of humans, wildlife, and ecosystems. While overcoming missing markets often requires public action, governments frequently fail to take appropriate measures. Limited resources, limited information, and limited political commitment regularly impede public action and mean that missing markets are allowed to persist. In what follows, we'll take a closer look at some especially pernicious and persistent missing markets, paying special attention to their implications for people living in extreme poverty.

Outdoor air pollution is an important environmental problem that's closely related, yet distinct from climate change. Research shows that 7.3 billion people, or 94 percent of the global population, live in areas exposed to unsafe levels of air pollution. Air pollution is especially severe in low- and middle-income countries due to their rapidly developing industrial sectors, slash-and-burn agricultural practices, and less stringent air quality regulations. Of the population that's exposed to excessive air pollution, roughly 80 percent reside in these countries. Poor air quality has severe consequences for human health. Four million people die each year from outdoor air pollutants and many others suffer from cardiovascular, respiratory, and neurological diseases.[16] Much like the climate, the non-excludability of clean air means that it's neither abundant in supply nor available for purchase.

Water suffers from similar issues. Over 80 percent of global wastewater is not safely treated before it's released into the environment. One consequence of this is that roughly two billion people across the world use a drinking water source that's contaminated with human feces, putting them at risk of contracting cholera, dysentery, typhoid, and polio.[17] Water pollution has especially grave implications for children. UNICEF estimates that seven hundred children under the age of five die each day from diarrhea due to exposure to unsafe water. In addition, approximately 144 million children under five worldwide are stunted, partly as a result of the lasting consequences of waterborne illnesses.[18] Similar to air pollution and climate change, these issues stem largely from the non-excludability of water resources.

But how can water be a nonmarket good when we sometimes pay for it? Water is more complicated than many other natural resources and can be priced in certain situations. For example, somebody can extract water from its source and sell it in bottles. Or, authorities can assign rights to use a source of water and allow users to trade those rights (as in Australia's Murray-Darling Basin). In its natural state—especially in large lakes, rivers, and aquifers—water is nevertheless non-excludable and vulnerable to the tragedy of the commons. Especially in developing countries, people rely heavily on open-access water resources and excessive pollution can have detrimental effects on human health, fishery production, and agricultural yields, among other things.

Non-excludability is by no means confined to environmental goods and services. For example, it can be costly or impossible to exclude people from certain infrastructure investments, such as roads, bridges, dams, sanitation facilities, or even communication technologies. Let's consider roads in more detail. Roads are physically accessible to anybody that wishes to use them and it can be prohibitively costly to install barriers, checkpoints, or tolls to restrict access. Even if access could be restricted, it's difficult to monitor and enforce exclusions without incurring significant administrative costs. The result of this non-excludability is that it's typically impractical to charge people for using a road and, as such, markets for roads tend to be missing.

Roads are especially lacking, in quantity and quality, in developing countries, in part because governments have limited capacities to intervene and directly provide transportation infrastructure. While upper-middle-income countries have an average of 1.04 kilometers of road per square kilometer of surface area, lower-income countries average about one-tenth this amount. Further, some estimates show that only about 18 percent of roads are paved in lower-income countries, with only 16 percent of roads paved in sub-Saharan Africa. These infrastructure issues severely constrain economic growth. For example, sub-Saharan Africa could increase annual growth by about 1.7 percentage points if brought up to the global median of infrastructure development.[19]

Barriers to entry are arguably the most important factor limiting some types of infrastructure investment. For example, building and maintaining broadband internet networks is extremely expensive and requires substantial up-front investments in planning and engineering, laying fiber optics or other cables, and building transmission towers, among other things. While developing countries have made progress toward expanding high-speed internet access in recent years, coverage is still far from complete. The International Telecommunications Union estimates that roughly 24 percent of people in the least developed countries still aren't covered by broadband internet. And this statistic masks some important disparities. Approximately 85 percent of people in South Sudan, 76 percent of people in Niger, and 60 percent of people in Guinea aren't covered by broadband internet.[20]

Quality education is another critical service that suffers from missing markets. Many developing countries have made considerable progress toward achieving universal primary education in recent decades, but it's become abundantly clear that "schooling ain't learning."[21] Roughly 125 million children worldwide don't attain functional literacy or numeracy after attending four years of school. Even upon completing primary school, millions of children don't have the basic competencies in reading or math needed to continue their education. In cross-country comparisons of standardized test scores, it's been shown that the average student in a low-income country performs worse than 95 percent of students in high-income countries.[22] What's the explanation for this "global learning crisis"?

The World Bank has argued that there are four immediate causes of the learning crisis: children arrive in school unprepared to learn, teachers lack the skills or motivation to be effective, resources commonly fail to reach classrooms, and poor management and governance often undermine schooling quality. These systemic issues in turn stem from a basic misalignment between the interests of education "consumers" (such as students and parents) and "producers" (including politicians, private schools, and teachers). In particular, rather than focusing on improving learning outcomes, politicians act to preserve their positions in power, private schools focus on the pursuit of profit, and teachers seek to maintain employment and protect their incomes. In other words, producers simply aren't held accountable to consumers.[23]

A critical reason why producers aren't held accountable is that consumers lack information. For example, parents frequently lack information about the performance of schools, the resources schools are entitled to receive, or the potential gains from different policies to improve learning. Such limited information weakens the ability of consumers to hold schools and teachers directly accountable, and also weakens their voices relative to policymakers and politicians. If parents and children had better information about schools, they could make more informed choices about which schools to attend and this would pressure lagging schools to improve quality. Better information could also lead to more effective oversight of schools and would further allow consumers to capably lobby governments for improved policies.[24]

Stated differently, markets for education in developing countries are constrained by asymmetric information, which can lead to both moral hazard and adverse selection. Moral hazard arises because schools have limited incentives to provide high-quality education when quality isn't fully observed by parents. Adverse selection arises because parents can't effectively evaluate different schooling options, which can lead them to select schools based on observable attributes. For example, low-quality schools may remain in the market because parents select them over high-quality schools due to their lower fees. The end result of these forces is that high-quality schools are either exceedingly scarce or missing altogether in many areas of the developing world.

The existing evidence largely supports this explanation of the learning crisis. For example, Tahir Andrabi and his coauthors conducted an interesting experiment in Pakistan where they gave parents in randomly selected villages report cards, which included information on the test scores of their children and the average test scores of all schools in their village. They found that students in both private and public schools in the treated villages witnessed increased test scores, with an additional gain of 42 percent over the control villages. The authors argued that these changes emerged because more informed parents placed increased pressure on schools, both through direct parent-school interactions and through increased competition in the market for education.[25]

Finally, it's important to note that the quality of healthcare in developing countries is similarly plagued by asymmetric information. Approximately 8.6 million people in low- and middle-income countries die each year from treatable conditions, with five million of these deaths corresponding to situations where patients sought medical assistance but received low-quality care. Mirroring the case of education, many believe that these quality issues are due to a misalignment of interests between "producers" and "consumers" of healthcare. Producers evidently aren't held accountable for their actions and a major reason for this is that consumers lack information about the quality of care that they receive.[26] According to a comprehensive review of the literature, this explanation is consistent with the evidence, as healthcare providers "certainly do behave such that we can suspect market failures due to asymmetric information."[27]

Overcoming Missing Markets

Cash transfers rely heavily on markets for poverty alleviation, but this approach is only effective to the extent that people can buy what they need to pull themselves out of poverty. In short, cash transfers inherit the limits of markets and we've seen that markets fail to deliver many goods that are vital to human well-being. Safe blood, clean air, clean water, quality education, and quality healthcare are just a few leading examples. There are many others. Though much of our discussion has focused on developing countries, many of the same issues affect more developed countries, albeit to a lesser extent. For example, healthcare providers are more likely to be held legally liable for poor care in high-income countries, which can mitigate the consequences of asymmetric information.

Ironically, market failures provide a major justification for giving people cash in the first place. One argument for cash transfers is that credit markets are imperfect and systematically exclude poor households, largely because they lack the collateral to obtain loans. When this is the case, cash transfers can give people the resources to make profitable investments to alleviate their poverty. Another argument for cash transfers is that insurance markets similarly exclude poor households and, as such, giving people money can help smooth income fluctuations and improve their welfare. In both these cases, market failures serve to rationalize cash programs, but advocates tend to neglect the fact that other types of market failures severely constrain what cash can accomplish.

Supporters of cash transfers frequently respond to these critiques by claiming that cash programs can actually help communities overcome certain market failures. To be clear, supporters don't usually claim that cash programs can help communities overcome *all* market failures. They instead tend to put forward a more narrow argument, which is that cash transfers can be used to pay for some non-excludable goods, most notably public goods. To make this concrete, let's say that some community suffers from low agricultural yields due to the poor maintenance of their irrigation infrastructure. In this case, supporters might argue that beneficiaries of a cash program could simply pool their money to pay for maintaining the irrigation infrastructure. Is this plausible?

The free-rider problem is unfortunately a major impediment to this kind of resource pooling. Let's revisit this problem by considering a community that only consists of two farmers, which we'll call A and B.[28] Assume that each farmer receives a $10 cash transfer, which they can either use to help maintain the irrigation system or keep for their own private consumption. As a public good, the irrigation system is both non-excludable and non-rival, which means that both farmers will benefit from increased crop yields when any one farmer contributes to maintaining the system. Let's say that when one farmer contributes to maintaining the system they both receive a benefit equal to $8.

From a societal perspective, it's optimal for both farmers to contribute to maintaining the system. In this case, each farmer receives a net benefit of $6 (the benefit of $16 minus the cost of $10). The farmers will nevertheless fail to reach this outcome. To see why, take the perspective of farmer A. If farmer B contributes, farmer A either contributes and receives a net benefit of $6, or doesn't contribute and receives a net benefit of $8. If farmer B doesn't contribute, farmer A either contributes and incurs a net loss of $2, or doesn't contribute and receives nothing. No matter what farmer B does, farmer A is always better off if he or she avoids contributing. And farmer B faces the exact same incentives, which means that neither farmer will want to contribute.

This is the free-rider problem: while it's socially optimal for both farmers to contribute to maintaining the irrigation system, neither farmer has an incentive to do so. As a result, contrary to the arguments of cash transfer supporters, we wouldn't expect cash transfers to be used to finance public goods. This is obviously a simplified example, but the logic extends to more complicated situations. In general terms, the basic issue is that people don't fully take into account the benefits others receive from their contributions to public goods and they therefore neglect to make socially beneficial investments. But are people really that selfish? Do people really completely ignore the effects of their actions on others?

Benedikt Herrmann and his coauthors implemented an interesting cross-country experiment that provides insights into these questions.[29] The researchers conducted experiments using sixteen different participant pools across fifteen countries with widely different socioeconomic and cultural backgrounds. This included participants from East Asia, the Middle East,

Europe, and several English-speaking countries (including the United States and Australia). They had people in each participant pool play a public goods game, which is a stylized version of situations that require cooperation to achieve socially beneficial outcomes in the presence of free-rider incentives. Each participant pool was divided into groups of four people and each of these groups played the public goods game.

In these games, each group member received twenty tokens and had to decide how many tokens to keep for themselves and how many to contribute to a hypothetical group project. For each token devoted to the group project, all group members were awarded 0.4 tokens. The incentives in this game mirror our example of the irrigation system. It's socially optimal for all group members to contribute all of their tokens, as this gives each person a payoff of thirty-two tokens (because when eighty tokens are contributed, each person receives 80×0.4 tokens). However, each person had an incentive to free ride, given that contributing a token yielded a benefit of only 0.4 tokens. If all participants were purely self-interested, nobody would contribute anything to the group project and each person would receive a (suboptimal) payoff of twenty tokens.

The researchers incorporated two additional elements in these experiments to make them better reflect real-world situations. First, participants were able to "punish" others in their group if they disapproved of their behavior. Specifically, any group member could sacrifice up to ten tokens, with each token serving to reduce the payoff of another member by three tokens. This reflects the real-world possibility of sanctioning inappropriate behavior through social exclusion, shaming, or even ridicule. Second, given that many social interactions occur repeatedly, the researchers had participants play the public goods game for ten rounds. This further allowed them to understand how punishment affects contributions in subsequent rounds.

What did they find? In the first period of the game, average contributions across the sixteen participant pools varied widely, ranging from a low of about six tokens in Athens to a high of roughly sixteen tokens in Boston. What happened in subsequent rounds depended heavily on whether participants were allowed to punish. Average contributions fell dramatically after the first period when participants weren't allowed to punish, but were more or less stable in the presence of punishment. Even with punishment, no participant pool was able to fully overcome the free-rider problem and many pools fell well below the optimal contribution of twenty tokens. Note, however, that all pools exhibited average contributions well above zero, which conflicts with what we'd expect if people were purely self-interested.

Across a variety of countries, people therefore demonstrate a capacity to cooperate, just not to the extent that they can fully overcome the free-rider problem. But these experiments don't provide direct evidence about cash transfers and one could argue that communities receiving cash transfers experience heightened cooperation. In particular, recipients of cash transfers are less vulnerable to income poverty and income fluctuations, which may improve their sense of belonging in their community, make them more likely to trust their neighbors, and increase their confidence in the future. If this is the case, we'd expect communities receiving cash programs to have greater levels of social cohesion and therefore a greater capacity to overcome the free-rider problem.[30]

Orazio Attanasio and his coauthors tested this idea by comparing two neighborhoods in Colombia—Pozón, which had received cash transfers from the program Familias en Acción, and Ciénaga, which had not. In both of these neighborhoods, they had people play a public goods game very similar to that described above. The primary difference in their game was that participants were given just one token and they had to decide whether to keep the token for themselves or contribute it to a common project. Their estimates showed that Familias en Acción significantly increased cooperation, as the people of Pozón were more likely to contribute to the common project than the people of Ciénaga, by roughly 23 percentage points.[31]

These estimates should be approached with caution—neither the neighborhoods nor the participants were randomly selected—but let's take them at face value. One issue is that the participants from Pozón were still far from overcoming the free-rider problem. Specifically, after receiving cash payments, only 33 percent of participants chose to contribute to the common project. An additional, deeper issue is that it's not clear that the cash transfers themselves improved cooperation. As part of the program, beneficiaries were invited to attend "care follow-up meetings" where they discussed hygiene, nutrition, and other health-related issues facing their community. The authors viewed these meetings as the primary channel through which the program facilitated cooperation, but such meetings clearly aren't a necessary feature of cash programs.

There are other studies showing that cash transfers can improve social cohesion, but there are also studies showing the opposite effect.[32] In Chapter 4, we saw several examples of cash programs that had unintended consequences for social cohesion. These examples are further supported by a study conducted by Sara Pavanello and colleagues, who undertook a qualitative analysis of several unconditional cash programs implemented in Yemen, the West Bank and Gaza, Kenya, Uganda, and Mozambique. The authors found evidence of negative effects on social cohesion in many of these countries, most notably Yemen, Kenya, and the West Bank and Gaza.[33]

Targeting-related issues were critical in all of these cases. For example, in the West Bank and Gaza, the majority of beneficiaries and community stakeholders reported feelings of envy, jealousy, and resentment between beneficiaries and nonbeneficiaries. These feelings stemmed from uncertainty about the criteria used to target the programs, which left community members confused about who was deemed eligible for the program and why. Such feelings were less pronounced in Uganda and Mozambique, and the authors attributed this fact to the categorical targeting procedures used for those programs. Uganda's Senior Citizen Grant, for example, targeted the elderly and many stakeholders agreed that this was fair because the elderly "are weak, poor, cannot farm and do business with ease like other categories of people do."[34]

Overall, it's then clear that the impacts of cash transfers are constrained by market failures and these programs, at best, play a limited role in helping communities overcome market failures. In fact, we've now seen several instances where cash programs have had detrimental effects on the social cohesion that's so vital for overcoming market failures. Targeting emerges yet again as an important concern. While programs that use categorical targeting appear less likely to compromise social cohesion, we know from Chapter 4 that these methods often lead to relatively high targeting error rates. The evidence thus suggests that cash transfers face a troubling tradeoff between reaching the poor and promoting social cohesion.

CHAPTER 7

The Diversity of Need

FOR MANY CHILDREN with disabilities, attending school isn't an option. Especially in less developed countries, schools regularly lack accessible classrooms, qualified teachers, and appropriate assistive technologies. While cash programs often aim to benefit children by giving families the resources to finance education, children with disabilities can be left behind because they're limited by these nonfinancial barriers to schooling. In other words, many children with disabilities face a *conversion failure,* whereby they struggle to attend school even when their families have adequate resources. Francis Kamuhanda is a rare but illustrative success story whose experiences show that truly inclusive education requires more than tackling financial barriers.

Francis was born to a humble family in the western Ugandan village of Kacungiro in 1976.[1] In the days following his birth, people flocked to the Kamuhanda family's home to meet their newborn baby boy and to congratulate them on their new addition. The visitors, however, were met with a surprise. Francis had been born with polio and, as a result, his right leg was weak and shorter than his left leg. "Oh no," some lamented, "your child has a deformed leg. It's a pity that you lost such a handsome boy." Some visitors not only felt pity for Francis but speculated that his family was cursed or had done something horrible to deserve such a fate.

Francis and his parents were resilient and refused to succumb to the stigma. When Francis was three years old, his mother split bamboo into two pieces and fastened them onto Francis's leg so that he could walk on his own. As Francis became more independent with his new leg calipers, he also became more exposed to the discriminatory attitudes of other people in his village. Most vividly, he wasn't called by his name, but rather by derogatory terms like *kalema* (disabled), *mugulupa* (damaged), and *mwiga* (crippled). Francis refused to let these insults go unpunished. As a defense mechanism, he would carry rocks in his pockets to hurl at those who made derogatory remarks, regardless of their age or status in the village.

School was particularly challenging for Francis. Due to his limited mobility, the long walk to his local elementary school was onerous and he often received canings as punishment for being late. To make matters worse, he was bullied over his disability and many of his peers refused to sit next to him because they feared that he was somehow contagious. While Francis regularly returned home dispirited, his parents placed a high value on education and continually encouraged him to work hard. He listened and it eventually paid off. When he became one of the top three students in his class, his peers started to befriend him, recognizing that he was an excellent study partner. Francis's work ethic also paid dividends in other areas, as he gained regard for his skills in soccer, gymnastics, and volleyball.

Francis continued to excel in secondary school and his dedication to his studies earned him one of the top scores on Uganda's national examinations, and a full scholarship to study at Makerere University in the capital of Kampala. His arrival in Kampala was bittersweet, as he was overwhelmed by the sheer number of people with disabilities begging in the streets. Feeling compelled to do something, he joined the Makerere University Disabled Students Association and began advocating for people with disabilities. Soon, he began to exert influence through radio, television, and visits to government ministries.

In one visit, Francis met Florence Nayiga Ssekabira, who was then Uganda's minister of state for elderly and disability affairs. Francis directly challenged Florence for not doing anything to help people with disabilities. Florence listened carefully and eventually asked Francis what plan he had for dealing with the problem. But Francis didn't have an answer. In the following weeks, however, as he reflected on the question, he repeatedly recalled how his own mother had urged him to excel in his studies because physical labor was an unlikely career path for a disabled person. Building on that sound advice, Francis formulated a plan to provide inclusive education for the many people with disabilities who were left behind by Uganda's education system.

Francis went back to Florence with his idea and she liked it—so much that she offered up land she owned some twenty miles south of the city as a site for an experimental school with specialized support for disabled children. Shortly after Francis graduated in 2002, Sure Prospects enrolled nine students with disabilities and began operating under an avocado tree on Florence's land in Entebbe. The school immediately confronted two problems. First, people in the community started referring to Sure Prospects as "the disabled school," a label that carried the stigma Francis wanted to avoid. Second, as the school grew remarkably fast—quintupling in size within the first year—the increasing operational costs became unaffordable with its tuition-free model.

In response to these challenges, Francis innovated. To confront the stigma associated with the school and help children with disabilities better integrate into "mainstream" society, Francis began admitting students without disabilities. And to cover the school's costs and continue providing free service to children with disabilities, he charged the students without disabilities for their tuition. The school initially implemented a 10:1 ratio—enrolling ten students without disabilities for each student with a disability—and this ratio was reduced as the school grew further. At present, Sure Prospects resides in a multi-classroom building with over four hundred students and uses a 3:1 ratio to fund the education of more than a hundred children with disabilities.

Sure Prospects offers a solution to a critical problem in Uganda: children with disabilities disproportionately lack access to adequate schooling. According to a 2019 household survey commissioned by the Ugandan government, 83 percent of school-aged children without disabilities attend school, whereas only 74 percent of children with disabilities do so. And these numbers mask important disparities by type of disability. For example, less than 40 percent of children with communication or self-care difficulties attend school. Furthermore, of the children with disabilities who are in school, only 15 percent attend fully inclusive schools, special schools, or dedicated units within mainstream schools. This means that 85 percent of enrolled students with disabilities lack access to school-based special education services.[2]

There are many reasons for the infrequent school attendance of children with disabilities. Parents often avoid sending children with disabilities to school because they assume they aren't able to learn or fear they'll be mistreated. Getting to and from school can be an insurmountable obstacle for many children, particularly those with mobility-related impairments. Schools commonly lack appropriate accommodations, including accessible classrooms, qualified teachers, or adequate assistive technologies. Addressing these barriers is largely beyond the scope of any individual- or household-level intervention, which means that "implementing a fully inclusive education system requires systemic changes to curriculum, pedagogy and funding models."[3] Sure Prospects is a step in this direction.

One way to view these issues is through the lens of conversion factors, discussed in Chapter 2. Recall that the means-ends distinction is a central part of the capability approach and stresses that understanding well-being requires looking at what people ultimately value (their ends) rather than the resources available to them (their means). Conversion factors are the personal, social, and environmental elements that influence a person's ability to translate the means of well-being into valued ends. Disability is an example of a conversion factor: at any given level of income, a child with a disability is less likely to obtain an adequate education than a child without a disability. Such conversion failures are widespread and frequently cause the most vulnerable people to be left behind or even harmed by social programs.

To clarify how such failures complicate the outcomes of cash transfer programs, this chapter takes a close look at three conversion factors in particular. First, it offers a deeper discussion of *disability*-related issues, which factor into areas of well-being that extend well beyond education. Then it turns to the relationship between income and *malnutrition*, highlighting how infectious diseases, environmental toxins, and limited nutritional awareness can interrupt this relationship. Finally, it discusses some vulnerabilities associated with *old age* and explains how cash programs can have grave consequences for elderly people when these vulnerabilities are left unchecked. A common theme throughout the chapter is that alleviating poverty in vulnerable groups typically demands more than giving people money.

Disabling Poverty

Disability is a complex issue and even basic definitions are contested. Historically, it has been understood in terms of a medical model that emphasizes the individual and views disability as resulting from certain impairments that require medical treatment. In the 1970s, an alternative social model emerged in response to concerns that the medical model placed too much emphasis on clinical diagnosis and invited a partial, dehumanizing view of people with disabilities. The social model instead views disability as a form of social oppression, which results from social arrangements that fail to account for people with impairments. This model, too, has its critics, with some expressing concern that it risks overemphasizing the social and thus neglects people's specific experiences living with impairments.[4]

In response to these debates, many international organizations, including the World Health Organization (WHO), have adopted a "hybrid" or "interactional" view of disability.[5] Specifically, the WHO views disability in terms of people's inability to function in certain ways, which includes limitations related to body function or structure (such as blindness), difficulties carrying out everyday activities (such as walking), and problems participating in social life (such as attending school). The WHO emphasizes that a disability isn't simply an attribute of a person, but rather the result of the *interaction* between an individual's health condition and the broader socioeconomic environment. This view of disability means that improving the lives of people with disabilities requires both medical interventions and creations of more inclusive social arrangements.[6]

In line with this definition, the WHO has argued that measuring disability cannot be as simple as identifying people with specific impairments while overlooking the environmental factors that constrain people's ability to function. Instead, the WHO and other international organizations have adopted a tool that measures people's abilities to function along six critical dimensions: seeing, hearing, walking, cognition, self-care, and communication. A straightforward questionnaire asks people about their experience in each of these domains (for example: *Do you have difficulty seeing, even if wearing glasses?*) and then aggregates the responses into a measure of disability. Using this measure, the 2011 *World Report on Disability* estimated that roughly 15 percent of the global population could be classified as disabled.[7]

People with disabilities are at increased risk of being income poor, in part because physical and mental impairments can limit their abilities to work. Even when impairments don't preclude work, people with disabilities can face limited employment opportunities due to discrimination and restricted access to transportation, among other challenges. It's also true, as already noted, that children with disabilities are less likely to attend school, which reduces their employment opportunities in adulthood. While statistics on the relative income poverty of people with disabilities are somewhat scarce, the United Nations compiled data from nine countries and found that people with disabilities were disproportionately poor in every country. And the differences were substantial in some cases. In Uganda, for example, the poverty rate was 12 percentage points higher for people with disabilities than for those without disabilities.[8]

Understanding the relative deprivation of people with disabilities, however, requires looking well beyond income and expenditure levels. One critical issue is that people with disabilities bear extra costs associated with healthcare, transportation, assistive products, and modified residences. This means that, at any given level of income, people with disabilities are unlikely to enjoy the same standard of living as people without disabilities. Using data from the United Kingdom, Asghar Zaidi and Tania Burchardt estimated the additional income people with disabilities require to attain the same standard of living as people without disabilities. They found that people with disabilities required somewhere between 1.1 and 7.7 percent more income for each unit increase on a twenty-two-point disability severity score.[9]

The extra costs associated with disability are clearly sizable, but an exclusive focus on costs masks another issue: even if people with disabilities could be compensated for their extra costs, many would still be disadvantaged by the difficulty of accessing certain goods. Looking at data from seven developing countries, the United Nations found that, on average, 13 percent of people with disabilities had been refused entry into a school or preschool because of their disabilities. Even when people with disabilities were able to attend school, around 17 percent stopped attending for nonfinancial reasons, such as issues with transportation or problems communicating with teachers.[10]

Healthcare is another area where people with disabilities experience systematic exclusion. Looking at data from thirty-seven countries, the United Nations reported that people with disabilities are more than three times likelier than people without disabilities to be unable to access healthcare when they need it. Importantly, nonfinancial barriers play a critical role in limiting healthcare access. In a sample of thirty-five countries, 70 percent of disabled people with unmet healthcare needs reported nonfinancial reasons for their lack of access. As with education, even when people with disabilities are able to access healthcare, they experience difficulties. For example, people with disabilities are more likely to report that their doctor didn't listen to them, treat them with respect, or involve them in treatment decisions.[11]

People with disabilities thus experience many forms of conversion failure and this has immediate implications for cash transfer programs. The first issue to note here is an abstract one, but no less important. Recall that the WHO definition of disability states that disability results from the interaction of a person's health condition and socioeconomic environment. In line with the social model, this definition emphasizes that disability is at least partly a social phenomenon, in that certain social arrangements (such as schooling) systematically exclude people with impairments. Exclusionary social arrangements are a key source of the relative impoverishment of people with disabilities—and this implies that to alleviate poverty among people with disabilities, social arrangements must be altered to be more inclusive.

Cash transfers conflict with this basic idea. Cash programs attempt to alleviate poverty by intervening at the individual or household level rather than by addressing broader social problems. Cash transfers are insensitive, then, to the needs of people with disabilities at a basic, conceptual level and this creates scope for practical problems. Service points, such as administrative offices, are often inaccessible to people with disabilities. Means-testing procedures overlook the fact that people with disabilities bear extra costs, implying that disabled people with marginally higher incomes or expenditures can be excluded despite their greater needs.[12] Conditional cash programs often include stipulations (such as school attendance) that many people with disabilities simply can't meet.[13]

This neglect of the social side of disability has especially important implications for disability grants. As one study explains:

> Assessment for a grant requires an emphasis on the individual with an impairment. The question an assessment has to answer is individual and categorical: "Does this person qualify for a grant or not?" This flies in the face of arguments which correctly point out that there is no neat distinction between the "disabled" and the "nondisabled," and also that disability is contextual and fluctuating according to social and environmental conditions.[14]

In short, because the complexity of disability makes it extremely challenging to identify recipients for cash grants, these programs frequently misclassify people. As one example, when Sophie Mitra conducted an analysis of South Africa's Disability Grant based on self-reported disability status, she found that 34 percent of recipients were actually ineligible, and 42 percent of eligible people were excluded.[15]

Another issue related to conversion failures is that they can mute the impacts that cash transfers have on people with disabilities. In India, for instance, some parents reported that they diverted education stipends intended for disabled children to their nondisabled siblings, often because they couldn't find schools that would accommodate their disabled children. Similarly, in a survey of recipients of South Africa's Care Dependency Grant, researchers found that 37 percent of beneficiary children were not attending school. For over 80 percent of these children, disability was reported as the main constraint and this was primarily due to a lack of adequate education facilities.[16] These findings confirm that people with disabilities have difficulties converting cash benefits into improved educational outcomes.

A more rigorous way to understand how cash transfers affect people with disabilities is to look at proper impact evaluations. While evaluations that specifically look at the effects of cash on people with disabilities are extremely scarce, one study by Richard de Groot and others provides interesting insights.[17] These researchers examined the impact of Lesotho's Child Grant Programme, a cash transfer program targeting poor households with children. The evaluation focused on an expansion of this program by which half of the "electoral divisions" within five districts were randomly assigned to a treatment group and the other half to a control group. The authors used this randomization to estimate the impact of the cash transfer scheme on people with disabilities.

Their findings were mixed, and in some places concerning. On the one hand, the Child Grant Programme showed beneficial effects. It reduced the frequency of extreme food shortages for households with and without people with disabilities. It also increased the frequency with which people with disabilities consulted a healthcare provider over a three-month period. On the other hand, the results showed that people with disabilities were left behind in critical ways. While Lesotho's program reduced food insecurity for children living in households without any disabled members, it showed no significant effect on children in households with disabled members. Similarly, it increased school enrollment for children without disabilities, but didn't do the same for children with disabilities.

These results clearly show how disability can mute the effects of cash transfers. And it's not just that people with disabilities sometimes fail to benefit from cash transfers; they can also be outright harmed. Most notably, disability grants are commonly tied to the health conditions of recipients and the benefits may lapse if a person's condition improves. These stipulations create a perverse incentive, especially for family caregivers, to keep the grant recipients in poor health so that they continue receiving benefits. Toward this end, caregivers may neglect the health of grant recipients, withhold their medications, or even forego a hospitalization or institutionalization that would entail a loss of benefits.

Gabrielle Kelly documented precisely these issues in her qualitative study of disability assistance in South Africa.[18] For example, Kelly reported the following remark from a nurse at a psychiatric facility:

> Sometimes what they do is they don't take grant medicine because they need to . . . even the families don't give the tablets because he must stay sick or she must stay sick so that they can get the grant.[19]

Similarly, Kelly documented that because South Africa's Social Assistance Act of 2004 stipulates that grants must lapse six months after a patient has been admitted to a state institution, several hospitals struggled to keep patients for extended periods of time. While it's not clear how common these issues are in South Africa (or elsewhere), her findings show that cash alone is insufficient for improving the well-being of many people with disabilities.

Worm Wars

The World Economic Forum is largely known for its annual meeting that convenes high-profile people from around the world in Davos, Switzerland, to discuss pressing global issues. While the gathering is mostly a serious affair, the 2008 meetings were marked by a surreal moment in which Cherie Blair, wife of the former British prime minister Tony Blair, dressed up as an intestinal worm and chased around several other attendees who were pretending to be schoolchildren. Gene Sperling, former economic advisor to the Clinton administration, played along as well, pretending to be a teacher rushing to get deworming medicine for the children.[20]

Blair's antics were an attempt to promote "Deworm the World," an initiative that works with governments across the globe to help deliver mass deworming programs to school-age children. Though such a campaign may seem mundane or uncontroversial, deworming initiatives have been at the center of a heated debate in the global health community in recent years. The catalyst for this debate was an influential study by Edward Miguel and Michael Kremer that examined the effects of a school-based deworming program in Kenya.[21] Miguel and Kremer found that the program not only had dramatic effects on treated students (including reducing their school absenteeism by roughly 25 percent) but also improved the health and schooling outcomes of children who didn't get treatment, by reducing the transmission of infections. When both the direct and the indirect effects were considered, Miguel and Kremer claimed that mass deworming campaigns were one of the most cost-effective development interventions to date.

The study ignited a movement to deworm the world. Yet some questioned the validity of the results. Most notably, a group of epidemiologists at the London School of Hygiene and Tropical Medicine took another look at Miguel and Kremer's analysis and identified several issues, such as unexplained missing data and critical coding errors. When the researchers fixed these issues, they found that many key results were less pronounced and that the indirect effects of the program effectively disappeared. These new results led many to question whether mass deworming programs were really as cost-effective as they initially appeared to be.[22]

The ensuing debate, dubbed "the worm wars," proved to be complicated and contentious. While some disagreement persists about the cost-effectiveness of mass deworming campaigns, both sides agree on a few things. For one, there's broad agreement that intestinal worms are a major health issue that affects a surprisingly large share of the global population. Soil-transmitted helminths alone affect an estimated 1.5 billion people or 24 percent of the world's population.[23] There's also broad agreement that children have a particularly high risk of infection due to their immature immune systems, lack of hygiene, and frequent play in contaminated water and soil.

Further, few disagree that the consequences of infection can be especially grave for children. Soil-transmitted helminths, for example, can lead to suppressed appetites, the malabsorption of nutrients, and even the loss of iron and protein as the worms feed on host tissues.[24] The resulting nutritional deficiencies can have lasting effects on children, leading to physical and cognitive impairments that may be irreversible. In addition, as highlighted by the Miguel and Kremer study, intestinal worm infections can prevent children from attending school, which can have long-term consequences for their education and employment outcomes. These facts taken together indicate that controlling the prevalence of intestinal worms in children really is an urgent health matter.

Above all, the worm wars highlight the critical relationship between infectious diseases and child development, especially child nutrition. Intestinal worm infections and other common infectious diseases—such as pneumonia, diarrheal diseases, malaria, and HIV—can be both consequences and causes of malnutrition. That is, malnutrition can make a child more susceptible to infection through weight loss, lowered immunity, and mucosal damage, and infectious diseases can lead to malnutrition through suppressed appetites, the malabsorption of nutrients, and the diversion of nutrients for the immune response.[25] The latter channel is notable because it points to a conversion failure: even relatively affluent and well-fed children can suffer from malnutrition if they are afflicted with untreated infectious disease.

Infectious diseases aren't the only source of failures to convert resources into beneficial developmental outcomes. Another is that children are far more sensitive than adults to toxic chemicals in the environment, in part because of their greater intake of food and fluids per pound of body weight. Mycotoxins, which are naturally occurring toxins produced by certain molds and found in many common foods, are a major concern in this regard as they've been shown to cause stunting in young children.[26] Similarly, pesticide exposure has been linked to endocrine-system disruption, neurodevelopmental delays, cancer, and even death in children.[27]

There are also many non-income barriers to the adoption of good nutrition practices. Consider breastfeeding. Recognizing its health benefits for children—such as protection against diarrheal and respiratory-related diseases—several international organizations recommend exclusive breastfeeding for the first six months. Despite this guideline, estimates show that only 42 percent of children are exclusively breastfed during this period. Unsurprisingly, the barriers to breastfeeding are nonfinancial. UNICEF states that the leading barriers to better practices include unfounded beliefs in the benefits of breastmilk substitutes, cultural taboos against breastfeeding, and difficulties faced by mothers who work outside the home.[28]

Given all the potential sources of conversion failure, we wouldn't expect a strong association between increases in incomes or wealth and better developmental outcomes. And this is precisely what the evidence shows. Several studies have examined the relationship between affluence and child development, from both a macro- and micro-level perspective. Macro-level studies typically focus on the cross-country relationship between per-capita income growth and anthropometric indicators.[29] For example, in one well-cited study, Rasmus Heltberg reported that a 10 percent increase in income per capita was associated with a 2 percent reduction in stunting. From these results, he concluded that "economic growth on average is slow in bringing about stunting reduction."[30]

Micro-level studies point to similar conclusions. A study led by Caitlin Brown, for example, used household survey data from thirty countries in sub-Saharan Africa to look at the incidence of malnutrition among women and children at different wealth and expenditure levels.[31] They concluded that most of Africa's nutritionally deprived women and children were not, in fact, found in the most economically disadvantaged households. Specifically, they discovered that roughly 75 percent of underweight women and undernourished children were not in the 20 percent of households with the lowest wealth levels. They reported similar results about the incidence of malnutrition in households with different levels of expenditure.

An interesting feature of this study was that the authors examined in detail why the relationship between malnutrition and affluence was so weak. Their results suggested that common health risks were a leading explanation. In particular, they looked at disease exposure—as measured by the incidence of diarrhea, blood in the stool, and fever—for children at different locations in the wealth distribution. While they found wealthier households to be somewhat less vulnerable to disease, the strength of the relationship was weak. As a result, the authors concluded that "health risks are clearly spread quite widely across the distribution of households in all countries studied."[32] These findings thus show that affluence provides only limited protection against disease and malnutrition.

Evaluations of cash transfer programs echo these findings. James Manley and his coauthors, for example, conducted a review of 129 studies analyzing the impacts of cash transfers on child nutritional outcomes.[33] The studies included in the review came from a variety of regions—including sub-Saharan Africa, Latin America, and South Asia—and covered several different types of cash programs. Summarizing the results of these programs, the authors focused on five primary anthropometric measures of nutritional status: height-for-age, weight-for-age, weight-for-height, incidence of stunting, and incidence of wasting. They also looked at some secondary outcomes (such as dietary diversity), but we'll focus here on the primary ones.

An especially large number of studies looked at height-for-age. Of the seventy-seven different estimates reviewed by Manley's team, only eleven were positive and statistically significant. Interestingly, of these eleven significant effects, only two related to an unconditional cash program and both these estimates were from a single study.[34] Further, thirty-two of the seventy-seven estimates pointed to negative effects on height-for-age, with two of these estimates showing statistical significance. The results of the individual studies thus showed mixed effects, and when the authors calculated a combined effect across all studies they found it to be positive but "small in size."[35]

The results from the other primary outcomes were similar. Consider weight-for-height, an outcome we would expect to be particularly responsive to cash transfers because of its high sensitivity to recent lifestyle changes. Manley and his coauthors compiled forty different estimates on weight-for-height and found that only five were positive and statistically significant. In addition, of these forty estimates, nineteen showed a negative sign and two were negative and statistically significant. Finally, much like in the case of height-for-age, the combined effect on weight-for-height had a positive sign, but was small in magnitude. The results from this review suggest the simple conclusion that cash transfers just aren't that powerful for fighting malnutrition.

In response to this, one could argue that it's simply challenging to bring about reductions in malnutrition, and that other programs have been similarly ineffective. This, however, would be incorrect. Emily Keats and several coauthors reviewed the evidence on the effectiveness of various interventions for addressing maternal and child malnutrition.[36] Their review identified twelve different interventions that showed "strong evidence for implementation," given their notably beneficial impacts on outcomes like stunting and wasting. Examples included complementary feeding education, zinc supplementation, small-quantity lipid-based nutrient supplementation, ready-to-use supplementary food, family planning, and insecticide-treated bed nets for malaria control.

This is not to say that there's some other intervention that will always outperform cash. The sheer prevalence of conversion issues related to child nutrition suggests that malnutrition can be caused by a variety of factors, such as the presence of infectious diseases, toxic chemicals in the environment, and limited awareness of good nutrition practices. According to UNICEF, addressing the multiple causes of malnutrition requires a multipronged approach, combining effective interventions to simultaneously stimulate demand for healthy food options, strengthen the supply of nutritious foods, and improve children's food environments.[37] Cash transfers are, at best, one part of this solution.

Our Aging World

The world's population is gradually and irreversibly aging. The share of the global population aged sixty-five or older is expected to increase from roughly 10 percent in 2021 to around 17 percent in 2050. In absolute terms, the number of older people is projected to more than double over the same period, growing from 761 million to approximately 1.6 billion. Much of this growth will be concentrated in developing regions, as the fastest growth in older populations over the next three decades is expected to occur in western Asia, northern Africa, and sub-Saharan Africa. In these regions, the number of older people is expected to roughly triple between 2021 and 2050.[38]

Population aging is the result of a demographic transition that began in Europe and North America in the early nineteenth century and then emerged on a global scale in the middle of the twentieth century. This demographic transition leads to population aging through three primary channels. First, populations are "aging from the bottom" as falling fertility rates reduce the number of younger people. Second, populations are "aging from the top" as improved health expands human lifespans and increases the number of older people. Finally, populations are aging through a "cohort effect" by which cohorts of people entering old age are larger than the cohorts that preceded them. This effect is usually created by multiple factors, including reductions in mortality at younger ages, higher fertility rates in the past, and historical inflows of migrants.[39]

While population aging is the result of major successes in improving living conditions around the world, it also presents challenges. For one, older people are at a heightened risk of falling into income poverty. People typically work less as they age and many at advanced ages stop working altogether, whether because they retire, are physically unable to work, or are pushed out of the labor force due to age-based discrimination. In developing countries, for example, estimates show that 23.2 percent of older people live in low-income households, compared to 16.1 percent of working-age people. Income poverty in developing countries is especially pronounced among those aged eighty and older, as 25.5 percent of them live in low-income households.[40]

Another challenge is that aging populations face distinct health risks. Older people have particularly high risks of contracting noncommunicable diseases, including heart disease, cancer, diabetes, and dementia. Disability is also a critical issue, as older people often experience hearing loss, vision loss, back and neck pain, and depressive disorders, to name a few. The special health risks of older populations typically lead to dramatic changes in demand for healthcare services as populations age, most notably for long-term care services. For example, in Japan, the number of older people needing care is expected to increase from 8.3 to 14.4 percent of the total population between the years 2020 and 2065.[41]

Responding to the health needs of older populations requires not only increasing the availability of certain types of care, but also taking measures to ensure that care is accessible. Older people with limited mobility frequently have difficulties traveling to healthcare facilities, especially if they live in rural areas with poor transportation infrastructure. Stigma associated with certain health conditions, such as dementia, often prevents older people from seeking care and is commonly considered a major hindrance to early diagnosis. Low education levels among older people can also be a barrier to accessing care, as less educated people have lower health literacy and are less likely to seek care when needed. In short, older people commonly experience health-related conversion failures.

Cash transfers, especially old-age grants, are regularly used to promote the well-being of older populations, but the presence of these conversion failures raises important questions. How effective are cash transfers in protecting the health of older populations? Most critically, what role can cash programs play in promoting the longevity of older populations? The answer to the latter question depends on the relationship between income and mortality. On the one hand, we might expect people with higher incomes to live longer lives, in part because they're able to consume healthier diets and afford better healthcare. On the other hand, it's possible that higher incomes contribute to increased obesity and more sedentary lifestyles, which in turn increase mortality risks.

The evidence on this question, derived from contributory and noncontributory pension plans, is concerningly mixed. Robert Jensen and Kaspar Richter looked at the health effects of a failure of the contributory Russian state pension system in 1996, which left fourteen million of its thirty-nine million pensioners unexpectedly without payments for a prolonged period.[42] They found that the pension crisis had a significant impact on the mortality of male pensioners, as men living in households with suspended payments were nearly 6 percentage points more likely to die in the two years following the crisis. The authors argued that the effects could have been more dire, as many households with suspended payments cushioned the shock by increasing their labor supply or selling off assets to replace their lost income.

Other evidence on contributory pensions tells a different story. In one well-known paper, Stephen Snyder and William Evans looked at the mortality effects of a "notch" in social security benefits in the United States.[43] Specifically, in 1977, the United States government changed the way payments were calculated for new beneficiaries and this substantially decreased the payments made to recipients born after January 1, 1917. Snyder and Evans found that older people receiving lower payments had mortality rates that were roughly 2 percent *lower* than those receiving higher payments. This effect was statistically significant, and the authors argued that it was due to the fact that people receiving lower payments worked more and thus experienced less social isolation.

The evidence on contributory pensions then shows that increased income can have both positive and negative effects on mortality. But what about noncontributory programs? The best evidence on this question comes from a small number of studies conducted in Mexico. One of these, conducted by Tania Barham and Jacob Rowberry, looked at the mortality effects of Mexico's Progresa program and found that it reduced mortality among older people.[44] As previously described, this pioneering program was one of the first poverty-alleviation programs to give poor households cash subject to conditions. Recipients were required to send their children to school, obtain regular preventive healthcare for all family members, and ensure that at least one family member attended regular health education sessions.

The program began in 1997 in a limited number of poor, rural localities and rapidly expanded thereafter, reaching about 40 percent of rural families by the year 2000. Barham and Rowberry used this rollout period to examine the effect of the program on the mortality of people aged sixty-five and older. Analyzing municipality-level data, they found that Progresa, on average, reduced mortality rates by 4 percent. Looking in more detail at specific causes of death, they found that Progresa significantly reduced mortality related to infectious disease, diabetes, poor nutrition, and anemia. The program didn't appear, however, to have any effect on deaths due to certain cardiovascular diseases, such as heart disease, stroke, and hypertension.

Kevin Feeney looked at a different Mexican program, colloquially known as 70 y Más, which is a noncontributory pension program for people aged seventy and older.[45] The program began in 2007 by giving cash payments to age-eligible people living in localities with fewer than twenty-five hundred inhabitants. The program expanded to all localities with fewer than twenty thousand people in 2008, and then again to localities with fewer than thirty thousand people in 2009. Between 2007 and 2009, enrollment in 70 y Más roughly doubled, growing from 1.03 million people in 2007 to 2.2 million people in 2009. The program covered roughly half of people seventy and older by 2009. During this period, eligible people were given cash payments every two months equivalent to amounts between 20 and 40 percent of their income.

Similar to Barham and Rowberry, Feeney used the rollout of 70 y Más to understand how the program affected the mortality of pensioners. In contrast to Barham and Rowberry, however, Feeney found that the pensions led to a significant 5 percent increase in mortality in 70 y Más localities. These excess deaths, he discovered, were largely due to increases in circulatory diseases, such as heart disease and diabetes. Feeney further looked into the behavioral changes behind the rise in mortality rates and identified two factors. First, 70 y Más led to increased consumption of foods high in fat and cholesterol, thereby putting people at greater risk of circulatory diseases. And second, the program increased rates of retirement among the eligible population, which may have promoted more sedentary lifestyles.

The fact that 70 y Más increased mortality rates is sobering, but not altogether surprising. Other studies of cash programs have shown that cash can increase the risk factors associated with chronic diseases. A study led by Jef Leroy, for example, examined the health effects of Mexico's Programa de Apoyo Alimentario (Food Support Program), which provided poor households with cash or in-kind food transfers.[46] It found that women receiving cash transfers experienced significantly greater weight gain than the control group and that this effect was most pronounced among women who were already obese. A similar analysis by Ian Forde and others showed that Colombia's Familias en Acción (Families in Action) program led to significant increases in the body mass indexes and odds of obesity for women receiving cash transfers.[47]

But why did the studies of Progresa and 70 y Más arrive at such different conclusions? A possible explanation is that the older people receiving Progresa had better healthcare than those receiving 70 y Más. Note that Progresa targeted localities with adequate access to healthcare, while 70 y Más didn't have a similar requirement.[48] Also, a condition of Progresa's transfers was that all family members must have regular checkups, whereas 70 y Más was an unconditional program. And given that Progresa emphasized cash transfers to families with children, the older people covered by the program were more likely to live in multigenerational homes—where they could experience the additional benefits of being less socially isolated and receive care from co-residing family members.

There are no simple fixes when the effect of rising incomes is to heighten mortality risks. Reducing people's incomes would be objectionable for many reasons, most notably because it would sacrifice the other, beneficial effects of having more money. It's tempting to argue that the problems with 70 y Más could be remedied by restructuring the program to be more like Progresa. But this would lead to the exclusion of the most vulnerable older people, particularly those living outside multigenerational homes and those without adequate access to healthcare. The critical issue raised by conversion failures is that cash alone isn't sufficient to improve the well-being of some of the most vulnerable groups of people. Specifically, giving people money while neglecting broader health- or education-related reforms can mean that vulnerable groups are left behind, or even outright harmed.

CHAPTER 8

Transformative Change

THE GATES FOUNDATION is one of the largest charitable organizations in the world. In 2016, Bill Gates announced that the foundation was making a big investment in a new initiative: chickens. More specifically, Gates wanted to increase the proportion of rural families in sub-Saharan Africa raising improved breeds of chickens from 5 to 30 percent. Gates explained that chickens are a wise investment for poor families, as they're easy to take care of, they earn a good return, they're a great source of nutrition, and the income they generate could empower women. "It's pretty clear to me that just about anyone who's living in extreme poverty is better off if they have chickens," Gates wrote. "In fact, if I were in their shoes, that's what I would do—I would raise chickens."[1]

Christopher Blattman responded to Gates with an open letter criticizing the idea of giving so many poor families chickens.[2] To begin with, Blattman questioned the economics of the initiative. Gates had claimed that a family receiving five hens could breed them and soon be earning a thousand dollars a year or more selling chickens at the going rate of five dollars each. Blattman, however, argued that if roughly a third of families were selling chickens, the increase in supply would put downward pressure on the price. To the extent the prevailing cost of chickens fell, a family would make less income, diminishing the effectiveness of the initiative. "Giving away chickens," Blattman argued, "probably works best if we give them to just a few of the poor."[3]

Relatedly, Blattman expressed skepticism about Gates's belief that giving away chickens would be a great investment of the foundation's resources. Blattman referenced a study in the journal *Science* that reported on programs set up in six different countries to equip poor families with free livestock and basic training in caring for the animals. The researchers found that, on average, these programs cost $1,700 per recipient to administer but increased the earnings of recipient households by just $80 per year. With returns that low, it would take over twenty years to recoup the initial investment, assuming the same yields seen in the three-year horizon of the study were sustained. In short, Blattman thought it likely that the Gates Foundation's return on chickens would be modest, and lower than alternative investments it could make.

Blattman proposed that instead of giving people chickens, Gates should consider giving them cash. His argument was that cash is not only easier and cheaper to give out than chickens, but also more versatile and likely to yield a higher return. To support the assertion, Blattman referenced one of his own studies examining a program that gave Ugandan women a one-time grant of $150 plus some business training and supervision. All told, that program cost $843 per household to implement, but because the treated women subsequently earned $202 more per year than the control group, its rate of return was much higher than that of livestock grants.

While this suggested a better use of Gates Foundation resources, Blattman acknowledged that there was not enough evidence to unequivocally advocate for cash over chickens. He therefore suggested that Gates invest in a large-scale study to compare several different types of investments, including both cash and chickens: "It would be straightforward to run a study with a few thousand people in six countries, and eight or twelve variations, to understand which combination works best, where, and with whom."[4] More broadly, Blattman argued that the future of poverty alleviation must involve the use of randomized trials to compare different programs and find out which are most cost-effective. Funding studies like the one he suggested would be "the best investment we could make to fight world poverty."[5]

Blattman's open letter to Gates was only the beginning of the debate. Shortly after its publication, Harvard economist Lant Pritchett responded with a criticism of Blattman's ideas for fighting poverty.[6] In an online post, Pritchett cautioned against taking such a narrow view of what it means to fight poverty and placing excessive emphasis on individual- or household-level interventions for poverty alleviation. Pritchett argued that this view neglects the systemic or structural issues that play a critical role in producing and reproducing global poverty. Rather than micro-level interventions, Pritchett said, the focus should be on national development, which entails promoting productivity growth, state capacity, democratic accountability, and equal treatment for all citizens.

In support of his argument, Pritchett pointed out that many developing countries simply don't have the resources to eradicate income poverty through redistributive programs. He calculated that, across the world's "least developed" countries, average gross domestic product per capita is just $2,566. Thus, even if resources could be equally distributed in these countries, this would leave everyone well below the poverty line of the United States (approximately $7,500 per person). Pritchett thus argued: "The only solution to world poverty is vast increases in the productivity per person which would be the result of sustained economic growth that is broadly shared and increases in national development."[7] Stated differently, eradicating poverty would require systemic or structural transformation.

Even if the focus was primarily on alleviating more extreme forms of income poverty (as we might say, "dollar a day" poverty), Pritchett argued that national development has a proven track record. He cited China, Vietnam, Indonesia, and India as the most recent success stories, each of which has managed to reduce income poverty from over half their population to much lower levels. He argued that these successes were produced not by micro-level interventions but rather by sustained growth in economic productivity. This claim, Pritchett noted, is supported by research from Aart Kraay showing that income poverty rates and average consumption levels are "almost perfectly inversely correlated" over long growth spells.

Ultimately, Pritchett's concern was that Blattman is preoccupied with making big contributions to small questions rather than small contributions to big questions. To illustrate the problem with this, Pritchett discussed the case of India, where policy reforms contributed to growth accelerations in 1993 and 2002 that augmented gross domestic product by $3.5 trillion. A research program that could make such growth accelerations even 1 percent more likely could still claim $35 billion in value. This is speculative, but Pritchett's point is that accumulated knowledge about big questions could indirectly contribute to policy reforms with immense payoffs in terms of economic growth and poverty reduction. "Research that plays only a small, uncredited, role in an historically epic story," he wrote, "might still be better value for money than the questions where researcher gets a leading part."[8]

Blattman and Pritchett clearly hold two very different views of what it means to fight global poverty. While Blattman emphasizes individual- or household-level interventions, Pritchett instead claims that structural interventions are vital for improving the well-being of people living in poverty. This chapter will examine their competing views and discuss precisely how cash transfers are situated within this broader debate. It will show that cash programs are strongly oriented toward an individualist rather than a structuralist view of poverty. It will then discuss an important concern with the individualist orientation of cash—that neglecting the structural causes of poverty means that cash programs prioritize palliative or incremental progress over more transformative change.

Two Views on the Causes of Poverty

Theories on the causes of poverty can be broadly classified into two basic types: individualist and structuralist. The individualist view, arguably the dominant view in poverty research, locates the presence and persistence of poverty in individual attributes. The critical feature of this view is that, to explain why a particular person is poor, one focuses on that person's traits rather than examining social relations or the broader social context. Traits may be acquired through *monadic* processes that are nonsocial in nature (often noted by the phrase "born that way") or through *relational* processes that entail interactions with others (perhaps described as "picked up at school"). In either case, however, the individualist view attributes poverty to the characteristics of the poor themselves.[9]

One leading individualist view of poverty emphasizes that poor households are prevented from investing in productive activities by their limited assets or wealth. Having limited assets often means that poor households have, for example, limited access to credit because they lack the ability to meet the collateral requirements of traditional lenders. Similarly, poor households typically have limited access to insurance, which can cause them to allocate their assets toward low-return investments to reduce their exposure to risk. This asset-based view was explicitly promoted by Christopher Blattman in his open letter to Bill Gates: "In the past ten years, we have learned a simple lesson: The poor generally have good investment opportunities but little access to capital."[10]

Another individualist view emphasizes how some important psychological consequences of living in poverty can lead to behaviors that inhibit escapes from poverty. One theory, for example, is that poverty causes stress and negative affective states that cause people to act in shortsighted and risk-averse ways.[11] A related theory claims that people living in poverty can be overwhelmed with difficult financial decisions, which impedes their cognitive functioning and leads to compromised decision-making. For example, a study led by Anandi Mani involved repeated interviews with Indian sugarcane farmers and found evidence of diminished cognitive performance before harvest (when they were relatively poor) as compared to after harvest (when they were relatively rich).[12]

A further individualist theory, popularized by the work of Gary Becker, highlights the role that differences in human capital (such as education) play in generating income poverty. The basic idea is that differences in earnings correspond to differences in productivity, as more productive workers earn high wages while less productive workers are either unemployed or channeled into low-wage jobs. In turn, productivity is determined by a person's education, training, and skills, which themselves are products of investment decisions made by people and their families earlier in life. While investment decisions can be influenced by both monadic and relational processes—such as preferences, information, costs, and norms—the theory ultimately places individual attributes at the forefront of explanations of poverty.[13]

The structuralist view, by contrast, emphasizes that poverty is a deeply social phenomenon that can't be completely explained by individual attributes. According to the structuralist view, individualism commits the fallacy of composition, incorrectly assuming that a property of a part is automatically true of the whole. For example, while a given person might escape income poverty by increasing their level of education, it doesn't follow that poverty can be eradicated with widespread advances in educational achievements. Generalized increases in education don't necessarily alter the occupational structure of society, and persistently limited job opportunities may mean that some people remain unemployed and poor despite their improved education. Instead, the structuralist argues that eradicating poverty requires altering the patterns of social arrangements.[14]

One well-known structural theory, known as dependency theory, focuses on how countries are integrated into the global economic system. In this body of theory, the global economy is partitioned into core and periphery economies, with the economies in the periphery being conditioned by those in the core. A critical feature of this relationship is that periphery economies largely export *primary* products to the industrialized core, and import *manufactured* products from it. According to the work of Rául Prebisch and Hans Singer, one issue with this relationship is that the price of primary products tends to decline relative to the price of manufactured products over the long term. The structure of the global economy then perpetuates poverty and underdevelopment in the periphery through an ongoing transfer of income from the periphery to the core.[15]

Institutions—the established practices and organizations that govern social interactions—form a critical part of the social structure.[16] One of the most popular theories of why some countries experience deep poverty and inequality centers on the role that political institutions play in the process of economic development. Daron Acemoglu and James Robinson, for example, argue that countries with more inclusive (often democratic) political institutions are characterized by broad distributions of political power, which in turn facilitate the creation of economic institutions that are beneficial to the majority of people. In contrast, countries with more extractive (often authoritarian) political institutions are associated with highly concentrated political power and therefore extractive economic institutions that primarily benefit the elites.[17]

Yet another group of theories with a structural orientation claims that the rules governing how certain populations are partitioned has important implications for their prosperity. The fact that European colonial powers, for instance, partitioned Africa with little regard to preexisting ethnic divisions has contributed to lasting political violence, instability, and poverty in many countries. Similarly, in the United States, Native Americans were placed on reservations according to tribal affiliations with little regard for the fact that decision-making had traditionally occurred at the sub-tribal level. Estimates show that reservations that combined multiple sub-tribal bands are roughly 30 percent poorer than those not subjected to forced coexistence.[18] Similar analyses have shown that residential segregation in the United States has contributed to the impoverishment of Black Americans.[19]

This is far from an exhaustive listing of all the individual and structural theories of poverty, but perhaps sufficient to convey the basic ideas behind the two views. Critically, not all theories can be neatly categorized into these two camps, as some studies combine individualist and structuralist elements in productive ways.[20] Nevertheless, most accounts reveal an emphasis on either individualism or structuralism, whether by their focus on certain parts of a theory or in their ultimate policy recommendations. The main point here is that individualist accounts locate the origins of poverty in individual attributes, and structuralist accounts concentrate on the stable patterns in social arrangements that create "the 'empty places' of poverty into which individuals get slotted."[21]

There's no unambiguously correct way to view poverty. The appropriate viewpoint almost certainly depends on the place, time, and dimension of poverty being considered. In line with Lant Pritchett's arguments, it's nevertheless true that structural changes have much greater *potential* for reducing poverty than changes in individual attributes. One way to build on Pritchett's claims in this regard is to consider natural experiments where different structures or institutions have been imposed on particular countries or groups of countries. Perhaps the most famous natural experiment—analyzed in detail by Daron Acemoglu, Simon Johnson, and James Robinson—occurred in 1948 when the Korean Peninsula was divided into North and South Korea at the 38th parallel.[22]

North and South Korea were remarkably similar before the division in terms of culture, geography, and economic conditions. After the division, however, the countries organized themselves in very different ways, with the North adopting a model of Soviet-style socialism and the South embracing markets and incentives to develop their economy. Though the North and South had roughly the same level of income per capita in 1948, the subsequent decades saw a dramatic divergence in the economic performance of the two countries. By 2000, income per capita in South Korea had reached $16,100, whereas in North Korea income per capita had stagnated at around $1,000. The average South Korean thus became roughly sixteen times richer than the average North Korean within the historically short span of fifty years.

According to Acemoglu and coauthors, there was "only one plausible explanation for the radically different economic experiences of the two Koreas after 1950: their very different institutions led to divergent economic outcomes."[23] Though well-being comparisons based on income or expenditures should be approached with caution, it's useful to consider how the impacts of these institutional changes compare with what can be accomplished through individual interventions. Pioneered by the Bangladesh-based nonprofit BRAC in 2002, the Targeting the Ultra Poor program has been widely acclaimed for its large and persistent impacts. Its multifaceted approach—including providing households with assets, cash, and trainings—has been shown to produce sustained increases in income of roughly 35 percent.[24] The program's effects, however, are still far from the sixteen-fold difference of the Korean case.[25]

These comparisons are imperfect and one major concern is that the Korean experiment is historically anomalous. In other work, Acemoglu, Johnson, and Robinson examined the economic effects of institutional quality in a larger sample of countries. A well-known study by these authors exploits the fact that European colonial powers adopted inclusive institutions in some colonies and extractive institutions in others, partly due to differences in the disease environments of the colonies. Using this fact to develop credible causal estimates, the authors found that institutional quality has a surprisingly large effect on economic performance. For example, their estimates suggest that improving Nigeria's institutions to the level of Chile's could lead to a sevenfold increase in Nigeria's income per capita.[26]

Another way to see the transformative effect of structural changes is to look at qualitative, historical accounts of major poverty-reduction episodes. Consider China, which over the last four decades has seen a more than hundredfold increase in its income per capita and has successfully ushered a billion people out of extreme income poverty. According to Mark Koyama and Jared Rubin, China's success in reducing poverty is the result of the economic growth that followed the market-oriented reforms initiated by Deng Xiaoping in 1979.[27] Though China remained politically centralized during this time, Deng adopted a strategy of "good rule means legitimate rule" and sought to establish his legitimacy by promoting broad-based economic growth.

The adoption of more inclusive economic institutions was central to this strategy. Through the decollectivization of agriculture and the revival of household farming, China saw grain output rise by nearly one-third in the early 1980s. Around the same time, China began opening up to foreign trade and investment, in part through special economic zones that experimented with market-oriented economic policies. Further, in the 1990s, China embarked on a privatization campaign, which led to the restructuring of the state-owned sector and the provision of legal protections for private enterprises. The lesson here isn't that market reforms are essential for poverty alleviation, as the appropriate reforms generally depend on the context. Rather, the lesson is that "institutions are of critical importance" in the story of China's success.[28]

Providing perhaps the best evidence on the transformative potential of structural change comes from estimates of the returns to international migration. Rather than focusing on how people in a given place are affected by a certain structural change, this evidence instead examines what happens when people move to an entirely new structural setting. Michael Clemens, Claudio Montenegro, and Lant Pritchett compared the wages of immigrant workers in the United States to workers in their home countries with similar observable traits.[29] They found that, on average, the earnings of immigrant workers were 6.84 times greater than those of similar people working in their home countries. For some countries, the returns to migration were extremely high, with immigrants from Nigeria, Yemen, and Haiti earning 16.31, 15.11, and 14.25 times their home-country counterparts, respectively.

One problem with these estimates is that immigrant workers may differ from home-country workers in ways that are unobservable (for example, in terms of skill or work ethic). Clemens's team recognized this issue and used several different methods to adjust their estimates for unobservable differences between workers. Their preferred estimates showed that the earnings of immigrant workers were still at least 5.65 times greater on average than the earnings of the corresponding home-country workers. As with the evidence discussed above, there are certainly aspects of these comparisons that are disputable, but the conclusion seems inescapable. That is, when viewed in light of the 35 percent income gains from Targeting the Ultra Poor, it's evident that structural interventions possess the potential for truly transformative change whereas individual interventions are more palliative in comparison.

Cash as Individualism

Cash transfers would appear to have a strong individualist orientation given that they focus assistance on the individual or household level. Is this a fair characterization? To what extent do cash programs neglect structural issues? One way to see more clearly the theory of poverty underlying cash programs is to look at the "theory of change" informing them. A theory of change is essentially a conceptual model that describes the changes expected from a program and the mechanisms through which these changes will come about. One well-known review of the evidence on cash programs, conducted by Francesca Bastagli and others, provides an especially comprehensive theory of change that is useful to consider in detail.[30]

This theory of change exhibits "a strong focus on individual- and household-level outcomes" that the authors classify into three types: first-order, second-order, and third-order outcomes.[31] First-order outcomes refer to the income and expenditure effects that immediately follow on receipt of cash. Specifically, a household receiving money can spend it, save it (or use it to pay off debts), or invest it in various ways. The investment channel is especially notable, as receiving a cash transfer can increase a household's access to credit (because, for example, the reliable payments can act as collateral), which can further facilitate investment. In addition, given that many poor households lack insurance, cash transfers can reduce the distress sale of assets following an adverse shock.

Second-order outcomes refer to behavioral changes that occur as a result of the first-order effects. Bastagli and her coauthors highlight several possible second-order effects. While cash transfers can improve health and education outcomes directly by helping to cover the costs of schooling and healthcare, they can also do so through second-order effects. For example, cash can improve the nutritional status of children and make households less reliant on child labor, both of which can improve school enrollment and attendance.

Receiving cash can also have second-order effects on labor-market participation, as a steady stream of income can either disincentivize work or facilitate it by improving the health and education of household members.

Third-order effects in a theory of change tend to occur in the medium and long term. Increased school enrollment and attendance can improve child learning, cognitive development, and grade progression. Improved access to healthcare can lead to reductions in maternal and child mortality, and also reduce the prevalence of stunting or wasting in children. Cash transfers can also improve mental health in the medium and long term by promoting positive affective states (such as self-esteem and dignity) and mitigating negative ones (such as stress and anxiety). Finally, cash programs can lead to improvements in social capital by increasing participation in community events or contribution-based networks such as savings groups.

While individual and household outcomes are the clear focus of this theory of change, Bastagli and her coauthors also mention some possible meso- and macro-level effects of cash transfers. Regarding meso-level effects, they emphasize that cash programs can have impacts on the local economy, either by affecting labor markets through changes in local labor supply, or by affecting markets for goods and services through increased demand. They also argue that cash programs can "shake up" local social relations in beneficial ways (for example, by prompting better integration of poor households) or in ways that are harmful (for example, by engendering conflict between recipients and non-recipients). With respect to macro-level effects, the authors suggest three potential changes: reductions in aggregate income poverty and inequality; increased aggregate productivity and growth; and potentially improved state-citizen relationships.

Lastly, Bastagli and her colleagues' explanation of the theory of change points to several program details and contextual factors that can influence the nature of a cash program's impacts. Several program details can influence the success of any given program, including the level and timing of the transfers, the use of conditions, the targeting procedure, and the addition of complementary interventions (such as improvements in the supply of local services). The authors also mention various contextual factors at the household, community, and country levels that can mediate a program's impacts. These include initial household wealth, household size and composition, existing social norms or institutions, local infrastructure, government capacity, the presence of conflict, and other factors.

The obvious conclusion to draw from this theory of change is that it is strongly individualist. The core idea of the framework is that cash transfers alleviate poverty by altering individual or household attributes in the form of improved physical, human, and even social capital. To be clear, the framework doesn't completely neglect structural issues. The theory of change mentions, for example, that cash transfers potentially alter state-citizen relationships and possibly change the structure of local labor markets. Further, the framework acknowledges that some structural factors (such as social norms and institutions) can influence the nature and extent of a program's impacts. These structural considerations play only an ancillary role, however, in the theory of change.

While this theory of change is comprehensive, one could argue that it doesn't actually pertain to a real-world cash program. Do the theories of change from actual programs feature structural issues more prominently? Consider Mexico's Oportunidades program (previously called Progresa), a pioneering conditional cash transfer program that served as the blueprint for many others. Martina Ulrichs and Keetie Roelen examined the program's theory of change and summarized its core aim as an attempt "to break the intergenerational cycle of poverty through compliance with certain conditions that promote the investment in human capital formation, based on the theory of accumulation of human capital as a recipe for the eradication of poverty."[32] Oportunidades was, in other words, based on an individualist (human capital) theory of poverty.

Regarding education, for example, the basic idea behind the theory of change was that higher levels of education led to reduced poverty in the future through improved access to better-paying, high-skilled jobs. The key problem was that poor households underinvested in education, either because they misunderstood the long-term benefits of education or because they depended heavily on the income generated by working children. Oportunidades attempted to remedy these issues by providing poor households with reliable incomes and setting conditions that children must go to school. Importantly, note that this theory of change implicitly assumes that the education system works sufficiently well, that labor markets function adequately, that there are no major constraints on social mobility, and that skilled work is appropriately rewarded.

According to Ulrichs and Roelen, the program's theory of change neglects the structural factors constraining poor households, especially in indigenous populations. One such factor is that indigenous populations have limited access to high-quality education and healthcare, because they tend to live in remote locations and because they face language barriers when accessing services. Moreover, job opportunities are severely limited in indigenous regions, and migrants experience limited opportunities due to labor-market discrimination and persistent social exclusion. Oportunidades therefore failed to address the disadvantages of indigenous people because it was "predicated on an individualistic understanding of what causes poverty and what needs to be done to overcome it."[33]

An individualist ideology is, in fact, more deeply embedded in cash programs than these examples would suggest. To see this, consider the intellectual context in which cash transfers are situated. Anton Jäger and Daniel Zamora Vargas, in *Welfare for Markets,* provide an intellectual history of cash transfers, tracing how the concept of development has been redefined in recent decades.[34] Until the mid-1970s, in part due to the influence of dependency theory, national economic development was viewed as essential for eradicating global poverty. The primary impediment to national development, in this view, was the structure of the global economy and the economic dependence of the developing world on industrialized nations. Proponents of these ideas argued that overcoming this dependence required a bold strategy: state-led industrialization.

Planned industrialization in many countries proceeded through *import substitution industrialization,* which attempted to reduce dependency on foreign imports via the substitution of locally produced manufactured goods. It typically entailed tariff and non-tariff trade barriers, incentives for domestic industries, price controls, currency manipulation, and other policies. This inward-looking strategy, however, largely failed. In particular, many countries were plagued by shortfalls of domestic demand, persistently uncompetitive manufactured goods, and problems with overvalued currencies. By the mid-1970s, the apparent failure of import substitution industrialization created scope for a wholesale redefinition of development that broadly dismissed economic dependence as the root cause of global poverty.

Jäger and Vargas argue that the redefinition of development consisted of two ideological shifts, largely initiated by the World Bank during Robert McNamara's presidency in the 1970s. First, McNamara reoriented the World Bank's agenda toward improving the absolute incomes of the poor and, in doing so, abstracted from the economic processes and structural issues creating poverty in the first place. Second, the World Bank increasingly rejected state-led industrialization in favor of a more market-oriented approach to development. This approach prescribed cuts to public spending, an enlarged scope of private sector activity, suspending price controls, and a focus on agricultural exports rather than industrial development. In short, the prevailing ideology shifted from a structuralist understanding of poverty coupled with state-led development to an individualist understanding of poverty coupled with market-led development.

Beginning with Mexico, the new orthodoxy was expressed throughout the developing world in the form of structural adjustment loans. By 1982, in the wake of falling oil prices and rising American interest rates, Mexico's debt had become unsustainable and the country faced imminent default. The International Monetary Fund and the United States Treasury Department responded to the crisis by granting Mexico currency loans and a debt restructuring deal, but only under the condition that the Mexican government implement drastic market-oriented reforms. These included cuts in public spending, the privatization of public assets, the dismantling of price controls, and eventually trade liberalization. By the early 1990s, nearly all Latin American countries and over thirty countries in sub-Saharan Africa were subject to similar reforms.

The effects of these market-oriented reforms were detrimental and many countries saw dramatic increases in poverty. Income poverty rates in Mexico, for example, increased from 23.5 percent to 38.9 percent by 1994.[35] First in Mexico and then elsewhere, cash transfer programs emerged as a tool for coping with the adverse effects of market-oriented reforms. According to Jäger and Vargas, rather than challenging the notion of market-led development, cash transfers instead complemented it by attempting to alleviate poverty through assimilating the poor into local, national, and global markets.

Progress in the fight against poverty therefore became a matter of reforming people rather than the economic system. It is in this regard that an individualist ideology is deeply embedded in cash transfer programs.

Cash as Palliative

Uganda's 2011 presidential election was one of the most expensive in the country's history. President Yoweri Museveni, seeking an unprecedented fourth elected term after abolishing term limits in 2005, spent hundreds of millions of dollars on his campaign, in large part by misappropriating state funds. According to election observers and opposition leaders, Museveni devoted a substantial portion of his campaign resources to illegal vote buying, sometimes personally handing out envelopes stuffed with cash in return for voters' support. Museveni's tactics contributed to his victory, but opponents understandably questioned the fairness of the election. Kizza Besigye's opposing campaign, for example, declared that "an election that has been marred with lots of bribery and intrigue cannot be trusted."[36]

Vote buying and other forms of clientelism are particularly effective when constituents are poor, which suggests that cash transfers could lessen the dependence of voters on favors from the ruling party and possibly increase support for opposition parties. Financial independence through cash transfers could also promote more educated, engaged, and critical citizens who act upon their political ideals rather than succumbing to clientelism. Further, financial independence could make voters more willing to hold governments accountable for their actions and more likely to punish underperforming incumbents electorally.[37] In short, while cash transfers are thoroughly individualistic, one might argue that they can disrupt the status quo by promoting political transitions, strengthening democracy, and creating scope for structural change. Does the evidence support this claim?

Christopher Blattman, Mathilde Emeriau, and Nathan Fiala looked at Uganda's Youth Opportunities Program to see if the one-time cash grants awarded in 2008 affected political behavior during Uganda's 2011 elections. While 88 percent of the control group reported that they voted to reelect Museveni, the treated group appeared marginally less supportive, with 84 percent doing so. Similarly, whereas 4 percent of the control group said they had joined the opposition or actively worked to get opposition parties elected, 7 percent of the treated group reported such political activity. The researchers believed this increased support for the opposition was most likely due to the greater financial independence afforded by the cash transfer program, although they weren't able to determine the precise mechanism.[38]

This study lends support to the idea that cash transfers can disrupt the status quo, but a broader look at the literature reveals that cash programs almost always have the opposite effect, or no effect at all. On the one hand, the "incumbent support hypothesis" suggests that cash programs should increase electoral support for the ruling party, either because voters reward incumbents for increasing their wealth or because they view the implementation of cash programs as a signal of the government's competence. On the other hand, cash programs may have no electoral effect whatsoever, given that they commonly allocate resources based on objective rules that give incumbents no discretion over implementation. This lack of discretion would lead voters to expect to receive identical treatment regardless of who is in office.[39]

Victor Araújo compiled thirty-five high-quality estimates from ten different studies of the electoral effects of (conditional) cash transfer programs.[40] Only five of the thirty-five estimates displayed a negative sign—indicating that cash transfers reduced support for incumbents—and none of these five were statistically significant. By contrast, thirty of the thirty-five estimates indicated that cash transfers increased support for the incumbent, and sixteen of these estimates displayed statistical significance. Araújo additionally calculated a combined (or weighted average) effect across all the estimates, which was positive—a further corroboration of the incumbent support hypothesis. The broader literature shows, then, that rather than disrupting the status quo, cash programs tend to perpetuate it by bolstering support for ruling parties.

What could possibly explain the anomalous result from the Uganda program? Blattman and his coauthors allowed that it was "possible that this result is unique to Uganda or even this context," and named some possible reasons why:

> We would expect context to play a huge role in any treatment effect of a policy on political behavior, and any number of factors could influence

the recipient's reaction to YOP: the nature of the program, the issues at play in this election, or the fact that these are largely first- and second-time voters.[41]

They emphasized that the nature of the program might be especially important. While other cash programs commonly provide recurring transfers, this one was a one-time grant and, as a result, the ruling party couldn't repeatedly claim credit for the program. This could have changed the political interpretation of the program, making the ruling party's role less salient to voters.

The political channel appears to be an unlikely path for transformative change, but there are still other channels worth considering. For example, one could argue that cash transfers facilitate broader economic transformations by expanding aggregate demand and consequently creating new employment opportunities, particularly in nonagricultural sectors. Evidence of this is limited and mixed, with the most rigorous evidence tending to suggest little or no aggregate employment effects. One of the most comprehensive studies on this issue was led by Dennis Egger and looked at the aggregate effects of a large-scale cash program implemented in rural Kenya.[42] This study concluded that the program had no discernible employment effects, but its finding is worth discussing in more detail.

Beginning in 2014, the nonprofit organization GiveDirectly selected 653 villages in Siaya county in western Kenya to participate in a cash transfer program. Of these, 328 were randomly assigned to a treatment group and the remainder were assigned to the control group. All households in the treatment villages that passed a simple means test were given cash transfers in three installments. Under many cash programs, the transfers are too small to drive aggregate economic effects, but in this case the payments were quite large. Specifically, the transfers amounted to about 75 percent of average annual expenditure for recipient households and over 15 percent of annual gross domestic product in the treated areas. The magnitude of the transfers combined with the experimental design make this an especially relevant case study.

On average, recipient households in this GiveDirectly program experienced a 13 percent increase in expenditures, Egger and his coauthors found. Interestingly, their analysis showed that these expenditure increases translated into large revenue gains for businesses in both treated and control areas, with the latter effect due to people making purchases outside of their villages. While these revenue gains were concentrated in the manufacturing and retail sectors, they weren't accompanied by any noticeable changes to firm investment behavior, including any employment creation. The authors put forward a simple explanation for this finding: businesses were operating with considerable excess capacity and were thus able to expand production without hiring additional labor. Accordingly, these results show that there's no necessary link between cash transfers and anything resembling structural economic change.[43]

In contrast to the weak evidence for the political and economic channels, there is compelling evidence that cash transfers can influence cultural traditions. Recall from Chapter 5 that many cultures practice matrilocality or patrilocality, meaning that a couple resides with either the bride's or the groom's parents after marriage. These traditions provide an important form of informal insurance because they ensure old-age support for parents in the absence of pension plans or savings mechanisms. A married couple residing with the bride's family, for example, provides financial and other forms of support to her parents in their later years. Cash transfers, especially support for the elderly, potentially undermine this institution by serving as a substitute for the financial support provided by children.

In an interesting analysis, Natalie Bau looked at the cultural implications of pension programs in Indonesia and Ghana, and found evidence for precisely this effect.[44] In the case of Indonesia, for example, Bau considered a program called Astek, which was a contributory pension scheme founded in 1977. She used geographic variation in the rollout of the program to estimate its effect on the practice of matrilocality, and found that women from traditionally matrilocal groups who had been more exposed to the program in childhood were less likely to practice matrilocality as adults. For the reasons discussed above, Astek reduced the prevalence and transmission of matrilocality in Indonesia. Bau found similar results in Ghana.

As mentioned in Chapter 5, however, the erosion of cultural traditions in this case had an important unintended consequence. In the context of matrilocal societies, for example, the practice of matrilocality gives parents an additional incentive to invest in their daughters, because parents eventually reap some of the benefits of those investments. Bau found that Astek diminished this incentive and, as a result, traditionally matrilocal women who were more exposed to the program as children had significantly lower educational outcomes than women who were less exposed to Astek. Naturally, the program had no effect on the educational outcomes of men from traditionally matrilocal groups, meaning that Astek reduced the relative standing of women in terms of their educational achievements.

What conclusions can be drawn from all this? This chapter's examination of two primary theories of poverty—the individualist and the structuralist views—has shown that interventions with an individualist orientation tend to be palliative rather than transformative. It has also become evident that cash transfers are thoroughly individualist, which would suggest that cash programs are also palliative. Some theories of change nevertheless claim that there are mechanisms through which cash programs can have transformative effects. Based on evidence discussed here, particularly regarding the political and economic channels, this is unlikely to be the case. In fact, regarding the political channel, it has already been established that cash transfers are more likely to perpetuate the status quo than to disrupt it.

Cash transfers are thus palliative, with the possible exception that they may undermine certain cultural institutions such as matrilocality or patrilocality. Even this exception proves to be problematic given that changing such cultural traditions can have unintended consequences for investments in children, especially in girls. Importantly, these effects point to a more general lesson, which is that many of the issues associated with cash transfers, especially their unintended consequences, stem from the fact that these programs don't meaningfully engage with the structural issues that constrain people living in poverty. As an example, recall that the individualistic orientation of Oportunidades meant that the program largely failed to address the structural disadvantages of indigenous Mexicans.

Previous chapters have offered many similar examples. Chapter 7 showed that social arrangements frequently fail to accommodate people with impairments, with one critical implication being that cash transfers have limited effects on the schooling of children with disabilities. Chapter 6 discussed the issue of missing markets and provided examples of goods (including blood, water, clean air, and others) that are critical to human well-being but can't be bought or sold. Chapter 5 focused on the allocation of resources within households and showed how cash transfers can interact with prevailing gender norms to produce harmful effects on both women and children. All these examples illustrate the dangers of neglecting structural factors when attempting to alleviate extreme poverty.

Returning then to the Blattman-Pritchett debate, who's right? The arguments in this chapter clearly lend support to Pritchett's claims that transformative change is difficult to bring about without interventions that address systemic or structural issues. Yet the process of engineering transformative change is challenging and uncertain, and may face steep political resistance. Seen in this light, Blattman's argument isn't unreasonable, and there may be situations where palliative measures like well-designed cash programs are appropriate uses of resources. Whether to take a more transformative or palliative approach to poverty alleviation is a complicated matter, but one thing is clear: the decision is not one to be made by academic economists. This is the subject of Chapter 9.

CHAPTER 9

Paternalism Revisited

ANTHONY KALULU, FOUNDER of the nonprofit Uganda Community Farm, has lived much of his life in and around extreme poverty.[1] Over the years he has become increasingly critical of cash transfers because, in his experience, many of the investments people want and need to escape poverty can't be made by giving money to individuals or households. His perspective contrasts starkly with much of the rhetoric surrounding cash transfers, which emphasizes that granting cash gives people full flexibility to decide for themselves how to best alleviate their poverty. Kalulu's own story highlights the flaws in this rhetoric and ultimately points to the need for alternative poverty-alleviation strategies that avoid imposing decisions on people living in poverty.

Kalulu grew up in a small hut in eastern Uganda with his mother, who worked to make ends meet by distilling alcohol. After dropping out of secondary school in 1998, he moved to Uganda's capital, Kampala, where he picked up odd jobs for several months before being hired by a motorcycle garage. Though this provided steady employment, Kalulu was still extremely poor. So when the government announced an opportunity for tuition-free teacher training in 2001, Kalulu enrolled immediately. Two years later Kalulu found a job as a teacher, yet his government salary was still so low that he often went to class hungry and was regularly ridiculed by his students for his worn-out clothing. He came to fear teaching, so much so that he quit in 2011.[2]

Kalulu had trouble finding a new job and was left nearly starving while living in a small, rented room in eastern Uganda. His teacher training had nevertheless stimulated his creativity and he eventually arrived at a different pathway out of poverty, not only for himself but for others in his community. In 2014, he founded the Uganda Community Farm with the goal of providing people living in poverty, particularly women and youth, with the necessary materials (such as seeds, fertilizers, and pesticides) for setting up

| 157

small-scale farming operations. Following a small crowdfunding campaign in 2015, Kalulu bought ten acres of land for him and his farmers to work, and shortly thereafter built a storage facility with the help of some student volunteers.[3] In the years since, the arrangement has helped hundreds of poor Ugandans diversify their incomes and experience greater food security.

Though Uganda Community Farm has come a long way since its founding, it still faces a critical challenge: the farmers are constrained by a lack of access to reliable markets beyond their community. The solution Kalulu envisions is to build an onsite facility capable of processing various crops—including maize, sorghum, cassava, and several fruits—into intermediate and finished food products that meet the quality standards of modern agricultural value chains. With such processing capacity in place, Uganda Community Farm could be a supplier to a variety of industries producing consumer products, from yogurt makers to breweries to pharmaceutical companies. Anthony is convinced that this facility offers him and his fellow farmers a real opportunity to sustainably escape poverty.[4]

Kalulu's attempts to secure funding, however, have met with resistance. Most tellingly, in 2021, he personally reached out to about a hundred philanthropists active on social media and asked if they'd post about his nonprofit's funding efforts. Only one agreed. Among those who declined, one replied with a simple question that spoke volumes: "Why do you think your project is more effective compared to the others?"[5] The message stuck with Kalulu because it succinctly summarized a major impediment to his ability to get funding for his agro-processing plant. The global development community, he realized, was increasingly focused on funding projects that were or could be deemed "effective" through rigorous impact evaluations, typically randomized controlled trials.[6]

While prioritizing effectiveness may seem reasonable, consider Kalulu's perspective. Not only is it extremely difficult to credibly evaluate a large-scale project like an agro-processing facility, such projects take years to build and scale up operations, meaning that they're unlikely to show impacts within the short time horizons specified by donors. Perhaps more importantly, using effectiveness as a metric for allocating resources strongly privileges scientific knowledge and leaves little room for the kind of rich, local knowledge that Kalulu possesses. It's a top-down approach by which, according to Kalulu, members of the global development community "have only pushed their own predetermined solutions which aren't rooted in the lived experiences of the extreme poor."[7]

Kalulu has become a vocal critic of the global development community and has frequently directed his criticisms at one of its leading causes: cash transfers. He disagrees with the common claim by advocates of cash programs that they place all spending decisions in the hands of people living in poverty. He argues that many of the investments people need to escape extreme poverty—access to markets, clean water, or better schools and healthcare—are collective and can't be made by giving money to individuals or households. For example, building an agro-processing plant following a cash program would require households to pool their resources, which Kalulu views as a near impossibility.

His skepticism isn't unfounded, as it comes from his own experiences with resource pooling. In particular, his community has three boreholes, initially installed with outside funding, which require frequent servicing and repair. To pay for this maintenance, each household in the community has been asked to contribute 5,000 Uganda shillings each year. Many households, however, regularly fail to pay their fair share, even following harvests when their ability to pay is less of a problem.[8] According to Kalulu, this "free-rider problem" means that many collective investments are beyond the reach of even the most generous cash transfer programs. In effect, then, cash transfers are a top-down form of intervention because they implicitly reject important investments that people living in poverty might want.

Kalulu isn't alone in his desire for collective investments. In a poll run in Tanzania, voters were asked whether they'd rather see available resources directly distributed to households in the form of cash transfers, or spent by the government on public needs such as healthcare, education, and infrastructure. Two-thirds of respondents said they'd prefer spending for public needs.[9] In a similar survey, people living in Bihar, India, echoed these sentiments. Out of some 3,800 respondents, 86 percent favored investments in public health and nutrition over cash transfers.[10] In Mongolia, too, nearly 80 percent of respondents to a poll said they'd prefer public investments oriented toward long-term social and economic development over direct disbursements of cash.[11]

The key point here is not that collective investments are always right or better than cash transfers, but that cash programs impose important decisions on people living in poverty. The unifying theme of the last several chapters is that these decisions are wide-ranging and deeply consequential. We've seen that cash programs target some households while leaving others behind; direct resources to some household *members* rather than others; prioritize market goods over nonmarket goods; neglect the unique needs of some of the most vulnerable people; and privilege an individualist rather than a structuralist approach to poverty. Is it ever justifiable to impose these decisions on people living in poverty?

"There's just a fundamental problem with development, which is that it involves outsiders, often foreigners, deciding what's good for you," says Rory Stewart, the former president of GiveDirectly. By contrast, with cash transfers, "it's their dignity, it's their choice on what they do."[12] Stewart is alluding to in-kind transfers and claiming that they are paternalistic because they impose decisions on people living in poverty. He's correct that imposing decisions on the poor is problematic and that in-kind transfers are generally paternalistic. But he's incorrect that cash transfers aren't similarly paternalistic. The next section will discuss this argument in more detail, and the remainder of the chapter will make the case for a more radical, alternative approach to decentralizing decision-making in the fight against global poverty.

The Paternalism of Cash

Poverty-alleviation programs can be classified into three basic groups: centralized, semi-decentralized, and radically decentralized. Centralized programs, such as in-kind transfers, leave little or no opportunity for beneficiaries to participate in important program decisions. While semi-decentralized programs give beneficiaries substantive decision-making responsibilities, these responsibilities remain limited in some ways. Cash transfers are best classified as semi-decentralized, as they give people control over their personal spending, but still impose many other decisions on people living in poverty. Radically decentralized programs leave virtually all program decisions up to the poor, giving them control over types of investment, implementation details, and financial management.

To understand the paternalism of cash transfers, it's first helpful to see exactly why cash transfer advocates view centralized, in-kind programs as paternalistic. While there's no consensus definition of paternalism, philosopher Douglas MacKay offered one definition that helps to clarify this argument. According to his definition, policymaker A acts paternalistically toward citizen B by implementing program C when:

1. C aims to improve B's good or well-being;
2. C is implemented without B's consent; and
3. A's implementation of C is motivated by a negative judgment or expresses a negative judgment of B's self-governance or decision-making abilities.[13]

The third part of this definition is critical, and it's important to clarify the distinction between a program that is *motivated* by a negative judgment of people's decision-making abilities and a program that *expresses* a negative judgment of those abilities. In particular, even if a program wasn't explicitly motivated by any negative judgment, it's still possible that the program is paternalistic because it implicitly expresses a negative judgment. Philosopher Nicolas Cornell illustrated this point with an example of a father who buys a business suit for his daughter.[14] While the father genuinely believes the daughter will enjoy the suit, the truth is that she feels no need for it because she's not interested in working in an office setting. The father's gift in this case isn't explicitly motivated by any negative judgment, but Cornell argued that the gift does implicitly express a negative judgment about his daughter's ability to make good life choices. Thus, the father's good intentions don't excuse him of paternalism, because the gift is experienced by his daughter as ignoring or dismissing her preference.

The second part of the definition, which relates to consent, also requires some clarification. A person's consent to an otherwise paternalistic program or policy can render it non-paternalistic. For example, if a person agrees that it is better to receive in-kind food transfers rather than cash, perhaps because that person lacks confidence in making decisions about how to use money wisely, the policymaker doesn't act paternalistically by complying with this preference. The reason for this is that when we interact with others in consensual ways we recognize their status as competent, self-governing citizens. MacKay made the critical point that consenting to a program or policy requires more than just obeying it or accepting its benefits. Rather, consent requires an explicit act of authorization, such as supporting it in a referendum.

Cash transfer advocates rightly claim that in-kind transfers commonly fit our definition of paternalism. The central argument is that in-kind transfers are motivated by the negative judgment that people can't be trusted to make "wise choices about how to spend their money."[15] Though policymakers often make these judgments quite explicitly, this isn't necessary for paternalism. As in the father-daughter example, in-kind transfers can also be paternalistic because they implicitly disregard people's preferences for other goods or services (such as housing, clothing, and agricultural inputs) that could alleviate their poverty. Treating these preferences as unworthy of consideration is an implicit negative judgment of people's decision-making abilities.[16]

Cash transfers are paternalistic in a similar way. Most obviously, when they are *conditional* they tend to be paternalistic because they compel people to comply with program requirements such as sending children to school. These conditions are typically motivated by the negative judgment that poor households underinvest in human capital because they're either misinformed about the returns to these investments or too shortsighted to make optimal investments.[17] This was precisely the motivation for the use of conditions in Mexico's Oportunidades program, discussed in Chapter 8. There may nevertheless be exceptional situations where conditions wouldn't be considered paternalistic. Policymakers, for instance, may attach conditions to programs because they simply believe that recipients have a civic obligation to do certain things, such as working or volunteering.[18]

The more interesting case is *unconditional* cash transfers, where paternalism is expressed in at least three different ways. First, we've already seen that unconditional cash transfers are commonly motivated by appealing to scientific evidence that demonstrates their effectiveness. As Anthony Kalulu's story illustrates, this appeal to scientific evidence marginalizes local actors and their knowledge about the nature and causes of poverty in their communities. The effectiveness motivation therefore makes an implicit negative judgment about the ability of people living in poverty to identify effective ways to address their own poverty. Importantly, the effectiveness motivation also implicitly discredits the decision-making abilities of people with different values, like those that prefer interventions that reduce inequality even if this sacrifices effectiveness.

Effectiveness is also commonly used as a criterion for choosing the implementation details of cash programs. Targeting procedures like the proxy means test are often justified on the basis of scientific evidence demonstrating their relative effectiveness at reaching poor households. Similarly, cash programs typically direct resources toward women in the household because the evidence suggests that this is the most effective way to improve the well-being of children. Much like the case where effectiveness is used for program selection, using effectiveness for choosing implementation details neglects local knowledge and values about the appropriate ways to administer a program. People living in poverty may have good reasons to prefer program structures that deviate from the scientific evidence, and disregarding these preferences is paternalistic.

The second way that cash transfers are paternalistic relates to the fact that they're routinely motivated by the argument that cash is less prone to corruption than other benefits (such as in-kind food transfers). The basic idea behind this argument is that cash programs can deliver benefits directly to the poor, bypassing inefficient government bureaucracies and opportunistic middlemen. According to GiveDirectly cofounder Paul Niehaus, the corruption issue was one of the main reasons for starting the organization:

> That all got started when I was in graduate school, and some of us at the time were starting to think about what could be done to reduce corruption or "leakage" from anti-poverty programs. . . . That was the question that really set GiveDirectly in motion.[19]

Taking these arguments at face value, it's evident that cash programs embody a decision to circumvent governments rather than engage with them. Corrupt or not, there are nevertheless several reasons why people living in poverty might prefer programs with stronger government involvement.

People may want structural reforms (for example, property rights reform) or nonmarket goods (for example, clean air), both of which are generally provided by governments. People may want interventions that address the unique needs of vulnerable populations—such as quality schooling for disabled children—many of which can only be supplied by governments. People may also prefer other interventions precisely because they better deal with corruption. For example, in the early 2000s, Indonesia began experimenting with replacing fuel subsidies with targeted cash transfers to poor households. Many people, however, opposed the reforms because cash transfers relied more heavily on corrupt local government officials for their implementation.[20] Once again, cash transfers express a negative judgment about people's decision-making abilities by disregarding these preferences.

Regarding the third way that cash is paternalistic, recall that cash transfers are often motivated by the idea that they give people more choice relative to in-kind transfers. That is, rather than being directly provided goods, people can either use cash to buy those same goods or use it to buy something they believe is more useful. This argument subtly neglects the fact that cash transfers take one important option away from beneficiaries, which is the option to be directly provided goods instead of having to obtain them via local markets. People living in poverty may prefer to avoid markets, perhaps because they live in remote areas, have limited mobility, or fear that inflation will erode the value of their benefits.

Reetika Khera conducted an in-depth study of people's preferences between cash and in-kind transfers across nine Indian states.[21] Of the roughly twelve hundred respondents, she found that over two-thirds preferred in-kind transfers. The respondents who preferred in-kind transfers cited many different reasons for their preference, but difficulties accessing markets and price inflation were among the leading concerns. One notable concern was that some especially vulnerable people—the elderly, disabled, or women—would struggle to convert cash into goods because of constraints on their physical mobility. For instance, a sixty-year-old tribal woman named Aetwaribhai said, "It is very difficult to get rice in the market. I am too old to go and search for rice."[22] Disregarding these preferences is paternalistic.

Is this paternalism morally wrong? MacKay rightly argued that people with sufficient capacity or competence to form preferences, make decisions, and act on those decisions should be viewed as equal and autonomous citizens. As equal and autonomous citizens, people have the right to demand that their preferences, decisions, and actions are respected by others. That is, sufficiently competent citizens possess an equal dignity that demands respect from others. Paternalistic policies or programs are morally wrong because they express a negative judgment about people's decision-making abilities and thus fail to respect their equal dignity. In fact, according to MacKay, there are two separate types of wrongs associated with this indignity.

One type of wrong is due to the fact that paternalistic programs effectively treat people as incapable, which disrespects their status as *autonomous* citizens able to make good decisions regarding their well-being. Another type of wrong is that paternalistic programs treat people as inferior because the policymaker, either explicitly or implicitly, occupies a superior position by dismissing the preferences or decisions of people living in poverty. This disrespects people's status as *equal* citizens. The main motivations behind cash transfers are thus paternalistic because they implicitly express a negative judgment about people's decision-making abilities, and this paternalism is morally wrong because it fails to respect people's status as autonomous and equal citizens.

There are, however, some caveats to this conclusion. As in the case of conditional programs, an unconditional program wouldn't necessarily be paternalistic if it were motivated by a basic belief that people have a right to some minimum income level. Certain factors might also affect the degree to which a paternalistic program was wrong, such as the number of beneficiaries that were sufficiently competent decision-makers or the number of people that had publicly consented to the program.[23] The idea that wrongness is a matter of degree suggests that cash programs could still be justifiable if the wrong were outweighed by competing considerations. Just as paternalistic seatbelt laws might be considered permissible based on their life-saving benefits, could cash transfers be similarly permissible? Answering this question requires weighing the promises and perils of radical decentralization in terms of alleviating poverty.

The Promises of Decentralization

Olivio Dutra of Brazil's Partido dos Trabalhadores became mayor of Porto Alegre in 1989 and immediately began experimenting with a radical form of democratized public decision-making. Dutra's administration implemented a participatory budgeting process that directly involved Porto Alegre's citizens in decisions about the city's spending. Popular assemblies were a key feature of this process and were organized within each region of the city to give citizens the opportunity to vote on local investment priorities and elect delegates to manage later stages in the budgeting process. In these later stages, the delegates were responsible for finalizing the investment priorities of each region and then ultimately reconciling the priorities of each region into a feasible budget for the city.[24]

Porto Alegre's experiment with participatory budgeting is one of the most well-known and successful examples of radical decentralization, which seeks to delegate major public decisions to local citizens. Relative to cash transfers, radical decentralization imposes fewer decisions on people living in poverty, primarily by empowering them to choose the investments their communities receive. While cash transfers can and should be an available option in these processes, radical decentralization creates scope for communities to alternatively choose investments in education and health, public infrastructure, property rights reform, in-kind transfers, or other priorities. In short, radical decentralization is a non-paternalistic alternative to cash transfers because it both eliminates the role of the external policymaker and creates a public forum for soliciting consent.

But what are the benefits of radical decentralization in terms of alleviating poverty? In *Development as Freedom,* economist and philosopher Amartya Sen outlined three basic benefits of decentralized, democratic approaches to fighting poverty.[25] First, he argued that decentralization has a *direct* role in reducing poverty because it immediately expands people's capabilities to participate in political life. Second, he argued that decentralization has an *instrumental* role in reducing poverty because it leads to the formulation of policies or programs that better leverage local values and knowledge. Finally, Sen argued that decentralization has a *constructive* role in poverty alleviation, as public debate and discussion can help develop people's understanding of their values and priorities. Each of these benefits will be discussed in more detail below.

Regarding the direct value of decentralization, Porto Alegre's popular assemblies clearly illustrate that the democratic approach to poverty alleviation creates opportunities for people to deliberate about and act upon their goals. Stated differently, radical decentralization directly enhances people's agency. Rutger Claassen's work, discussed in Chapter 2, is especially clear about the relationship between agency and human capabilities. Specifically, Claassen rightly argued that agency is a kind of capability, as being an agent entails having the capability to deliberate and act. If we accept the view that poverty is a lack of capabilities rather than a lack of income, it becomes evident that decentralization directly alleviates poverty by expanding people's agency-oriented capabilities.

We can take this a step further. Claassen distinguished between two broad types of agency: participational and navigational agency. While participational agency refers to a person's ability to act within existing social practices or institutions, navigational agency refers to a person's ability to move between or even reform social practices. He argued that navigational agency was especially critical for a just society because it limits coercion by ensuring that people participate voluntarily in social practices by virtue of their ability to move between them. His three basic capabilities, which include political liberties, are precisely those required to be a navigational agent.[26] Accordingly, beyond claiming that decentralization expands people's agency in general terms, we can further say that decentralization expands people's navigational agency by giving them more opportunities to participate in political life. This is the direct value of radical decentralization.

With respect to the instrumental value of decentralization, delegating decisions to people living in poverty can lead to the creation of better programs or policies. There are at least two channels through which this occurs. First, decentralized decision-making can lead to interventions that are more responsive to local *values,* particularly by empowering the poor to choose interventions that are more in line with how they define or conceptualize poverty. Second, decentralization better incorporates local *knowledge* about the nature of poverty in particular places (for example, who is poor and why), which can lead to interventions that more directly address the primary constraints to escaping poverty in those places. Radical decentralization thus uses local values and knowledge to develop "best fit" policies rather than relying on one-size-fits-all, "best practice" policies.

How vital are local values and knowledge to poverty alleviation? One way to understand the importance of local values is to consider the research on community-based targeting. Recall from Chapter 4 that community-based targeting allows community members or local leaders to select beneficiaries for poverty-alleviation programs, often through community assemblies where people meet to discuss and rank their neighbors on the basis of need. The research on community-based targeting shows quite clearly that local conceptions of poverty are both rich and highly variable across communities. More specifically, this literature shows that the household rankings produced through community-based targeting are frequently at odds with rankings based on household income or expenditure levels.

A study led by Michael Hillebrecht, for example, analyzed the results of a community-based targeting scheme conducted in the department of Nouna in Burkina Faso.[27] It found that the households selected by communities weren't the poorest in terms of expenditures, as roughly 67 percent of the expenditure poor were excluded from the community beneficiary lists. To explain these results, Hillebrecht's team showed that local definitions of poverty were simply different from the standard income- and expenditure-oriented definitions, with communities adopting more holistic and multidimensional definitions of poverty. Specifically, the community-based targeting procedures weighted illness, illiteracy, and female headship more strongly than expenditures when selecting beneficiaries.

The community-based targeting literature also highlights the value of local knowledge for poverty alleviation. In one influential paper, Harold Alderman examined Albania's Ndihma Ekonomike program, which delegated targeting decisions to local elected officials.[28] Alderman was especially interested in whether these officials used their unique knowledge of their communities to improve the targeting of assistance beyond what could be accomplished by the central government. For example, local officials might know that some households experienced idiosyncratic shocks, such as illness or crop failure, which left them with lower consumption levels than indicated by a proxy means test. Alderman found that officials did have local knowledge and that this knowledge led to the poorest households receiving somewhere between 12 and 19 percent greater benefits.[29]

The instrumental benefits of local knowledge go well beyond targeting decisions. Amartya Sen, for example, argued that one reason famines are virtually nonexistent in democracies is because democracy creates channels for local knowledge to be passed on to policymakers. Another Nobel laureate, Elinor Ostrom, similarly argued that decentralized governance of common-pool resources is often successful precisely because local users have better knowledge about the local ecosystem, the behavior of the resource, and the social dynamics of resource use.[30] Yuen Yuen Ang, in *How China Escaped the Poverty Trap,* showed that China's delegation of power to local officials was critical to its success in fighting poverty because the approach capitalized on local knowledge.[31] Overall, it's evident that local values and knowledge are essential to creating effective policies and programs.

Turning to the constructive value of decentralization, the point of empowering citizens to participate in public decisions isn't just to integrate people's existing preferences into policymaking. Rather, the idea is to create opportunities for citizens to reflect on their priorities, learn from others, and ultimately update their beliefs. Stated differently, public discussion invites people to "construct" their preferences. This constructive aspect of decentralization can have direct and instrumental benefits, as it can both deepen people's agency and help them make more informed choices about the appropriate policies to implement. The three benefits of decentralization are thus complementary and, according to Sen, "no evaluation of the democratic form of governance can be complete without considering each."[32]

The constructive value of decentralization is nicely illustrated by a democratic experiment conducted in 2015 in Tamale, Ghana. Tamale is Ghana's third largest city by population and one of the fastest-growing cities in West Africa. In the years preceding the experiment, Tamale had experienced increasingly severe issues with disease and food insecurity, due in part to the government's inability to provide sufficient water, sanitation, and hygiene infrastructure for the city's growing population. To help devise solutions to these problems, researchers from the University of Development Studies and Stanford University convened a representative sample of 208 people from Tamale to deliberate about possible policy responses. During the two-day deliberations, participants reviewed briefing materials, participated in small discussion groups, and attended plenary sessions with experts.[33]

The deliberations revolved around a list of forty policy proposals compiled by an advisory committee with input from focus groups and key informant interviews. Both before and after the deliberative event, all participants rated the proposals on a ten-point scale with higher scores representing interventions they deemed more important. The deliberations produced substantial opinion changes. The ratings for twenty-eight of the forty proposals showed statistically significant changes following deliberation, and the aggregate ranking of eighteen of the forty proposals changed by five or more positions.[34] These results demonstrate clearly that decentralized decision-making can help people sharpen their values and priorities through learning, reflection, and public discussion.

We've now seen that cash transfers can and should be viewed as paternalistic—and that this paternalism is morally wrong because it violates people's right to be treated as autonomous and equal citizens. Though this wrong could be viewed as a decisive argument for radical decentralization over cash transfers, one could still argue that the relative poverty-alleviation effects of decentralization must be fully considered before making any final judgment. The discussion in this section, however, shows that decentralization is a promising approach to poverty alleviation due to its direct, instrumental, and constructive benefits. Additional evidence for this will be presented in Chapter 10, but first we need to take a closer look at decentralization and its problems.

The Perils of Decentralization

Participatory budgeting in Porto Alegre was remarkably successful, as it effectively incorporated the poor into public decision-making, it redistributed spending toward the city's poorest areas, and it reduced clientelism in public spending, among other things. In 2004, the Partido dos Trabalhadores (Brazil's Workers' Party) nevertheless lost the mayor's office to José Fogaça of the rival Partido Popular Socialista, in part because Fogaça promised to further improve the participatory budgeting process. But despite the popularity of participatory budgeting, Fogaça and subsequent mayors ultimately prioritized other approaches to infrastructure and service provision. As a result, only 42 percent of the investment projects approved through participatory budgeting were completed in the decade following 2004, marking a stark contrast with the 82 percent completion rate in the decade prior.[35]

The government's declining commitment to participatory budgeting highlights an important issue with radical decentralization, which is that it can be challenging to build and sustain deliberative processes without deeper political reforms. In the context of existing political structures, public officials have limited incentives to support deliberative processes because, by definition, these processes reduce their power as decision-makers. Decentralization can reduce their ability to allocate resources for their own benefit, diminish the value of their training and expertise—and perhaps still leave them accountable for the outcomes of decisions made deliberatively. Sociologist Peter Evans refers to this as the "marriage problem" because these incentives frustrate any attempt to marry deliberative institutions with existing political structures.[36]

Another issue, which David Crocker refers to as the "autonomy objection," is that people may not actually want increased decision-making responsibilities.[37] They may want to maintain past traditions of hierarchical decision-making rather than replace them with more democratic procedures. There can be many reasons for a lack of demand for decentralization. People may simply value tradition, for example, or they may dislike politics and be content to let elites govern, or they may find that the costs of participation are too high. Regarding the costs of participation, deliberative procedures are not only time-consuming, but they can also impose important psychological costs on participants by requiring them to publicly discuss sensitive matters (for example, their beliefs, problems, or needs).

Even if people do want to engage in deliberative decision-making, some observers have argued that people have a limited capacity to do so. This "capacity problem" may result from people's limited analytical abilities, as their causal reasoning processes may be imperfect, they may have difficulties internalizing abstract forms of evidence, or they may hold fast to flawed schemas or representations of reality. These issues can be compounded by inabilities to weigh arguments in unbiased ways. For example, people may fall prey to "motivated reasoning" wherein they accept evidence that coincides with their existing beliefs and reject information that challenges those beliefs. Finally, beyond individual cognitive shortcomings, capacity issues can result from problems with the dynamics of group discussion.[38]

An issue with group dynamics is that discussion can influence a group to move toward more extreme positions in the direction of the group's original tendencies. There are two main explanations for this. First, people's desire to be perceived favorably by other group members might cause them to adjust their positions in the direction of the dominant view once they hear what others believe. Second, a group's original tendencies can be amplified by discussion, as a disproportionate amount of the arguments will support those tendencies and people may respond by adjusting their positions further in the direction of the original tendencies. While such polarization doesn't necessarily lead to misguided group decisions, there are legitimate concerns that it can have adverse effects, such as fueling hatred or extremism.[39]

Arguably the most common criticism of radical decentralization is what can be termed the "inequality objection." This criticism holds that economic, political, and social power is unequally distributed and that decisions made through deliberative processes will reproduce rather than counteract these inequalities. That is, deliberative procedures can be "captured" by local elites. People with greater wealth or political influence can use their power to influence group decisions to their benefit. People with higher levels of education may excel in debates and thus have the ability to dominate group discussions. Further, people who are privileged based on certain aspects of their identity—such as gender, race, or sexual orientation—may be permitted more speaking opportunities while less privileged people are relegated to the margins.

Even when less privileged groups are given adequate speaking opportunities, their arguments may be marginalized in more subtle ways. People from less privileged backgrounds, especially those with less formal education, may be more likely to voice their positions in impassioned or emotional ways rather than through rational and dispassionate discussion. In particular, instead of emphasizing reason and evidence, marginalized groups may be more inclined to rely on personal testimony, rhetoric, or storytelling when advancing their arguments. To the extent that deliberative procedures place more weight on reason as opposed to emotion, we would then expect less privileged groups to have limited influence over group decisions.[40]

How decisive are these critiques? Regarding the marriage problem, while radical decentralization is not without political challenges, it's far from infeasible. Participedia—an open-source repository that tracks the global spread of experiments in deliberative governance—documents over 2,500 instances of participatory decision-making across roughly 160 countries.[41] The most well-known form of decentralized decision-making, participatory budgeting, has been implemented in around twelve thousand locations across over seventy countries around the world.[42] Many international development agencies have also invested heavily in participatory approaches. For example, as of 2018, the World Bank was supporting 190 participatory projects across nearly eighty countries.[43]

Decentralized decision-making is therefore no utopian idea and, in fact, the evidence suggests that "deliberative institutional experimentation is flourishing throughout the world."[44] There are also many examples of deliberative procedures that have proved to be remarkably durable and, in some cases, are accompanied by deep forms of institutionalization. Many nations (including Indonesia, the Philippines, Uganda, South Africa, and all Latin American countries) have national policy frameworks that support participatory approaches.[45] There are also several examples of countries—such as France, Italy, and Spain—where decentralized decision-making has been formalized through the adoption of specific laws.[46] Perhaps most prominently, in 1992, India passed a constitutional amendment that codified decentralized decision-making through village assemblies.[47]

The most convincing counterargument to the marriage problem is that it's not clear that the political challenges of decentralization are any more severe than those confronting cash transfers. In fact, the political challenges of implementing cash programs closely mirror those of more participatory approaches. Relative to centralized programs like in-kind transfers, cash programs also require public officials to relinquish decision-making power. Much like decentralization, cash transfers can face resistance from public officials when they believe that cash programs limit opportunities for clientelism or patronage, devalue their training or expertise, or leave them to be held accountable if recipients misuse their money. The marriage problem is hardly a decisive critique if cash transfers encounter similar political resistance.[48]

Regarding the autonomy objection, the rapid and widespread proliferation of decentralized decision-making suggests that popular demand for it is substantial. Participation rates are also encouraging. Reviewing the evidence on participatory development interventions, Susan Wong and Scott

Guggenheim found that participation in community meetings ranged from 40 to 70 percent of households.[49] Participation in deliberative procedures has further proven to be quite large in terms of absolute numbers. By some estimates, nearly a hundred thousand people took part in Porto Alegre's participatory budgeting process in 1996 alone.[50] In short, according to several leading deliberative theorists, "claims that most people do not want to participate in politics prove false once the possibility of participation in meaningful deliberation is offered."[51]

The autonomy objection fails for another reason. The only way to know whether people truly reject decentralized decision-making is to give them the opportunity to engage in public discussion about different forms of governance. Through this kind of public discussion, people can be informed about the alternative policymaking procedures available to their communities, and can be given the ability to deliberate about the arguments and counterarguments for each. While it's certainly possible that communities ultimately choose less democratic approaches to policymaking, clearly some level of democracy is necessary to arrive at legitimate decisions on these matters. In brief, what's most important isn't that people exercise their political functionings, but rather that they have the capability to do so.[52]

The capacity problem and the inequality objection similarly fail to withstand scrutiny. Both of these issues relate to the quality of public discussion, but the evidence suggests that people are fully capable of engaging in high-quality, inclusive deliberation. Regarding capacities, if the quality of deliberation were severely deficient, then we'd expect participants to be dissatisfied with the process. Wong and Guggenheim found that this is not the case, as decentralized decision-making "often turns out to be enormously popular."[53] More specifically, they found that people's satisfaction with decentralized decision-making is typically high, ranging from 82 percent in Myanmar to over 90 percent in Lao PDR. They also observed that decentralization was typically inclusive, with the quality of women's participation being "broadly positive" in nearly all cases they reviewed.[54]

There's also a sizable literature providing more direct evidence on the quality of public discussions. In their review of the literature, Andre Bächtiger and his coauthors listed several instances of high-quality deliberation.[55] In the well-known British Colombia Citizens' Assembly on Electoral Reform, members were able to exhibit knowledge about electoral systems at the level of many experts. Similarly, in Pittsburgh, Pennsylvania, participants in the Virtual Agora Project proved to be deeply engaged and produced a high level of reasoned opinion about problems in local public schools. Other examples—ranging from the transnational EuroPolis deliberative poll to the AmericaSpeaks town hall meetings—show that people regularly change their opinions during public discussion, generally in response to well-reasoned arguments rather than group pressures or motivated reasoning.

To be clear, there are certainly instances where participatory processes have been low-quality, exclusive, and subject to elite capture. Research shows, however, that these issues can be counteracted when participatory processes are well-designed. High-quality public discussion can be promoted through provisions of balanced information, expert testimony, oversight by trained facilitators, and other elements. The effect of institutional design is nicely illustrated by an experiment in Finland, which recruited people with extreme attitudes toward immigrants. The participants were put in like-minded groups, with some groups engaging in free discussion and others guided by trained facilitation and discussion rules. While free discussion led groups to become more extreme or polarized, guided discussion reversed those tendencies.[56]

Institutional design has similarly proven critical for the quality of participatory development programs. For example, Scott Fritzen analyzed Indonesia's Urban Poverty Project, which gave communities block grants and let community development boards decide how to use the funds for poverty alleviation.[57] While the first phase of the project placed little structure on the board selection process, the second phase emphasized electing boards democratically and also provided workshops on how to incorporate poor households into project activities. Fritzen found that the boards in the second-phase communities were less dominated by elites, more competent, and more attentive to the needs of poor households. High-quality design effectively counteracted the capacity and inequality problems.

To borrow a phrase from the influential development scholar Robert Chambers, this chapter has argued for "putting the last first" by placing decision-making power in the hands of people living in poverty.[58] We've seen that cash transfers are paternalistic and that radical decentralization avoids this paternalism by eliminating the role of the external policymaker and creating a forum for soliciting consent. We've further seen that decentralization has clear benefits—including direct, instrumental, and constructive benefits—in terms of poverty alleviation. Though none of the criticisms of decentralization should be taken lightly, the above discussion shows that these issues are surmountable. Because it puts the poor at the forefront of decision-making, decentralization is thus a promising alternative to cash transfers. Chapter 10 will discuss this approach in greater detail.

CHAPTER 10
Deliberative Democracy

IN EARLY 2015, A twenty-four-year-old street vendor from southern Tanzania, Hamisi Hamisi, had just been invited to participate in a two-day meeting about economic policy in the capital of Dar es Salaam. This kind of invitation was so uncommon in Tanzania that his family begged him not to go; they feared it might be a gathering organized by some kind of cult. "They were very, very scared," Hamisi later recalled, quoting their warning: "These researchers must be bad people who are going to take people for human sacrifice." Hamisi was nevertheless intrigued by the opportunity and, after speaking with a local official, decided to attend the meeting. "I convinced myself that it was worth the risk. If I took the trip and I ended up dying then it would be the day that God had written for me to die."[1]

Sizable deposits of natural gas had been discovered off Tanzania's southern coast in 2010, valued at roughly fifteen times the country's gross domestic product. Tanzanian policymakers immediately began considering the implications of this resource windfall and a critical debate centered on the question of how the eventual revenues should be spent. Should they be directly distributed to citizens in the form of cash transfers? Or should the government apply the revenues to large-scale initiatives in areas like public health, education, and infrastructure? To inform the government's decision, a group of researchers from the Center for Global Development and Stanford University took an innovative approach to consulting ordinary citizens like Hamisi.[2]

The researchers were guided by a simple question: If the people affected by the decisions were able to consider the issues under good conditions, what would they think? Common methods for gauging public opinion, such as opinion polls, weren't well-suited to answering this question. According to one of the researchers, Stanford's James Fishkin, "If you have ordinary polls people usually are not well-informed. You don't want to follow public opinion when the public just has a vague impression of sound-bites and headlines."[3] To avoid this problem, the researchers used a more sophisticated method known as *deliberative polling,* developed by Fishkin himself in the 1980s. Deliberative polls recruit a representative sample of citizens and solicit their opinions only after they've had the opportunity to review briefing materials, consult with experts, and engage in structured deliberations with one another.

Deliberative polling is a promising approach to decentralized decision-making for poverty alleviation. An interesting feature of the Tanzanian case was that the researchers embedded the poll in a broader experiment to better understand how it worked. The experiment began in 2015 with the recruitment of a nationally representative sample of about two thousand Tanzanian citizens. Because one objective was to understand the independent effects of information and deliberation on people's opinions, the researchers randomly assigned participants to two treatment groups. While the first group of approximately three hundred citizens was only provided with information, the second group of just over four hundred citizens was engaged in the full deliberative procedure. The remainder of the sampled citizens made up the control group.

The information treatment group was given detailed information about the gas discovery as well as the benefits and limitations of the various policy options. Because of concerns about limited literacy among Tanzania's population, the information was conveyed through a thirty-minute video, the script of which incorporated input from several stakeholders (such as industry representatives, civil society leaders, and officials from Tanzania's major political parties). The aim of the video was to give participants a balanced view of controversial alternatives informed by experiences from other places. For example, the video explained the idea of cash transfers by showing experiences from programs implemented in Mongolia, the United States, and South Africa.

The deliberation treatment group viewed the same informational video, but also attended a two-day deliberative event. At it, ordinary citizens like Hamisi attended four sessions, each focused on a different topic related to policy surrounding the natural gas discovery. The sessions consisted of two parts. For the first part of each session, participants were randomly assigned to twenty-five breakout group discussions led by trained facilitators.

The second part was a ninety-minute plenary gathering, where all participants convened to learn from a panel of experts. The panelists were selected to reflect diverse viewpoints and included academics, civil society leaders, and members of opposing political parties. One spokesperson from each breakout group was nominated to pose questions to the experts.

What did people think about how to use the resource windfall after the deliberations had been completed? Recall from Chapter 9 that 66 percent of Tanzanians preferred government spending on health, education, or infrastructure over cash transfers; this was the polling result for the control group. Interestingly, opposition to cash transfers was *more* pronounced in the treated groups. Specifically, 69 percent of the information group and 77 percent of the deliberation group opposed cash transfers.[4] The poll also included questions to elicit people's preferences on spending on social services (such as health and education initiatives) versus infrastructure (such as roads and electricity). While 61 percent of the control group expressed support for social services over infrastructure, this majority rose to 71 percent following deliberation.[5]

These results reinforce the idea that people can and often do prefer other interventions to cash transfers, even when they're informed and engaged. More to the point of this chapter, the results show the value of deliberation in decentralized decision-making. The researchers found not only that participating in deliberative events changed people's opinions, but that the opinion changes were driven by the process of deliberation, as opposed to being driven merely by access to better information. In fact, the impact on people's opinions of the information treatment alone was not statistically significant.[6] Deliberation, then, in addition to its direct value in deepening people's agency, advances the instrumental and constructive benefits of decentralization by sharpening people's views on appropriate interventions for promoting their well-being.

The experiment also shows that well-designed deliberative procedures aren't constrained by capacity or inequality problems. Less affluent deliberators experienced knowledge gains similar to richer deliberators and were no less likely to refine their views. People's opinion changes also weren't influenced by the initial majority views of their small groups. Similarly, people's opinion changes weren't influenced by the views of the more privileged members in their small groups: the initial views expressed by men, the relatively wealthy, and the more educated exerted no disproportionate influence on people's opinions.[7] Given that deliberative polling was specifically developed to counteract many of the concerns with deliberative decision-making, it should not surprise us that people were able to participate on a level playing field.

Despite the concerns of Hamisi's family, deliberative democracy is not a cult. Rather, it is an especially compelling way to decentralize decision-making in the fight against global poverty. To make the case for deliberative democracy, this chapter will focus on three basic democratic values—deliberation, equality, and participation—and show how attempts to realize any two of these values must undermine the realization of the third. This is the *democratic trilemma*. We'll then see that *microcosmic deliberation* is the most promising way to navigate this trilemma and consider the merits of several variants of this model. Finally, the discussion will turn to some practical details related to the variant that's best suited for developing poverty-alleviation strategies—namely, deliberative polling.

The Democratic Trilemma

Deliberation Day is an idealized model for democratic decision-making proposed by Fishkin and Bruce Ackerman.[8] Rather than using random samples of people, it would extend deliberative polling to an entire population by providing widespread access to briefing materials, small-group discussions, and consultations with experts. These deliberative exercises would be conducted throughout the course of a single day with the overall aim of giving everybody the opportunity to weigh important issues under good conditions. Deliberation Day is, however, impractical for large populations because it would be extremely costly, be challenging to organize, and require considerable institutional will.

Despite its practical barriers, Deliberation Day is a useful idea because it's a model of democratic decision-making that simultaneously realizes three key values: deliberation, equality, and participation.[9] Deliberation is "the act of weighing" and specifically refers to the process by which people consider competing arguments through discussions with each other. High-quality deliberation is critical for democratic decision-making because it's the basis for securing collective consent regarding policies or programs. To secure genuine consent, people must be adequately informed, exposed to competing views, and also given the opportunity to reflect on their beliefs. Deliberation Day clearly realizes the value of deliberation, particularly through facilitating small-group discussions where people have the opportunity to debate and reflect with each other.

Deliberation Day also realizes the second value, equality, by ensuring that people deliberate on equal terms and by counting any final votes equally. Equal voting power is often considered essential for political equality and requires that each citizen has an equal likelihood of being the decisive voter. Such political equality can be achieved in various ways. The most common way of achieving political equality has been to allow all citizens to vote and then to count their votes equally. An alternative method, most notably practiced in ancient Athens, is to choose voters through a lottery and then to count the votes of the selected citizens equally. Whether the voting process is direct or intermediated by a lottery is inconsequential for political equality, as in both cases each person still has an equal chance of being the decisive voter.

The final value is mass political participation, which refers to the extent of citizens' engagement in activities intended to influence politics or policy. Voting is the most common way people influence politics or policy, but participation also encompasses attending deliberations or demonstrations, signing petitions, and contributing money to political causes, among other things. Political participation in a population depends not only on how many people participate in political activities, but also on the degree to which any given person participates. The breadth of participation is, however, especially important for the legitimacy of democratic decisions, largely because it signals a form of mass consent. Deliberation Day realizes the value of participation by giving everybody the chance to deliberate and additionally provides stipends to incentivize participation.

While Deliberation Day realizes all three democratic values, feasible models of democratic decision-making inevitably fall short of this ideal. Specifically, the democratic trilemma holds that attempts to realize any two of the values will generally undermine achieving the third. Fishkin summarized the issue as follows:

> The challenge posed by the trilemma is not insuperable, at least in theory. We can imagine ways around it, but at great expense and with departures

from the range of reforms usually regarded as feasible. . . . But barring such a major departure from our usual political practices and constraints or barring some unforeseen new innovation or technology, we can reliably expect the trilemma pattern to hold. It has held throughout the long history of democratic experimentation. There has never, in other words, been an institution that reliably delivered political equality, deliberation, and mass participation simultaneously.[10]

The trilemma leaves us with a choice between three design alternatives, each of which realizes two of the democratic values. These alternatives are represented in Figure 10.1.

"Mass democracy" attempts to realize the values of political equality and mass participation, but in doing so sacrifices deliberation. To see why, imagine a referendum that puts some issue to a direct vote by all people, with each vote counted equally. While this referendum may realize the values of equality

	Equality	Participation	Deliberation
Mass democracy	+	+	−
Mobilized deliberation	−	+	+
Microcosmic deliberation	+	−	+

FIGURE 10.1. Options in the democratic trilemma

James Fishkin, *When the People Speak: Deliberative Democracy and Public Consultation* (Oxford, UK: Oxford University Press, 2009), Chart II, 46. Reproduced with permission from Oxford University Press.

and participation, the fact that many people participate on equal terms means that the influence of any single vote is small. As a result, people have little incentive to become informed about the issues and little incentive to deeply weigh the competing arguments. In the absence of any additional incentives, this "rational ignorance" leads to limited deliberation and produces results that fail to reflect informed and considered judgments. All forms of mass democracy, not just referenda, suffer from this deliberative deficit.

"Mobilized deliberation" takes a different approach by emphasizing participation and deliberation while sacrificing equality. Consider, for example, democratic decision-making through popular assemblies, like those held in Porto Alegre, Brazil. Such popular assemblies are open to everybody in the relevant population and are intended to facilitate deliberation. They suffer from "participatory distortion," however, in the sense that attendees are self-selected and thus unlikely to be representative of the population. Predictably, this skews results as decisions made through popular assemblies disproportionately reflect the views of the most active and able groups of people. The views of the rest are underrepresented, which means that mobilized deliberation comes at the expense of political equality.

The final alternative, "microcosmic deliberation," sacrifices mass participation to realize the values of equality and deliberation. There are many variants of microcosmic deliberation, but deliberative polling is a leading example. As we've seen in the case of Tanzania, deliberative polling strongly emphasizes informed and structured deliberation. Deliberative polling also promises political equality, as random sampling ensures that everybody has an equal chance at participating and all decision processes count votes equally. It's nevertheless logistically challenging to engage large portions of the population in these types of deliberative exercises, implying that deliberative polls must sacrifice mass participation. Like mass democracy and mobilized deliberation, microcosmic deliberation therefore also fails to satisfy all three democratic values.

Which alternative is best suited to developing poverty-alleviation strategies? The "right" answer to this question depends on the context and the specifics of the policy question, but there are some compelling reasons for giving microcosmic deliberation special consideration in any context. For one, deliberation is vital for realizing the benefits of radical decentralization. Recall that the direct benefit of decentralization results from expanding people's agency and we've seen that being an agent entails having the capability to deliberate and act. Any democratic procedure that lacks a deliberative component therefore fails to realize the full direct benefits of decentralization.

Deliberation is also crucial for promoting the instrumental and constructive benefits of decentralization. We've already seen examples from Ghana and Tanzania where deliberation led to substantial opinion changes. These examples most immediately show that deliberation is the primary channel through which decentralization helps construct people's preferences. They also highlight the instrumental benefits of deliberation, as policy decisions made on the basis of people's updated beliefs are arguably superior to those made on the basis of their raw opinions. For instance, in the case of Ghana, shared in Chapter 9, we saw that the rankings of eighteen of the forty policy proposals changed by five or more positions following deliberation. Because the updated rankings better reflect local values and information, it is reasonable to expect they will provide better guidance for developing poverty-alleviation strategies.

Political equality is just as essential as deliberation to realizing the benefits of decentralization, particularly for people living in poverty. A commitment to political equality is foundational for ensuring that all people are represented in democratic decision-making procedures. Political equality thus facilitates the direct benefits of decentralization by providing even the most marginalized groups with an equal capability to exercise their agency. A commitment to equality is also important for realizing the constructive benefits of decentralization. In particular, prioritizing equality involves structuring deliberations in a way that promotes equal participation, which in turn gives less privileged participants an equal opportunity to learn, debate, and update their beliefs.

There are at least two channels through which political equality promotes the instrumental benefits of decentralization. First, representative processes that count all votes equally lead to the adoption of policies that are responsive to the needs of all groups, most notably people living in poverty. Second, the presence of less privileged people in deliberations has been shown to affect the views of more privileged participants, making them more sympathetic to supporting the less well-off. This point is nicely illustrated by a deliberative exercise conducted in Australia about policies for promoting reconciliation with indigenous people. While deliberation moved all discussion groups to be more supportive of reconciliation policies, the groups with indigenous participants moved more in that direction because of stronger opinion changes among nonindigenous people.[11]

We can also consider the importance of political equality from a different perspective. Recall that the inequality objection explained in Chapter 9 is one of the most common criticisms of decentralization and raises the concern that deliberative exercises will be captured by local elites. Any democratic procedure that lacks a serious commitment to equality will be vulnerable to this objection. Specifically, mobilized deliberation sacrifices equality to realize the values of deliberation and participation. This, however, leaves mobilized deliberation vulnerable to criticism: because participants are inevitably self-selected, the people deliberating are often disproportionately informed, affluent, and politically active. A commitment to equality is crucial for mitigating such elite capture and preempting the inequality objection.

The main point here is that only one democratic alternative realizes the fundamental values of deliberation and equality, and that is microcosmic deliberation. Although it sacrifices mass participation, that value is less fundamental because a lack of mass participation doesn't distort decision-making in any predictable way. Stated differently, the values of deliberation and equality refer to the *quality* of the decision-making process whereas the value of participation refers only to the *quantity* of people participating. The reason for prioritizing quality over quantity is straightforward: because the criticisms of radical decentralization focus heavily on the quality of the decision-making process (for example, the inequality objection), the natural response is to prioritize the alternative that preempts those concerns.

While there are compelling reasons for favoring microcosmic deliberation when developing poverty-alleviation strategies, this still leaves many variants of microcosmic deliberation to choose among. Not all of the variants, however, realize the values of deliberation and equality to the same extent and we can use this fact to narrow down the options. Generally speaking, the various options can be classified into two groups based on whether they select participants *randomly* or *nonrandomly*. In the next section, we'll see that the variants using nonrandom selection often fail to fully realize the value of political equality, and this will lead to a closer look at the variants that instead use random selection.

Microcosmic Deliberation in Detail

Prior to the 1997 East Asian economic crisis, Indonesia had made substantial progress reducing income poverty, as poverty rates had fallen from over 50 percent in 1970 to under 20 percent in 1997. When that crisis hit, however, increased economic vulnerability and popular resentment of the Suharto regime boiled over into riots that ultimately forced the resignation of Suharto after thirty-two years in power.[12] As a result of the economic and political turmoil, Indonesia's gross domestic product shrank by 13.5 percent in 1998 alone and millions of people fell below the income poverty line, especially in rural areas. Desperate to counteract these trends, the new administration decided to rapidly scale up a pilot of a promising poverty-alleviation program: the Kecamatan Development Program (KDP).[13]

KDP took a radically decentralized approach to poverty alleviation that is known in the field of international development as "community-driven development." The program provided block grants to participating kecamatan, which are subdistricts of Indonesia that typically contain between ten and twenty villages. In each kecamatan, a forum was assembled of six elected representatives from each village, including the village head and at least three women, and put in charge of deciding how to use the funds to promote local development. Each forum chose from a list of projects put forth by the villages in the kecamatan, with each village submitting one general project and one project specifically targeted toward women.[14]

The two projects selected by each village were chosen through parallel village-level assemblies. The general project was selected in an assembly open to everybody in the village whereas the women's project was selected in an assembly only open to women. Though the assemblies were open to the public, they were disproportionately attended by people in leadership positions, including village heads, neighborhood heads, and people representing village groups. In these village-level assemblies, project facilitators presented lists of proposed projects gathered across several months of small meetings throughout the village.[15] Beyond a short "negative" list prohibiting proposals such as funding for military or paramilitary purposes, very few restrictions were placed on the types of programs people could suggest.[16]

By placing kecamatan forums at the forefront of decision-making, KDP is an example of microcosmic deliberation, specifically one that relies on selecting participants *nonrandomly*. This model has been widely acclaimed and has proliferated both inside and outside of Indonesia. Beginning in just forty-eight villages in 1997, the program scaled up rapidly within Indonesia and eventually reached all of the country's seventy-five thousand villages by 2014.[17] Many other countries have also implemented programs inspired by the kecamatan model, most notably Afghanistan, East Timor, Liberia, and the Philippines. By 2018, the World Bank alone was financing over 170 similar programs across seventy-nine developing countries.[18]

One reason for the success of the kecamatan model is that it has been effective. John Voss evaluated the second phase of KDP, which covered over thirteen hundred kecamatan between the years 2002 and 2007. He found that communities, given nearly unrestricted choice, overwhelmingly chose infrastructure projects—74 percent of the disbursed funds went to infrastructure activities related to tertiary roads, markets, and irrigation systems—and that these projects translated into various positive economic impacts. The poorest households in treated areas experienced consumption gains 11 percentage points greater than their counterparts in kecamatan receiving no planning or financial assistance. Similarly, Voss found that the proportion of households escaping income poverty in the poorest kecamatan was 9.2 percent higher. Both of these effects were statistically significant.[19]

The kecamatan model has also shown notable impacts in other countries. In a 2018 review of the literature, economist Katherine Casey summarized the evidence on seven different programs, including KDP. Casey found that the model routinely generated significant impacts on local public goods, including investments in clean water, sanitation, and electricity. In addition, Casey found evidence of significant effects on economic outcomes—such as increases in household assets, employment, and community-level market activity—although these effects were less pronounced. While some areas of benefit (such as social capital) showed little or no change, the overall picture was still fairly impressive, largely because many of the programs took place in challenging, conflict-affected areas.[20]

All of these evaluations focused on short- to medium-term impacts, but more recent research has examined the longer run. Casey and several coauthors revisited Sierra Leone's GoBifo project eleven years after it began to see whether the program had persistent effects. GoBifo began in 2005 and was structured similarly to KDP, with the program providing block grants and planning assistance to select communities. Casey and her colleagues found that the treated communities had a strong preference for investing in public goods and that these investments were remarkably durable. Relative to control areas that didn't receive any support, the treated areas had 40 percent more public goods after eleven years. Moreover, the treated communities showed significant long-term increases in economic activity, including greater numbers of petty traders, goods for sale, and new businesses.[21]

The Sierra Leone study suggests that microcosmic deliberation can produce lasting effects, which contrasts starkly with the limited long-run effects of cash transfers discussed in Chapter 3. Other evaluations support this conclusion. In an eight-year study of the Democratic Republic of Congo's Tuungane program, researchers found that treated communities' hospitals and schools were of significantly higher quality in the long run. Health facilities in the treated areas were also significantly better stocked with antibiotics, antimalarial pills, and anti-inflammatory tablets.[22] Similarly, a nine-year evaluation of Indonesia's Generasi program showed that it led to a lasting revitalization of local clinics known as *posyandu*. (The name combines three words to suggest an "integrated service post" providing a mix of services vital to the health of mothers and children in a rural area.) This resulted in significant increases in nutrition supplementation, infant weighing, and attendance at prenatal and parenting classes.[23]

While the kecamatan model is promising in many ways, it has some important limitations. Reviewing the evidence on radical decentralization, a study led by Howard White raised several issues, the most concerning of which is that community decision-making is often dominated by relatively privileged or elite groups (such as village heads, activists, or men). For example, women were found to be half as likely to be aware of a program in their community, and even less likely to attend or speak at meetings. The review further found that committee members were nearly three times more likely to be men than women. Though many programs had specific measures in place to counteract gender exclusion, frequently these measures either were not enforced or were insufficient for ensuring genuine representation. (In some cases, for example, women's meetings were dominated by elite women.)[24]

White's review covered several different types of decentralized programs, but the kecamatan model was no exception to these issues. The evidence on KDP, for example, shows that attendees of women's meetings were predominantly activists or relatives of village officials. Women's meetings were also sometimes used by other groups to advance their own projects, given that a project targeted to women had a greater chance of being selected by the kecamatan forums. Another issue with KDP was that village heads and other leaders exerted substantial influence on decision-making, sometimes by circumventing formal procedures. In West Java, one village head worked informally with other leaders to rally support for a market renovation project and then invited only the known supporters to program meetings.[25]

Despite the potential for elite domination in kecamatan-type programs, it's worth noting that community leaders are often elected representatives who act in the interests of their constituents. A program in the Philippines called Kalahi-CIDSS provides an interesting example. Julien Labonne and Robert Chase of the World Bank found that this program's resources routinely flowed to the poorest villages and that most of its projects reflected the preferences of community members. While elite domination didn't appear to distort project selection on average, Labonne and Chase found that elected leaders in more unequal villages tended to override community preferences in favor of their own projects. This was likely because village leaders were more powerful in unequal villages and therefore more able to impose their preferences.[26]

The kecamatan model shows that microcosmic deliberation can be effective, but is susceptible to elite domination—and we've seen that elites don't always respect the preferences of the broader community. Marginalized groups are often less informed about the program, less likely to attend or speak at meetings, and less likely to serve on program committees. In short, though the kecamatan model realizes the value of deliberation through its various decision-making bodies, it falls short in terms of fully realizing the value of equality. A deep commitment to political equality entails taking steps to make sure that community decision-making bodies are representative of the population, but this simply isn't guaranteed by selecting participants nonrandomly. A better alternative is to select participants randomly.

It's worth briefly considering a few of the many variants of microcosmic deliberation that select participants at random. All of them incorporate deliberative discussion among participants informed by experts, but they differ in terms of the number of participants, the nature of the event, and the output generated. The *citizens' jury* is one popular type of microcosmic deliberation that gathers a small number of citizens (an average of thirty-four people, according to one study) to discuss a pressing policy issue.[27] After a short learning period about the issue, the jurors call witnesses, hear testimony, and discuss the policy options. On average, participants meet for about four days over the course of five weeks, with the final output being a collective recommendation to policymakers.

Consensus conferences are another well-known variant of microcosmic deliberation. Developed by the Danish Board of Technology in 1987, these events typically gather an average of sixteen citizens for about four days. Consensus conferences strive for random selections of citizens, but participants are typically recruited through advertisements and the sample is only drawn from those volunteering to participate. After a weekend of preparatory meetings, the citizens hear presentations by experts, pose questions to the experts, and then deliberate about the policy in question. Participants are generally required to reach a consensus on their recommendations and to present these recommendations to the experts on the final day of the event. Members of the press and other stakeholders are typically invited to the final day, with the goal of making the recommendations public and promoting wider debate.

Planning cells, developed by Peter Dienel at the University of Wuppertal in the 1970s, are yet another popular variant. Their defining feature is that numerous randomly selected groups meet in different locations (such as many towns within a region), sometimes to consider different parts of a given policy problem. Each cell consists of twenty-four citizens on average and each event typically takes place over the course of three consecutive days. Like citizens' juries and consensus conferences, each cell begins with a short learning phase, followed by deliberation in small groups and a procedure for developing a final recommendation. While citizens' juries and consensus conferences are generally moderated by skilled facilitators, participants in planning cells deliberate in their small groups without facilitation.

These are only a few of the forms of microcosmic deliberation that rely on random sampling, but they illustrate how variants can differ in their numbers of participants, the nature of their deliberations, and the outputs of the events.[28] What design features are essential to fully realizing the value of political equality, particularly in high-poverty contexts? There are at least three. First, the number of participants must be large enough to constitute a (statistically) representative sample of the underlying population. Second, deliberations must be moderated by trained facilitators to promote the participation of marginalized groups. And finally, the process should avoid consensus decisions to protect vulnerable participants, especially poorer participants, from coercion.

Deliberative polling is the only variant of microcosmic deliberation that incorporates all these features. Unlike small-scale citizens' juries, for example, deliberative polls specifically recruit a large and statistically representative sample of the target population. Deliberative polls also strongly emphasize discussion in the presence of trained facilitators, which is not the case with planning cells and some other variants. Further, in contrast to variants like the consensus conference, participants in deliberative polls express their final views through secret ballots rather than through consensus statements. While deliberative polling may not always be the "right" variant, a strong claim can be made that it serves the values of deliberation and equality, which makes it worthy of serious consideration in any setting.

Designing Deliberations

Deliberative polling hasn't been widely used for developing poverty-alleviation strategies, but it's hardly a new idea and decades of experimentation offer valuable lessons. Since Fishkin developed the idea in the 1980s, deliberative polling has been applied more than 150 times in over fifty countries.[29] Unlike other models, which have mostly been implemented in more developed countries, deliberative polling has been implemented in a wide variety of places. This includes many applications in Africa, Asia, the Middle East, Oceania, and South America, as well as Europe and North America. Deliberative polling has also been used to address a variety of issues, shaping policy in response to environmental disasters, renewable energy, education and healthcare, unemployment, and many other challenges.

Throughout the years, deliberative polling has proven to be remarkably flexible in its geographic scope. Deliberative polls have been successfully conducted at various geographic levels, from small towns to entire countries and even internationally. The implication of this flexibility is that deliberative polling can be tailored to the most relevant geographic scale for a given poverty-alleviation strategy. In the case of Tanzania, the application was at the national level because the country required a national strategy for how best to use its natural gas revenues. By contrast, the polls implemented in Tamale, Ghana, occurred at the city level because the policy question was how best to respond to the city's growing problems with disease and food insecurity. Not only can polls be applied to any geographical scale, they can also be conducted in several areas at the same time.

Consider another African example: the Mount Elgon region of Uganda. Two districts in this region, Butaleja and Bududa, have faced numerous developmental challenges due to frequent natural disasters. A common policy response, however, has often been considered unattractive because the regions are very different. Butaleja is in the lowlands and subject to frequent flooding whereas Bududa is in the highlands and plagued by frequent landslides. In 2014, a team led by researchers at Makerere University thus conducted deliberative polls in both regions to develop tailored solutions for each. The polls showed that the participants in each region had distinct policy preferences, with Butaleja prioritizing drilling for clean water and Bududa prioritizing education interventions.[30] Perhaps more importantly, this example shows that deliberative polls are modular and can be implemented simultaneously across (potentially many) different places to inform localized policy solutions.

Another important design decision relates to setting the agenda for deliberative polls. How can one create a complete "menu" of policies or projects for the deliberators to consider? While there are various ways to set the agenda, one proven strategy is to use focus groups and key informant interviews to identify important issues and potential policy solutions. In Uganda, for example, focus groups and interviews identified environmental disasters as an especially critical issue, with resettlement management, land management, and population pressure as policy priorities. This information was then passed to an advisory group—composed of government officials, academic experts, and local NGOs—to determine the feasible policies in each of these areas. The end result was a list of thirty-six policy options for the deliberators to discuss and rank.[31]

This kind of agenda-setting process can be enriched in several ways. Most importantly, genuinely decentralized decision-making would go beyond letting people choose their preferred policies and also allow them to determine the implementation details. Say a community decides to build a new school or renovate an existing one. Should the community manage the construction themselves or should the project be delegated to a government ministry or private contractor? Or, say a community decides to distribute the available resources to households in the form of a cash transfer. How should the cash transfer be targeted and which household member should receive the transfer? As we've seen in the case of cash transfers, implementation issues can be controversial and any complete agenda would delegate these issues to the deliberators.

Like the agenda, the procedure for sampling participants must also be designed carefully. The ultimate goal is to understand what the *population* in a given place thinks about an issue and the sample must be large enough to support this inference. Small samples run a greater risk of being unusual or unrepresentative just by chance. Importantly, deliberative polls also emphasize diagnosing the quality of the deliberations by trying to understand how people's views change during the event. Did people's views polarize during the deliberations or move in the direction of more elite participants? Opinion changes can be evaluated by surveying participants before and after the deliberations, but the sample must be large enough for statistically valid conclusions. The number of participants necessary for this can nevertheless be calculated using standard sample size formulas.

At a minimum, the sample should be representative of key demographic groups, including different age, class, gender, and ethnic groups, to name a few. Some deliberative polls might also want to make sure that the sample is representative of people with different policy attitudes. Particularly when some subgroups are only a small fraction of the population, simple random sampling can be insufficient to guarantee that these groups are adequately represented. This issue, however, can be addressed with stratified random sampling. In this case, the population is divided into distinct subgroups, or strata, based on their demographic characteristics and then random samples are taken within each subgroup. As long as the size of each subgroup sample is proportionate to the target population, the final sample will be representative of all the relevant groups.[32]

Once the sample is recruited, it's important to ensure that everybody participates in the deliberations on a level playing field. There are at least three design features that can mitigate power imbalances: accessible briefing materials, skilled facilitation, and secret ballots. Regarding briefing materials, when deliberative polling is applied to high-poverty contexts, there are typically concerns that some participants are illiterate. Given that written briefing materials are inaccessible to these people, it's necessary to take an alternative approach. In Tanzania and Ghana, for instance, these issues were circumvented by presenting briefing materials in the form of videos. The videos were short, in the range of fifteen to thirty minutes, and used concrete examples to explain key issues.

With respect to facilitation, small-group discussions can devolve into platforms for more privileged or opinionated participants if they're not managed carefully. Deliberative polls preempt this issue by having each small-group discussion led by a facilitator who's been given a short training ahead of time. In these trainings, facilitators are taught to encourage everybody to talk, to make sure participants talk to each other, and to avoid expressing their own opinions, among other things. Finding facilitators can be challenging, especially in high-poverty contexts when many polls are conducted simultaneously. One option in this case is to use a strategy from Ackerman and Fishkin's Deliberation Day wherein facilitators are drawn randomly from the sample of deliberators and given additional stipends to serve in that role.

Finally, on the issue of secret ballots, deliberative polls explicitly avoid consensus statements or even public expressions of opinion (such as a show of hands during small-group discussions). The goal is to understand what people think under good conditions, and an important element of this is to minimize any social pressure to conform to the opinions of others. Consensus-seeking or public expressions of opinion often result in explicit or implicit pressure to conform to the majority, which undermines people's ability to independently form their own judgments. Deliberative polls avoid these issues by gauging people's post-deliberation views through secret ballots or confidential questionnaires. This strategy has proven to be remarkably successful and is one reason why the evidence routinely shows that deliberative polls are resistant to distortions.[33]

Even when the deliberations are well-designed, there may still be situations where the results are viewed as illegitimate because only a sample of the population participates. Deliberative polls, as we've seen, explicitly sacrifice mass participation and therefore can't claim to signal *actual* mass consent. One creative way to overcome this challenge is to link the deliberative exercises to a referendum. In this case, one would take the recommendations from the deliberative exercises and give the population an opportunity to vote on whether to accept or reject the proposal.[34] While this approach can provide a token of mass consent, the main risk is that the broader population is less informed than the deliberators, which could skew the results. Raising awareness through media campaigns and providing widespread access to briefing materials can, however, mitigate this risk.

This kind of hybrid approach was used in British Columbia's well-known Citizens' Assembly on Electoral Reform. In 2004, British Columbia's government convened a random sample of 160 citizens to deliberate about the Canadian province's electoral system. The deliberators met nearly every other weekend for one year and were tasked to consider alternatives to the existing "first-past-the-post" electoral system. The group voted overwhelmingly in favor of a new model known as the "single transferable vote" system where voters rank candidates from most to least favorite. The recommendation was then put to a referendum in 2005, which required 60 percent approval to pass. Many voters nevertheless reported limited awareness of the referendum question and it ultimately fell a few points short of the required percentage of votes.[35]

The above discussion shows that deliberative polling is both practical and flexible. As a result of various design features—including accessible briefing materials, skilled facilitation, and secret ballots—deliberative polls have proven to be resistant to elite domination and group polarization. Beyond enabling representative groups of citizens to participate on a level playing field, deliberative polls have also proved adaptable in their geographic scope. It is possible to implement polls at different geographic levels (covering a city, for example, or a sub-national region, or a whole nation), and possible to implement polls in many places at once. Overall, deliberative polling's feasibility and flexibility have allowed it to be applied successfully across a wide variety of policy issues in more and less developed countries.

The virtues of deliberative polling largely stem from its commitment to deliberation and political equality. To realize the value of deliberation, people must be adequately informed, exposed to competing views, and able to reflect on their beliefs. To realize the value of political equality, everyone must have an equal chance of being the decisive voter and be able to deliberate on equal terms. The design features of deliberative polls follow immediately from these commitments, which together allow people to make decisions under good conditions. Again, deliberative polling may not be the "right" model for every situation, but its emphasis on high-quality decision procedures makes it a promising starting point for any radically decentralized approach to fighting extreme poverty.

Conclusion

THE GLOBAL DEVELOPMENT community has a history of failed promises. Microcredit was once widely celebrated as the solution to global poverty, but enthusiasm waned as we learned that small loans aren't that transformative and are sometimes actually harmful.[1] Similarly, giving poor people legal titles to their land and homes was once held by many as the missing piece in the fight against poverty, yet it turns out that reducing poverty is more complicated than unlocking "dead capital."[2] Another prominent example is the Millennium Villages Project led by economist Jeffrey Sachs, which prescribed a combination of health, education, and agriculture interventions. Despite Sachs's promise to end poverty "once and for all," the project is largely viewed as a failure.[3]

Cash transfers have been similarly portrayed as the ultimate solution to poverty. For example, Facebook cofounder Chris Hughes argued in 2018 for a guaranteed income in the United States declaring that "we can be the generation that ends poverty in America."[4] Others have taken the rhetoric even further and ascribed almost supernatural powers to cash transfers. Recall the words of Nancy Birdsall, cofounder of the Center for Global Development, who said cash transfers are "as close as you can come to a magic bullet in development."[5] Former GiveDirectly president Rory Stewart, recalling the classic advice not to "give a man a fish" but rather teach him to fish, described the impact of cash transfers as "less like giving a fish and more like giving a . . . magic fish."[6]

Though many people working in international development have rightly become skeptical of "magic bullet" solutions, the hype around cash transfers still far exceeds what these programs can deliver. As with microcredit and land titling initiatives, the issue isn't that cash programs are necessarily bad, but rather that cash is just one of many tools in the fight against global poverty. Each has limits that are important to understand when determining the appropriate way to alleviate poverty in a given place or time. It's true that cash is a flexible solution and puts some important decisions into the hands of recipients. While cash transfers may be a step in the right direction of empowering people living in poverty, there is no one-size-fits-all solution.

To have a clear understanding of the limits of cash transfers, we've seen that it's important to have a proper definition of poverty. Although poverty has long been defined as a lack of income, there's now some agreement that this definition has severe shortcomings. Most critically, human diversity implies that any two people with the same means (for example, income) may have very different abilities to meet their ends (for example, being well-fed or well-educated). An income-based view can then fail to capture important dimensions of injustice. Because the capability approach focuses directly on the ends of well-being, it offers a broader view of poverty that recognizes the complex and multidimensional nature of human deprivation. In short, poverty is better defined as a lack of capabilities.

The capability approach highlights that expanding human agency is central to the fight against poverty. Roughly speaking, respecting people's agency means respecting their capability to make decisions for themselves. Amartya Sen summarized the basic idea as follows:

> In terms of the medieval distinction between "the patient" and "the agent" . . . [the capability approach] is very much an agent-oriented view. With adequate social opportunities, individuals can effectively shape their own destiny and help each other. They need not be seen primarily as passive recipients of the benefits of cunning development programs.[7]

The agent-oriented view entails treating people in poverty less like pawns on a chessboard (or patients) and more like chess players who can make strategic decisions and influence the game (or agents). Though agency may seem like an abstract idea, it has very practical implications for understanding cash transfers.

What this book has made clear is that cash programs have real limitations at each step between program launch and actually expanding people's capabilities. Targeting is prone to errors and can cause harmful effects by dividing communities into recipients and non-recipients. Households often allocate resources inequitably, generally to the detriment of women and children. Even if cash transfers land in all the right beneficiaries' hands, money still can't buy everything that matters to well-being, and members of vulnerable groups often face severe challenges in "converting" cash into well-being. Finally, programs that distribute cash to individuals don't address the structural causes of poverty and are thus unlikely to significantly transform people's capabilities.

The unifying theme of these limitations is that cash programs impose many decisions on people living in poverty that they might not make for themselves. For example, a person experiencing poverty may believe that having access to certain nonmarket goods (for example, clean water) is critical to their well-being, but cash programs deny this option by disbursing the required funds at the individual or household level. Ironically, cash advocates regularly claim that cash programs are anti-paternalistic, because they give recipients unfettered choice over what they do with their money.[8] This is false. While cash transfers may be less paternalistic than some alternative solutions (such as in-kind transfers), they still effectively narrow the choices available to people living in poverty—and in this sense can and should be viewed as paternalistic.

The way forward rests on a simple idea: the opposite of being subjected to paternalism is exercising agency. If we really respect people's ability to make decisions for themselves, then the natural alternative to cash transfers is deliberative democracy. The critical feature of the deliberative-democratic approach is that it doesn't prescribe any one-size-fits-all solution to global poverty, but rather a meta-solution that prescribes fair procedures for finding best-fit solutions for any given place or time. Deliberative democracy allows groups of people living in poverty to consider a wide array of options and choose whether available funds should be invested in, say, education, health, public infrastructure, property rights reform, or in-kind transfers. As cash is one possible tool in the fight against poverty, it should be an available option in any genuinely democratic procedure.

The critical analysis offered here is part of a broader critique of top-down or technocratic approaches to poverty alleviation. Rory Stewart phrased it nicely when he said, "There's just a fundamental problem with development, which is that it involves outsiders, often foreigners, deciding what's good for you."[9] Many past policy failures, such as the Millennium Villages Project, have been criticized not only because their outcomes fell short, but also because their designs largely ignored the voices of people living in poverty. Remarkably, despite a seeming commitment to the belief that people in poverty should be treated as agents rather than patients, the development community still regularly implements policies that fail to do that. It is a pervasive problem of which cash transfers are just a recent example.

While the deliberative-democratic approach to reducing poverty takes ending paternalism seriously, it's not a panacea. We've seen that it can be challenging to build and sustain deliberative procedures without deeper political reforms, as public officials have limited incentives to relinquish their decision-making powers. We've also seen that group decision-making can be polarizing, which raises concerns that deliberative procedures can fuel hatred or extremism. Further, we've seen that democratic processes can be "captured" by elites who use their political power to influence group decisions to their benefit. These issues shouldn't be ignored and democratic deliberations can easily go wrong if they aren't carefully designed.

Democratic approaches to poverty alleviation aren't yet widespread, but the idea is far from new. In fact, something along these lines was proposed in India to deal with the fallout from the Direct Benefit Transfer for Food Subsidy program described in Chapter 1. Karthik Muralidharan, an economist at the University of California San Diego, developed a proposal with some others to implement a "choice-based" reform in the state of Maharashtra.[10] Rather than having policymakers make the decision to provide people with in-kind or cash transfers, their proposal was to empower beneficiaries by giving them the choice between the two options. Though the available choices are limited, their proposal is a step in the right direction.

Other prominent examples include Porto Alegre's experiments in participatory budgeting, Indonesia's Kecamatan Development Program, and Tanzania's use of deliberative polling to inform policy related to natural gas revenues. Deliberative polls have been conducted more than 150 times in over fifty countries and experience shows that the model is both flexible and highly successful.[11] Most importantly, deliberative polls have proven to be resistant to issues like group polarization and elite domination, largely due to their emphasis on accessible briefing materials, skilled facilitation, and confidential questionnaires. These design features follow from a deep commitment to the values of deliberation and equality, and make deliberative polling an especially compelling model.

The simplicity of cash is seductive but, as this book shows, proponents of cash transfers face a difficult choice. They can hold either that people living in poverty should be treated as equals, or that they should be treated as agents rather than patients—but ultimately, they cannot hold both. If cash advocates believe that people should be treated as agents, they can't also uphold equality, because cash programs deny people living in poverty equal decision-making power. Similarly, if cash advocates are committed to treating people as equals, this commitment must apply to something other than agency—again, because cash programs don't give people equal decision-making power. Because equality and agency are foundational commitments in the fight against extreme poverty, the best way out of this situation is to reject cash transfers in favor of a more democratic alternative.

Notes

Chapter 1 · The Rise of Cash Transfers

1. See the chart, updated monthly, on GiveDirectly's website: https://www.givedirectly.org/financials/.
2. Rory Stewart, "Giving Cash to Africa Is the Best Thing the U.S. Can Do for Both Africa and Itself," *Time,* January 23, 2023.
3. Cecilia W. Dugger, "To Help Poor Be Pupils, Not Wage Earners, Brazil Pays Parents," *New York Times,* January 3, 2004.
4. Jahnavi Sen, "Why People Are Protesting against Jharkhand's Experiment with Direct Benefit Transfers," *The Wire,* March 1, 2018, https://thewire.in/rights/jharkhand-nagri-ration-pds-direct-benefit-transfer.
5. J. Sen, "Why People Are Protesting."
6. Jean Drèze, "Following the Grain Trail: On India's Public Distribution System," *The Hindu,* January 17, 2018, https://www.thehindu.com/opinion/lead/following-the-grain-trail/article6211200.ece.
7. Rohini Mohan, "In Ranchi's Nagri Block, Ration Rice Comes at a Heavy Price," *The Hindu,* March 10, 2018, https://www.thehindu.com/society/in-ranchis-nagri-block-ration-rice-comes-at-a-heavy-price/article23000824.ece.
8. "Social Audit of Direct Benefit Transfer (DBT) for Food Subsidy Pilot in Nagri, Ranchi, Jarkhand," technical report, Social Audit Unit, Rural Development Department, Government of Jharkhand, 2018. The report is no longer accessible online, but its "executive summary" section is reproduced in Jahnavi Sen, "If Jharkhand's Direct Benefit Transfer Experiment Isn't Working, Why Is It Still On?" The Wire, June 21, 2018, https://thewire.in/rights/jharkhand-direct-benefit-transfer-nagri-pds.
9. Drèze quoted in Mohan, "In Ranchi's Nagri Block."
10. Reetika Khera, "Cash vs. In-kind Transfers: Indian Data Meets Theory," *Food Policy* 46 (2014): 116–128, 121.
11. Stuti Khemani, James Habyarimana, and Irfan Nooruddin, "What Do Poor People Think about Direct Cash Transfers?" commentary, Brookings Institution, April 8, 2019, https://www.brookings.edu/articles/what-do-poor-people-think-about-direct-cash-transfers.
12. S. Anukriti, "Financial Incentives and the Fertility–Sex Ratio Trade-off," *American Economic Journal: Applied Economics* 10, no. 2 (2018): 27–57.
13. Shireen Santosham, Dominica Lindsey, and Altai Consulting, "Bridging the Gender Gap: Mobile Access and Usage in Low- and Middle-Income Countries," report, GSMA, February 26, 2015, https://www.gsma.com/solutions-and-impact/connectivity-for

-good/mobile-for-development/gsma_resources/bridging-gender-gap-mobile-access-usage-low-middle-income-countries/.
14. "Social Audit of 'Direct Benefit Transfer (DBT) for Food Subsidy' Pilot."
15. Jean Drèze, Nazar Khalid, Reetika Khera, and Anmol Somanchi, "Aadhaar and Food Security in Jharkhand: Pain without Gain?" *Economic & Political Weekly* (Mumbai) 52, no. 16, December 16, 2017, 50–59.
16. In the social insurance and health literature, universality generally refers to situations where everybody is technically covered by some program, even though they'll only be eligible for benefits if some event occurs (for example, illness or disability). Once again, this situation doesn't meet our definition of universality because eligibility is restricted to those people that experience the event. For additional discussion of universality, see Ugo Gentilini, Margaret Grosh, and Ruslan Yemtsov, "The Idea of Universal Basic Income," in *Exploring Universal Basic Income: A Guide to Navigating Concepts, Evidence, and Practices*, ed. Ugo Gentilini, Margaret Grosh, Jamele Rigolini, and Ruslan Yemtsov (Washington, DC: World Bank, 2020), 17–72.
17. Gentilini, Grosh, and Yemtsov, "The Idea of Universal Basic Income."
18. Nothing in the definition of a universal basic income requires people to receive equal amounts. The payment amount can vary by, say, age or geographical location of the recipient. For additional discussion, see Philippe Van Parijs and Yannick Vanderborght, *Basic Income: A Radical Proposal for a Free Society and a Sane Economy* (Cambridge, MA: Harvard University Press, 2017), ch. 1.
19. Ugo Gentilini and Margaret Grosh, "UBI as Social Assistance: Comparative Models and Instruments," in Gentilini et al., *Exploring Universal Basic Income*, 73–97.
20. For a more detailed comparison of guaranteed minimum income schemes and negative income taxes, see Robert A. Moffitt, "The Negative Income Tax and the Evolution of US Welfare Policy," *Journal of Economic Perspectives* 17, no. 3 (2003): 119–140.
21. Moffitt, "The Negative Income Tax."
22. Van Parijs and Vanderborght, *Basic Income*, ch. 1.
23. Keetie Roelen, Stephen Devereux, Abdul-Gafaru Abdulai, Bruno Martorano, Tia Palermo, and Luigi Peter Ragno, "How to Make 'Cash Plus' Work: Linking Cash Transfers to Services and Sectors," Innocenti Working Paper WP-2017-10, Office of Research, UNICEF, August 2017.
24. Joseph Hanlon, Armando Barrientos, and David Hulme, *Just Give Money to the Poor: The Development Revolution from the Global South* (London: Kumarian Press, 2010), ch. 2.
25. Joseph Persky, "Classical Family Values: Ending the Poor Laws as They Knew Them," *Journal of Economic Perspectives* 11, no. 1 (1997): 179–189.
26. Milton D. Speizman, "Speenhamland: An Experiment in Guaranteed Income," *Social Service Review* 40, no. 1 (1966): 44–55.
27. George Boyer, "English Poor Laws," *EH.net Encyclopedia*, May 8, 2002.
28. Aiqun Hu and Patrick Manning, "The Global Social Insurance Movement since the 1880s," *Journal of Global History* 5, no. 1 (2010): 125–148.
29. Stein Kuhnle and Anne Sander, "The Emergence of the Western Welfare State," in *The Oxford Handbook of the Welfare State*, ed. Francis G. Castles, Stephan Leibfried, Jane Lewis, Herbert Obinger, and Christopher Pierson (Oxford: Oxford University Press, 2010), 61–80.
30. Kuhnle and Sander, "The Emergence of the Western Welfare State."

31. Karl Widerquist, "Three Waves of Basic Income Support," in *The Palgrave International Handbook of Basic Income*, ed. Malcolm Torry (Cham, Switzerland: Palgrave Macmillan, 2019), 31–46.
32. Van Parijs and Vanderborght, *Basic Income*.
33. The phrase "quiet revolution" is commonly attributed to Hanlon, Barrientos, and Hulme, *Just Give Money to the Poor*, ch. 1.
34. Armando Barrientos, *Social Assistance in Developing Countries* (Cambridge: Cambridge University Press, 2013), ch. 1.
35. Santiago Levy, *Progress against Poverty: Sustaining Mexico's Progresa-Oportunidades Program* (Washington, DC: Brookings Institution Press, 2006), ch. 2.
36. Kathy Lindert, Anja Linder, Jason Hobbs, and Bénédicte de la Brière, "The Nuts and Bolts of Brazil's Bolsa Família Program: Implementing Conditional Cash Transfers in a Decentralized Context," SP Discussion Paper No. 0709, Social Protection, World Bank, May 2007.
37. Hanlon, Barrientos, and Hulme, *Just Give Money to the Poor*, ch. 3.
38. Lutz Leisering, *The Global Rise of Social Cash Transfers* (Oxford: Oxford University Press, 2019), ch. 5.
39. Gentilini, Grosh, and Yemtsov, "The Idea of Universal Basic Income."
40. Sigal Samuel, "Everywhere Basic Income Has Been Tried, in One Map," *Vox*, October 20, 2020, https://www.vox.com/future-perfect/2020/2/19/21112570/universal-basic-income-ubi-map.
41. Charlotte Bilo, Maya Hammad, Anna Carolina Machado, Lucas Sato, Fábio Veras Soares, and Marina Andrade, "How Countries in the Global South Have Used Social Protection to Attenuate the Impact of the COVID-19 Crisis?" *Policy in Focus* 19, no. 1 (2021): 7–10.
42. See Chapter 3 for a detailed discussion of this evidence.
43. Stewart, "Giving Cash to Africa."
44. Daniel Gerszon Mahler, Alaka Holla, and Umar Serajuddin, "Time to Stop Referring to the 'Developing World,'" Data Blog, World Bank, January 23, 2024, https://blogs.worldbank.org/en/opendata/time-stop-referring-developing-world.

Chapter 2 · Defining Poverty

1. Dylan Matthews, "The Big Drop in American Poverty during the Pandemic, Explained," *Vox*, August 11, 2021, https://www.vox.com/22600143/poverty-us-covid-19-pandemic-stimulus-checks.
2. Freedom House, *Freedom in the World 2010: The Annual Survey of Political Rights and Civil Liberties* (Washington, DC: Freedom House, 2010).
3. Amartya Sen, *Development as Freedom* (New York: Anchor Books, 1999), 72.
4. World Bank, *World Development Report 2000/2001: Attacking Poverty* (Washington, DC: World Bank, 2001), 15.
5. *The World Bank Poverty and Inequality Platform*, https://pip.worldbank.org, accessed March 18, 2024.
6. For an accessible overview of these works, see Ranil Dissanayake, "Between the Lines: A History of the Most Important Concept in Global Poverty," *Asterisk*, October 1,

2023, https://asteriskmag.com/issues/04/between-the-lines-a-history-of-the-most-important-concept-in-global-poverty.
7. Gordon M. Fisher, "The Development and History of the Poverty Thresholds," *Social Security Bulletin* 55, no. 4 (1992): 3–14.
8. World Bank, *World Development Report 1990: Poverty* (Washington, DC: World Bank, 1990).
9. Rob Konkel, "The Monetization of Global Poverty: The Concept of Poverty in World Bank History, 1944–90," *Journal of Global History* 9, no. 2 (2014): 276–300.
10. Konkel, "The Monetization of Global Poverty," 298.
11. Sanjay G. Reddy and Thomas Pogge, "How *Not* to Count the Poor," in *Debates on the Measurement of Global Poverty,* ed. Sudhir Anand, Paul Segal, and Joseph E. Stiglitz (Oxford: Oxford University Press, 2010), 42
12. For more detailed discussion, see Reddy and Pogge, "How *Not* to Count the Poor."
13. Reddy and Pogge, "How *Not* to Count the Poor."
14. Francisco H. G. Ferreira, Shaohua Chen, et al., "A Global Count of the Extreme Poor in 2012: Data Issues, Methodology and Initial Results," *Journal of Economic Inequality* 14 (2016): 141–172.
15. For example, see Dean Jolliffe, "Poverty, Prices, and Place: How Sensitive Is the Spatial Distribution of Poverty to Cost of Living Adjustments?" *Economic Inquiry* 44, no. 2 (2006): 296–310.
16. World Bank, *Poverty and Inequality Platform Methodology Handbook,* Edition 2024-09, 2024, ch. 2, https://datanalytics.worldbank.org/PIP-Methodology.
17. For additional discussion, see Anthony B. Atkinson, *Measuring Poverty around the World* (Princeton, NJ: Princeton University Press, 2019).
18. World Bank, *Poverty and Inequality Platform Methodology Handbook,* ch. 2.
19. Joachim De Weerdt, John Gibson, and Kathleen Beegle, "What Can We Learn from Experimenting with Survey Methods?" *Annual Review of Resource Economics* 12, no. 1 (2020): 431–447, 431.
20. Caitlin Brown, Rossella Calvi, and Jacob Penglase, "Sharing the Pie: An Analysis of Undernutrition and Individual Consumption in Bangladesh," *Journal of Public Economics* 200 (2021): 104460.
21. Asghar Zaidi and Tania Burchardt, "Comparing Incomes When Needs Differ: Equivalization for the Extra Costs of Disability in the UK," *Review of Income and Wealth* 51, no. 1 (2005): 89–114.
22. To some extent, "equivalence scales" can be used to adjust consumption or income estimates for differences in household size and composition. These adjustments, however, are typically crude and there's little agreement on which equivalence scales to use. For detailed discussion, see Angus Deaton, *The Analysis of Household Surveys: A Microeconometric Approach to Development Policy,* reissue with a new preface (1997; Washington, DC: World Bank, 2018).
23. United Nations, *The United Nations World Water Development Report 2023: Partnerships and Cooperation for Water* (Paris: UNESCO, 2023)
24. Deaton, *The Analysis of Household Surveys.*
25. Amartya Sen, "Equality of What?" Tanner Lecture on Human Values, Stanford University, May 22, 1979, https://tannerlectures.org/lectures/equality-of-what/.

26. The following discussion of the capability approach draws heavily on Ingrid Robeyns, *Wellbeing, Freedom and Social Justice: The Capability Approach Re-examined* (Cambridge: Open Book Publishers, 2017).
27. Martha C. Nussbaum, *Women and Human Development: The Capabilities Approach* (Cambridge: Cambridge University Press, 2000), ch. 1.
28. Amartya Sen, "Well-being, Agency and Freedom: The Dewey Lectures 1984," *Journal of Philosophy* 82, no. 4 (1985): 169–221, 201.
29. For a more detailed discussion of these issues, see Robeyns, *Wellbeing, Freedom and Social Justice*, ch. 3.
30. Ingrid Robeyns, "The Capability Approach: A Theoretical Survey," *Journal of Human Development* 6, no. 1 (2005): 93–114.
31. A. Sen, "Well-being, Agency and Freedom."
32. A. Sen, *Development as Freedom*.
33. Rutger Claassen, *Capabilities in a Just Society: A Theory of Navigational Agency* (Cambridge: Cambridge University Press, 2018), 53.
34. Nussbaum, *Women and Human Development*, ch. 1.
35. For a more detailed graphical representation of the capability approach, see Robeyns, "The Capability Approach."
36. Bryan Stevenson, *Just Mercy: A Story of Justice and Redemption* (New York: Spiegal & Grau, 2015), 18.
37. Amartya Sen, "Capabilities, Lists, and Public Reason: Continuing the Conversation," *Feminist Economics* 10, no. 3 (2004): 77–80.
38. Martha C. Nussbaum, "Capabilities as Fundamental Entitlements: Sen and Social Justice," *Feminist Economics* 9, nos. 2–3 (2003): 33–59.
39. Claassen, *Capabilities in a Just Society*.
40. For additional discussion, see Severine Deneulin and Lila Shahani, *An Introduction to the Human Development and Capability Approach: Freedom and Agency* (London: Earthscan, 2009), ch. 2.
41. The following draws heavily on Robeyns, *Wellbeing, Freedom and Social Justice*, ch. 4.
42. Bengt-Christer Ysander, "Robert Erikson: Descriptions of Inequality," in *The Quality of Life*, ed. Martha Nussbaum and Amartya Sen (Oxford: Oxford University Press, 1993), 84.
43. For a list of several applications, see Enrica Chiappero-Martinetti and José Manuel Roche, "Operationalization of the Capability Approach, from Theory to Practice: A Review of Techniques and Empirical Applications," in *Debating Global Society: Reach and Limits of the Capability Approach*, ed. Enrica Chiappero-Martinetti (Milan, Italy: Fondazione Feltrinelli, 2009), 157–201.
44. For example, see Heath Henderson and Lendie Follett, "A Bayesian Framework for Estimating Human Capabilities," *World Development* 129 (2020): 104872.

Chapter 3 · What the Evidence Shows

1. Sonya V. Troller-Renfree, Molly A. Costanzo, et al., "The Impact of a Poverty Reduction Intervention on Infant Brain Activity," *Proceedings of the National Academy of Sciences* 119, no. 5 (2022): e2115649119.

2. Troller-Renfree et al., "Impact of a Poverty Reduction Intervention," 5.
3. Jason DeParle, "Cash Aid to Poor Mothers Increases Brain Activity in Babies, Study Finds," *New York Times,* January 24, 2022.
4. For example, see Stuart Ritchie, "The Real Lesson of That Cash-for-Babies Study," *The Atlantic,* February 4, 2022.
5. Ritchie, "The Real Lesson of That Cash-for-Babies Study."
6. Ritchie, "The Real Lesson of That Cash-for-Babies Study."
7. Rory Stewart, "Giving Cash to Africa Is the Best Thing the U.S. Can Do for Both Africa and Itself," *Time,* January 23, 2023.
8. Francesca Bastagli, Jessica Hagen-Zanker, et al., "The Impact of Cash Transfers: A Review of the Evidence from Low- and Middle-income Countries," *Journal of Social Policy* 48, no. 3 (2019): 569–594. For another well-known review, see Tommaso Crosta, Dean S. Karlan, Finley Ong, Julius Rüschenpöhler, and Christopher Udry, "Unconditional Cash Transfers: A Bayesian Meta-analysis of Randomized Evaluations in Low and Middle Income Countries," Working Paper 32779, National Bureau of Economic Research, August 2024.
9. Sebastian Galiani, Paul Gertler, and Rosangela Bando, "Non-contributory Pensions," *Labour Economics* 38 (2016): 47–58.
10. Cally Ardington, Anne Case, and Victoria Hosegood, "Labor Supply Responses to Large Social Transfers: Longitudinal Evidence from South Africa," *American Economic Journal: Applied Economics* 1, no. 1 (2009): 22–48.
11. The ODI review also considered the impact of cash on time spent working, but a close inspection of the results again shows that none of the negative effects provide clear evidence that cash transfers reduced the labor supply of working-age adults.
12. Andrew Dabalen, Talip Kilic, and Waly Wane, "Social Transfers, Labor Supply and Poverty Reduction: The Case of Albania," Policy Research Working Paper 4783, World Bank, November 2008.
13. Rafael Perez Ribas, Fábio Veras Soares, Clarissa Teixeira, Elydia Silva, and Guilherme Hirata, "Beyond Cash: Assessing Externality and Behaviour Effects of Non-experimental Cash Transfers," Working Paper 65, International Policy Centre for Inclusive Growth, June 2010.
14. Sarah Baird, Francisco H. G. Ferreira, Berk Özler, and Michael Woolcock, "Conditional, Unconditional and Everything In Between: A Systematic Review of the Effects of Cash Transfer Programmes on Schooling Outcomes," *Journal of Development Effectiveness* 6, no. 1 (2014): 1–43.
15. These results are presented in Figure 5 of Baird et al., "Conditional, Unconditional and Everything In Between." The review actually presents results in terms of "odd ratios," which are difficult to interpret. Here, the implied effect on enrollment rates is calculated using the estimated odds ratio and the average enrollment rate of the control group across the six studies. Given that the confidence interval on the combined effect excludes zero, it's tempting to conclude that this effect is statistically significant. The confidence interval, however, gives us only the plausible range of values for the "grand mean" and doesn't tell us about the plausible range of actual treatment effects. The appropriate statistical test requires a prediction interval, which the study doesn't provide. For details, see Joanna IntHout, John P. A. Ioannidis, Maroeska M. Rovers, and

Jelle J. Goeman, "Plea for Routinely Presenting Prediction Intervals in Meta-analysis," *BMJ Open* 6, no. 7 (2016): e010247.

16. Frank Pega, Sze Yan Liu, Stefan Walter, Roman Pabayo, Ruhi Saith, and Stefan K. Lhachimi, "Unconditional Cash Transfers for Reducing Poverty and Vulnerabilities: Effect on Use of Health Services and Health Outcomes in Low- and Middle-income Countries," *Cochrane Database of Systematic Reviews*, no. 3 (2022).

17. As noted previously, interpretation of the confidence intervals on the combined effects will generally be avoided here because they're not prediction intervals. See IntHout et al., "Plea for Routinely Presenting Prediction Intervals in Meta-analysis."

18. Christopher Blattman, Nathan Fiala, and Sebastian Martinez, "The Long-term Impacts of Grants on Poverty: Nine-year Evidence from Uganda's Youth Opportunities Program," *American Economic Review: Insights* 2, no. 3 (2020): 287–304.

19. Adrien Bouguen, Yue Huang, Michael Kremer, and Edward Miguel, "Using Randomized Controlled Trials to Estimate Long-run Impacts in Development Economics," *Annual Review of Economics* 11 (2019): 523–561. For another review of dynamic effects, see Crosta et al., "Unconditional Cash Transfers."

20. M. Caridad Araujo, Mariano Bosch, and Norbert Schady, "Can Cash Transfers Help Households Escape an Intergenerational Poverty Trap?" in *The Economics of Poverty Traps*, ed. Christopher B. Barrett, Michael R. Carter, and Jean-Paul Chavas (Chicago: University of Chicago Press, 2018), 357–382.

21. The researchers also took a different approach to evaluating the program by comparing households just eligible for the program to those that were just ineligible. Here the focus is on the experimental results, because the alternative method is simply less credible and gives us information only about the impacts of cash bonuses on households near the eligibility threshold. The conclusions are nevertheless similar, albeit with some caveats.

22. Sarah Baird, Craig McIntosh, and Berk Özler, "When the Money Runs Out: Do Cash Transfers Have Sustained Effects on Human Capital Accumulation?" *Journal of Development Economics* 140 (2019): 169–185.

23. They did find a significant increase in age at first marriage and a significant reduction in anemia, though both effects were sensitive to some methodological choices.

24. Christopher Blattman, Stefan Dercon, and Simon Franklin, "Impacts of Industrial and Entrepreneurial Jobs on Youth: 5-year Experimental Evidence on Factory Job Offers and Cash Grants in Ethiopia," *Journal of Development Economics* 156 (2022): 102807.

25. Teresa Molina Millán, Tania Barham, Karen Macours, John A. Maluccio, and Marco Stampini, "Long-term Impacts of Conditional Cash Transfers: Review of the Evidence," *World Bank Research Observer* 34, no. 1 (2019): 119–159.

26. See Tables 2a and 2b in Molina Millán et al., "Long-term Impacts of Conditional Cash Transfers" for a concise summary of all the estimates. Note that most of the studies estimate effects for boys and girls separately. Given that the separate estimates for boys and girls are most often in agreement, to keep things simple, each pair of effects is treated as one "estimate" in summarizing the results. The gendered impacts of cash transfers are considered in later chapters.

27. The mixed effect here simply refers to a study that found no impacts for girls, but positive impacts for boys.

28. For an example of how inflation can undermine the benefits of cash programs, see Deon Filmer, Jed Friedman, Eeshani Kandpal, and Junko Onishi, "Cash Transfers, Food Prices, and Nutrition Impacts on Ineligible Children," *Review of Economics and Statistics* 105, no. 2 (2023): 327–343. For evidence on decreasing returns to household investments, see Florence Kondylis and John Ashton Loeser, "Intervention Size and Persistence," Policy Research Working Paper 9769, World Bank, September 2021. Finally, for detailed discussion on capacity constraints, see Jules Gazeaud and Claire Ricard, "Learning Effects of Conditional Cash Transfers: The Role of Class Size and Composition," *Journal of Development Economics* 166 (2024): 103194.
29. Hunt Allcott, "Site Selection Bias in Program Evaluation," *Quarterly Journal of Economics* 130, no. 3 (2015): 1117–1165.
30. Arnaud Vaganay, "Outcome Reporting Bias in Government-sponsored Policy Evaluations: A Qualitative Content Analysis of 13 Studies," *PLoS One* 11, no. 9 (2016): e0163702.
31. Eva Vivalt, "Specification Searching and Significance Inflation across Time, Methods and Disciplines," *Oxford Bulletin of Economics and Statistics* 81, no. 4 (2019): 797–816.
32. Getaw Tadesse, Gashaw T. Abate, and Tadiwos Zewdie, "Biases in Self-reported Food Insecurity Measurement: A List Experiment Approach," *Food Policy* 92 (2020): 101862.
33. For additional discussion, see Donal Khosrowi, "Trade-offs between Epistemic and Moral Values in Evidence-based Policy," *Economics & Philosophy* 35, no. 1 (2019): 49–78.

Chapter 4 · The Targeting Problem

1. Anne Della Guardia, Milli Lake, and Pascale Schnitzer, "Selective Inclusion in Cash Transfer Programs: Unintended Consequences for Social Cohesion," *World Development* 157 (2022): 105922.
2. Della Guardia, Lake, and Schnitzer, "Selective Inclusion in Cash Transfer Programs," 10.
3. Della Guardia, Lake, and Schnitzer, "Selective Inclusion in Cash Transfer Programs," 10.
4. Della Guardia, Lake, and Schnitzer, "Selective Inclusion in Cash Transfer Programs," 10.
5. Della Guardia, Lake, and Schnitzer, "Selective Inclusion in Cash Transfer Programs," 9.
6. Della Guardia, Lake, and Schnitzer, "Selective Inclusion in Cash Transfer Programs," 8.
7. Nora Lustig, Jon Jellema, and Valentina Martinez Pabon, "Are Budget Neutral Income Floors Fiscally Viable in Sub-Saharan Africa?" Working Paper 588, Center for Global Development, Washington DC, July 2021.
8. Rema Hanna and Benjamin A. Olken, "Universal Basic Incomes versus Targeted Transfers: Anti-poverty Programs in Developing Countries," *Journal of Economic Perspectives* 32, no. 4 (2018): 201–226.
9. Unless noted otherwise, the material in this section draws on David Coady, Margaret E. Grosh, and John Hoddinott, *Targeting of Transfers in Developing Countries: Review of Lessons and Experience* (Washington, DC: World Bank, 2004); and Margaret Grosh, Phillippe Leite, Matthew Wai-Poi, and Emil Tesliuc, *Revisiting Targeting in Social Assistance: A New Look at Old Dilemmas* (Washington, DC: World Bank, 2022).
10. Anders Jensen, "Employment Structure and the Rise of the Modern Tax System," *American Economic Review* 112, no. 1 (2022): 213–234.
11. Chris Elbers, Jean O. Lanjouw, and Peter Lanjouw, "Micro-level Estimation of Poverty and Inequality," *Econometrica* 71, no. 1 (2003): 355–364.

12. For additional discussion, see Grosh et al., *Revisiting Targeting in Social Assistance*, ch. 6.
13. Christopher Barrett and Daniel Clay, "How Accurate is Food-for-Work Self-targeting in the Presence of Imperfect Factor Markets? Evidence from Ethiopia," *Journal of Development Studies* 39, no. 5 (2003): 152–180.
14. Marina Dodlova, Anna Giolbas, and Jann Lay, "Non-contributory Social Transfer Programs in Developing Countries: A New Dataset and Research Agenda," *Data in Brief* 16 (2018): 51–64.
15. Grosh et al., *Revisiting Targeting in Social Assistance*, ch. 5.
16. We need to be somewhat careful with exclusion error rates because programs can achieve reduced exclusion errors simply by covering a larger share of the population. In our case, for any method involving a proxy means test or geographic targeting, the hypothetical program's coverage is fixed at 30 percent of the population. For demographic targeting, program coverage varies depending on the size of the demographic group, with the highest coverage achieved by targeting households with children (43 percent) and the lowest coverage by targeting widows (9 percent). With differences in coverage, it's often beneficial to also look at inclusion error rates, which capture the share of program beneficiaries that are not poor. For further discussion on the relationship between exclusion and inclusion error rates, see Hanna and Olken, "Universal Basic Incomes versus Targeted Transfers."
17. While the proxy means test and geographic targeting cover 30 percent of the population, the demographic methods vary depending on the size of the demographic group.
18. Caitlin Brown, Martin Ravallion, and Dominique van de Walle, "A Poor Means Test? Econometric Targeting in Africa," *Journal of Development Economics* 134 (2018): 109–124.
19. These results are from the most complete proxy means test in Brown et al., "A Poor Means Test?," which the researchers called the "extended" proxy means test. See Table 3. Note that results are presented for both fixed poverty lines and fixed poverty rates. Here, the results for the fixed poverty rates are cited because they're more favorable to the proxy means test. Further note that when fixing the poverty rate, the exclusion and inclusion error rates will be equal, so the authors refer only to the targeting error rate when presenting these results.
20. Stephen Kidd and Diloá Athias, "Hit and Miss: An Assessment of Targeting Effectiveness in Social Protection with Additional Analysis," Working Paper, Development Pathways, June 2020.
21. Vivi Alatas, Abhijit Banerjee, Rema Hanna, Benjamin A. Olken, and Julia Tobias, "Targeting the Poor: Evidence from a Field Experiment in Indonesia," *American Economic Review* 102, no. 4 (2012): 1206–1240.
22. For example, see Michael Hillebrecht, Stefan Klonner, Noraogo A. Pacere, and Aurélia Souares, "Community-based versus Statistical Targeting of Anti-poverty Programs: Evidence from Burkina Faso," *Journal of African Economies* 29, no. 3 (2020): 271–305.
23. See, for example, Maria Pia Basurto, Pascaline Dupas, and Jonathan Robinson, "Decentralization and Efficiency of Subsidy Targeting: Evidence from Chiefs in Rural Malawi," *Journal of Public Economics* 185 (2020): 104047.
24. Kidd and Athias, "Hit and Miss."
25. Puja Dutta, Rinku Murgai, Martin Ravallion, and Dominique van de Walle, *Right to Work? Assessing India's Employment Guarantee Scheme in Bihar* (Washington, DC: World Bank, 2014).

26. Kidd and Athias, "Hit and Miss."
27. Caitlin Brown, Rossella Calvi, and Jacob Penglase, "Sharing the Pie: An Analysis of Undernutrition and Individual Consumption in Bangladesh," *Journal of Public Economics* 200 (2021): 104460.
28. Heath Henderson and Lendie Follett, "Targeting Social Safety Net Programs on Human Capabilities," *World Development* 151 (2022): 105741.
29. Lisa Cameron and Manisha Shah, "Can Mistargeting Destroy Social Capital and Stimulate Crime? Evidence from a Cash Transfer Program in Indonesia," *Economic Development and Cultural Change* 62, no. 2 (2014): 381–415.
30. Cameron and Shah, "Can Mistargeting Destroy Social Capital and Stimulate Crime?"
31. Mulyadi Sumarto, "Welfare and Conflict: Policy Failure in the Indonesian Cash Transfer," *Journal of Social Policy* 50, no. 3 (2021): 533–551.
32. Cameron and Shah, "Can Mistargeting Destroy Social Capital and Stimulate Crime?"
33. See the literature review and associated references in Della Guardia, Lake, and Schnitzer, "Selective Inclusion in Cash Transfer Programs."
34. Deon Filmer, Jed Friedman, Eeshani Kandpal, and Junko Onishi, "Cash Transfers, Food Prices, and Nutrition Impacts on Ineligible Children," *Review of Economics and Statistics* 105, no. 2 (2023): 327–343.
35. Kathleen Beegle, Emanuela Galasso, and Jessica Goldberg, "Direct and Indirect Effects of Malawi's Public Works Program on Food Security," *Journal of Development Economics* 128 (2017): 1–23.
36. The treatment variations consisted of both altering the timing of the work and changing the structure of payments (that is, lump-sum payments versus payments disbursed over time).
37. Sarah Baird, Jacobus De Hoop, and Berk Özler, "Income Shocks and Adolescent Mental Health," *Journal of Human Resources* 48, no. 2 (2013): 370–403.
38. Dennis Egger, Johannes Haushofer, Edward Miguel, Paul Niehaus, and Michael Walker, "General Equilibrium Effects of Cash Transfers: Experimental Evidence from Kenya," *Econometrica* 90, no. 6 (2022): 2603–2643.
39. Manuela Angelucci and Giacomo De Giorgi, "Indirect Effects of an Aid Program: How Do Cash Transfers Affect Ineligibles' Consumption?" *American Economic Review* 99, no. 1 (2009): 486–508
40. Della Guardia, Lake, and Schnitzer, "Selective Inclusion in Cash Transfer Programs."
41. Lustig, Jellema, and Pabon, "Are Budget Neutral Income Floors Fiscally Viable?"
42. Brown, Ravallion, and Walle, "A Poor Means Test?"

Chapter 5 · Inequality within Households

1. Amartya Sen, "Missing Women," *BMJ: British Medical Journal* 304, no. 6827 (1992): 587.
2. John Bongaarts and Christophe Z. Guilmoto, "How Many More Missing Women? Excess Female Mortality and Prenatal Sex Selection, 1970–2050," *Population and Development Review* 41, no. 2 (2015): 241–269.
3. The following draws heavily on Aparajita Dasgupta and Anisha Sharma, "Missing Women: A Review of Underlying Causes and Policy Responses," June 20, 2022, *Oxford Research Encyclopedia of Economics and Finance*.

4. Yuyu Chen, Hongbin Li, and Lingsheng Meng, "Prenatal Sex Selection and Missing Girls in China: Evidence from the Diffusion of Diagnostic Ultrasound," *Journal of Human Resources* 48, no. 1 (2013): 36–70.
5. Seema Jayachandran, "Fertility Decline and Missing Women," *American Economic Journal: Applied Economics* 9, no. 1 (2017): 118–139.
6. Prashant Bharadwaj and Leah K. Lakdawala, "Discrimination Begins in the Womb: Evidence of Sex-selective Prenatal Investments," *Journal of Human Resources* 48, no. 1 (2013): 71–113.
7. Emily Oster, "Proximate Sources of Population Sex Imbalance in India," *Demography* 46, no. 2 (2009): 325–339.
8. Sonia Bhalotra, Abhishek Chakravarty, Dilip Mookherjee, and Francisco J. Pino, "Property Rights and Gender Bias: Evidence from Land Reform in West Bengal," *American Economic Journal: Applied Economics* 11, no. 2 (2019): 205–237.
9. For further discussion, see Eliana Carranza, "Soil Endowments, Female Labor Force Participation, and the Demographic Deficit of Women in India," *American Economic Journal: Applied Economics* 6, no. 4 (2014): 197–225.
10. For further discussion and references, see Dasgupta and Sharma, "Missing Women."
11. S. Anukriti, "Financial Incentives and the Fertility–Sex Ratio Trade-off," *American Economic Journal: Applied Economics* 10, no. 2 (2018): 27–57.
12. The following discussion of household models draws heavily on Pierre-Andre Chiappori and Maurizio Mazzocco, "Static and Intertemporal Household Decisions," *Journal of Economic Literature* 55, no. 3 (2017): 985–1045.
13. Technically speaking, when the weights don't depend on these other factors (that is, the weights are fixed at some constant level), the unitary model emerges as a special case of the collective model.
14. For details, see Martin Browning, Pierre-André Chiappori, and Yoram Weiss, *Economics of the Family* (New York: Cambridge University Press, 2014), ch. 3.
15. For further discussion, see Chiappori and Mazzocco, "Static and Intertemporal Household Decisions."
16. Chiappori and Mazzocco, "Static and Intertemporal Household Decisions."
17. Christopher Udry, "Gender, Agricultural Production, and the Theory of the Household," *Journal of Political Economy* 104, no. 5 (1996): 1010–1046.
18. For a review of this literature, see Alistair Munro, "Intra-household Experiments: A Survey," *Journal of Economic Surveys* 32, no. 1 (2018): 134–175.
19. Vegard Iversen, Cecile Jackson, Bereket Kebede, Alistair Munro, and Arjan Verschoor, "Do Spouses Realise Cooperative Gains? Experimental Evidence from Rural Uganda," *World Development* 39, no. 4 (2011): 569–578.
20. Tara Patricia Cookson, *Unjust Conditions* (Oakland: University of California Press, 2018).
21. Cookson, *Unjust Conditions*.
22. Maxine Molyneux, "Change and Continuity in Social Protection in Latin America: Mothers at the Service of the State," Gender and Development Programme Paper Number 1, United Nations Research Institute for Social Development, May 2007; Maxine Molyneux and Marilyn Thomson, "Cash Transfers, Gender Equity and Women's Empowerment in Peru, Ecuador and Bolivia," *Gender & Development* 19, no. 2 (2011): 195–212.
23. Molyneux, "Change and Continuity in Social Protection."

24. Francesca Bastagli, Jessica Hagen-Zanker, Luke Harman, Valentina Barca, Georgina Sturge, and Tanja Schmidt, "The Impact of Cash Transfers: A Review of the Evidence from Low- and Middle-income Countries," *Journal of Social Policy* 48, no. 3 (2019): 569–594.
25. Shalini Roy, Jinnat Ara, Narayan Das, and Agnes R. Quisumbing, "'Flypaper Effects' in Transfers Targeted to Women: Evidence from BRAC's 'Targeting the Ultra Poor' Program in Bangladesh," *Journal of Development Economics* 117 (2015): 1–19.
26. For another example of cash transfers reducing women's decision-making power, see Alan De Brauw, Daniel O. Gilligan, John Hoddinott, and Shalini Roy, "The Impact of Bolsa Família on Women's Decision-making Power," *World Development* 59 (2014): 487–504.
27. A thorough review of the literature can be found in Victoria Baranov, Lisa Cameron, Diana Contreras Suarez, and Claire Thibout, "Theoretical Underpinnings and Meta-analysis of the Effects of Cash Transfers on Intimate Partner Violence in Low- and Middle-income Countries," *Journal of Development Studies* 57, no. 1 (2021): 1–25.
28. Manuela Angelucci, "Love on the Rocks: Domestic Violence and Alcohol Abuse in Rural Mexico," *BE Journal of Economic Analysis & Policy* 8, no. 1 (2008), article 43.
29. Melissa Hidrobo and Lia Fernald, "Cash Transfers and Domestic Violence," *Journal of Health Economics* 32, no. 1 (2013): 304–319.
30. Marcelo Bergolo and Estefanía Galván, "Intra-household Behavioral Responses to Cash Transfer Programs: Evidence from a Regression Discontinuity Design," *World Development* 103 (2018): 100–118.
31. For other studies reporting adverse effects on women's formal employment, see Santiago Garganta and Leonardo Gasparini, "The Impact of a Social Program on Labor Informality: The Case of AUH in Argentina," *Journal of Development Economics* 115 (2015): 99–110; and Mariano Bosch and Norbert Schady, "The Effect of Welfare Payments on Work: Regression Discontinuity Evidence from Ecuador," *Journal of Development Economics* 139 (2019): 17–27.
32. Jacob Moscona and Awa Ambra Seck, "Age Set versus Kin: Culture and Financial Ties in East Africa," *American Economic Review* 114, no. 9 (2024): 2748–2791.
33. Natalie Bau, "Can Policy Change Culture? Government Pension Plans and Traditional Kinship Practices," *American Economic Review* 111, no. 6 (2021): 1880–1917.
34. An overview of the literature can be found in Gabriel Cepaluni, Taylor Kinsley Chewning, Amanda Driscoll, and Marco Antonio Faganello, "Conditional Cash Transfers and Child Labor," *World Development* 152 (2022): 105768.
35. Alberto Chong and Monica Yáñez-Pagans, "Not So Fast! Cash Transfers Can Increase Child Labor: Evidence for Bolivia," *Economics Letters* 179 (2019): 57–61.
36. Katia Covarrubias, Benjamin Davis, and Paul Winters, "From Protection to Production: Productive Impacts of the Malawi Social Cash Transfer Scheme," *Journal of Development Effectiveness* 4, no. 1 (2012): 50–77.
37. For a similar finding, see Ximena V. Del Carpio and Karen Macours, "Leveling the Intra-household Playing Field: Compensation and Specialization in Child Labor Allocation," in *Child Labor and the Transition between School and Work*, ed. Randall K. Q. Akee, Eric V. Edmonds, and Konstantinos Tatsiramos (Bingley, UK: Emerald Group Publishing, 2010), 259–295.
38. Debosree Banerjee and Stephan Klasen, "Conditional Cash Transfers to Mothers, Intra-household Allocations: The Role of Unobservability," *International Journal of Economic Policy Studies* 16, no. 1 (2022): 275–296.

39. Banerjee and Klasen, "Conditional Cash Transfers to Mothers," 293.
40. For a review of the literature, see Charlotte Ringdal and Ingrid Hoem Sjursen, "Household Bargaining and Spending on Children: Experimental Evidence from Tanzania," *Economica* 88, no. 350 (2021): 430–455. For a relevant meta-analysis, see Tommaso Crosta, Dean Karlan, Finley Ong, Julius Rüschenpöhler, and Christopher R. Udry, "Unconditional Cash Transfers: A Bayesian Meta-analysis of Randomized Evaluations in Low and Middle Income Countries," Working Paper 32779, National Bureau of Economic Research, August 2024.
41. Najy Benhassine, Florencia Devoto, Esther Duflo, Pascaline Dupas, and Victor Pouliquen, "Turning a Shove into a Nudge? A 'Labeled Cash Transfer' for Education," *American Economic Journal: Economic Policy* 7, no. 3 (2015): 86–125.
42. Ringdal and Sjursen, "Household Bargaining and Spending on Children."

Chapter 6 · When Markets Fail

1. Sheilla's story is documented in Max Bearak and Rael Ombuor, "Kenya's Blood Banks Are Running Dry after U.S. Ended Aid—and a Baby's Life Is at Risk," *Washington Post*, January 30, 2020.
2. Bearak and Ombuor, "Kenya's Blood Banks Are Running Dry."
3. World Health Organization, "WHO Global Consultation: 100% Voluntary Non-Remunerated Donation of Blood and Blood Components," meeting report, June 20, 2009, 33.
4. To be clear, sometimes donors who are found through informal channels (like social media) ask for payment, and in such cases there is a price for blood. For reasons explained, this is nevertheless a very risky way of getting blood, so this price actually applies to a differentiated good (that is, risky rather than safe blood).
5. Robert Slonim, Carmen Wang, and Ellen Garbarino, "The Market for Blood," *Journal of Economic Perspectives* 28, no. 2 (2014): 177–196.
6. For additional examples, see Alvin E. Roth, "Repugnance as a Constraint on Markets," *Journal of Economic Perspectives* 21, no. 3 (2007): 37–58.
7. Debra Satz, *Why Some Things Should Not Be for Sale: The Moral Limits of Markets* (Oxford: Oxford University Press, 2010).
8. When economists talk about efficiency, they're typically referring to Pareto efficiency, which is any situation where nobody can be made better off without making somebody else worse off.
9. This example is taken from Philip E. Graves, *Environmental Economics: A Critique of Cost-benefit Analysis* (Lanham, MD: Rowman and Littlefield, 2007).
10. Hee Eun Lee, Woo Young Kim, Hyo Kang, and Kangwook Han, "Still Lacking Reliable Electricity from the Grid, Many Africans Turn to Other Sources," Dispatch No. 514, Afrobarometer, April 8, 2022.
11. Shilpa Aggarwal, Brian Giera, Dahyeon Jeong, Jonathan Robinson, and Alan Spearot, "Market Access, Trade Costs, and Technology Adoption: Evidence from Northern Tanzania," *Review of Economics and Statistics* 106, no. 6 (2022): 1511–1528.
12. Chelsea Harvey, "Astonishing Heat Grips India and Pakistan," *Scientific American*, May 3, 2022.

13. "India Heatwave: High Temperatures Killing More Indians Now, Lancet Study Finds," *BBC*, October 26, 2022, https://www.bbc.com/news/world-asia-india-63384167.
14. "India Heatwave: High Temperatures Killing."
15. Bramka Arga Jafino, Brian Walsh, Julie Rozenberg, and Stephane Hallegatte, "Revised Estimates of the Impact of Climate Change on Extreme Poverty by 2030," Policy Research Working Paper 9417, World Bank, September 1, 2020.
16. Jun Rentschler and Nadia Leonova, "Air Pollution and Poverty: PM2.5 Exposure in 211 Countries and Territories," Policy Research Working Paper 10005, World Bank, April 18, 2022.
17. United Nations, *The United Nations World Water Development Report 2023: Partnerships and Cooperation for Water*, March 15, 2023.
18. UNICEF, "Reimagining WASH: Water Security for All," March 2021.
19. César Calderón, Catalina Cantú, and Punam Chuhan-Pole, "Infrastructure Development in Sub-Saharan Africa: A Scorecard," Policy Research Working Paper 8425, World Bank, May 2, 2018.
20. "Connectivity in the Least Developed Countries: Status Report 2021," International Telecommunications Union, Geneva, 2021.
21. Lant Pritchett, *The Rebirth of Education: Schooling Ain't Learning* (Washington, DC: Center for Global Development, 2013).
22. Naomi Hossain and Sam Hickey, "The Problem of Education Quality in Developing Countries," in *The Politics of Education in Developing Countries: From Schooling to Learning*, ed. Sam Hickey and Naomi Hossain (Oxford: Oxford University Press, 2019), 1–21.
23. World Bank, *World Development Report 2018: Learning to Realize Education's Promise* (Washington, DC: World Bank, 2018).
24. Barbara Bruns, Deon Filmer, and Harry Anthony Patrinos, *Making Schools Work: New Evidence on Accountability Reforms* (Washington, DC: World Bank, 2011).
25. Tahir Andrabi, Jishnu Das, and Asim Ijaz Khwaja, "Report Cards: The Impact of Providing School and Child Test Scores on Educational Markets," *American Economic Review* 107, no. 6 (2017): 1535–1563.
26. Margaret E. Kruk, Anna D. Gage, et al., "High-quality Health Systems in the Sustainable Development Goals Era: Time for a Revolution," *The Lancet Global Health* 6, no. 11 (2018): e1196–e1252.
27. Jishnu Das and Jeffrey Hammer, "Quality of Primary Care in Low-income Countries: Facts and Economics," *Annual Review of Economics* 6, no. 1 (2014): 525–553, 546.
28. This example is adapted from The CORE Team, *The Economy: Economics for a Changing World* (Oxford: Oxford University Press, 2019).
29. Benedikt Herrmann, Christian Thöni, and Simon Gächter, "Antisocial Punishment across Societies," *Science* 319, no. 5868 (2008): 1362–1367.
30. Francesco Burchi, Markus Loewe, Daniele Malerba, and Julia Leininger, "Disentangling the Relationship between Social Protection and Social Cohesion: Introduction to the Special Issue," *European Journal of Development Research* 34, no. 3 (2022): 1195–1215.
31. Orazio Attanasio, Sandra Polania-Reyes, and Luca Pellerano, "Building Social Capital: Conditional Cash Transfers and Cooperation," *Journal of Economic Behavior & Organization* 118 (2015): 22–39.
32. For a review of the literature, see Burchi et al., "Disentangling the Relationship."

33. Sara Pavanello, Carol Watson, W. Onyango-Ouma, and Paul Bukuluki, "Effects of Cash Transfers on Community Interactions: Emerging Evidence," *Journal of Development Studies* 52, no. 8 (2016): 1147-1161.
34. Pavanello et al., "Effects of Cash Transfers," 1154.

Chapter 7 · The Diversity of Need

1. This story was shared in personal correspondence from Francis Kamuhanda.
2. Maria Kett, *Situational Analysis of Persons with Disabilities in Uganda* (Kampala, Uganda: Ministry of Gender, Labour and Social Development, 2020).
3. Kett, *Situational Analysis of Persons with Disabilities*, 107.
4. For a full discussion, see David Cobley, *Disability and International Development: A Guide for Students and Practitioners* (New York: Routledge, 2018).
5. For detailed discussion of this approach, see Sophie Mitra, *Disability, Health and Human Development* (New York: Springer Nature, 2017).
6. Cobley, *Disability and International Development*.
7. World Health Organization and World Bank, *World Report on Disability* (Geneva, Switzerland: World Health Organization, 2011).
8. United Nations Department of Economic and Social Affairs, *Disability and Development Report 2018* (New York: United Nations, 2019).
9. Asghar Zaidi and Tania Burchardt, "Comparing Incomes When Needs Differ: Equivalization for the Extra Costs of Disability in the UK," *Review of Income and Wealth* 51, no. 1 (2005): 89-114.
10. United Nations, *Disability and Development Report 2018*.
11. United Nations, *Disability and Development Report 2018*.
12. Daniel Mont, "Estimating the Extra Disability Expenditures for the Design of Inclusive Social Protection Policies," *Frontiers in Rehabilitation Sciences* 4 (2023): 1179213.
13. For detailed discussion of these issues, see Kate Gooding and Anna Marriot, "Including Persons with Disabilities in Social Cash Transfer Programmes in Developing Countries," *Journal of International Development* 21, no. 5 (2009): 685-698.
14. Leslie Swartz and Marguerite Schneider, "Tough Choices: Disability and Social Security in South Africa," in *Disability and Social Change: A South African Agenda,* ed. Brian Watermeyer Leslie Swartz, Theresa Lorenzo, Marguerite Schneider, and Mark Priestley (Cape Town, South Africa: HSRC Press, 2006), 240.
15. Note that disability self-reports may suffer from measurement error, so these results should be interpreted with some caution. For detailed discussion, see Sophie Mitra, "Disability Cash Transfers in the Context of Poverty and Unemployment: The Case of South Africa," *World Development* 38, no. 12 (2010): 1692-1709.
16. Gooding and Marriot, "Including Persons with Disabilities."
17. Richard de Groot, Tia Palermo, Lena Morgon Banks, and Hannah Kuper, "The Impact of the Lesotho Child Grant Programme in the Lives of Children and Adults with Disabilities: Disaggregated Analysis of a Community Randomized Controlled Trial," *International Social Security Review* 74, no. 2 (2021): 55-81.
18. Gabrielle Kelly, "Disability, Cash Transfers and Family Practices in South Africa," *Critical Social Policy* 39, no. 4 (2019): 541-559.

19. Kelly, "Disability, Cash Transfers and Family Practices," 554.
20. "Cherie Blair Wants to Kill the World's Intestinal Worms," *Time*, January 25, 2008.
21. Edward Miguel and Michael Kremer, "Worms: Identifying Impacts on Education and Health in the Presence of Treatment Externalities," *Econometrica* 72, no. 1 (2004): 159–217.
22. Calum Davey, Alexander M Aiken, Richard J Hayes, James R Hargreaves, "Re-analysis of Health and Educational Impacts of a School-Based Deworming Programme in Western Kenya: A Statistical Replication of a Cluster Quasi-Randomized Stepped-Wedge Trial," *International Journal of Epidemiology*, 44, no. 5 (2015): 1581–1592, https://doi.org/10.1093/ije/dyv128. For further discussion, see Julia Belluz, "Worm Wars: The Fight Tearing Apart the Global Health Community, Explained," *Vox*, July 28, 2015, https://www.vox.com/2015/7/24/9031909/worm-wars-explained.
23. "Soil-transmitted Helminth Infections," fact sheet, World Health Organization, January 18, 2023, https://www.who.int/news-room/fact-sheets/detail/soil-transmitted-helminth-infections
24. "Soil-transmitted Helminth Infections."
25. Peter Katona and Judit Katona-Apte, "The Interaction between Nutrition and Infection," *Clinical Infectious Diseases* 46, no. 10 (2008): 1582–1588.
26. Andrew J. Prendergast and Jean H. Humphrey, "The Stunting Syndrome in Developing Countries," *Paediatrics and International Child Health* 34, no. 4 (2014): 250–265.
27. "Understanding the Impacts of Pesticides on Children: A Discussion Paper," technical report, UNICEF, January 2018.
28. UNICEF, *The State of the World's Children 2019: Children, Food and Nutrition: Growing Well in a Changing World* (New York: UNICEF, 2019).
29. For a review of the literature, see Mark E. McGovern, Aditi Krishna, Victor M. Aguayo, and S. V. Subramanian, "A Review of the Evidence Linking Child Stunting to Economic Outcomes," *International Journal of Epidemiology* 46, no. 4 (2017): 1171–1191.
30. Rasmus Heltberg, "Malnutrition, Poverty, and Economic Growth," *Health Economics* 18, no. S1 (2009): S85.
31. Caitlin Brown, Martin Ravallion, and Dominique van de Walle, "Most of Africa's Nutritionally Deprived Women and Children Are Not Found in Poor Households," *Review of Economics and Statistics* 101, no. 4 (2019): 631–644.
32. Brown, Ravallion, and van de Walle, "Most of Africa's Nutritionally Deprived," 642.
33. James Manley, Harold Alderman, and Ugo Gentilini, "More Evidence on Cash Transfers and Child Nutritional Outcomes: A Systematic Review and Meta-analysis," *BMJ Global Health* 7, no. 4 (2022): e008233.
34. Bridget Fenn, Tim Colbourn, Carmel Dolan, Silke Pietzsch, Murtaza Sangrasi, and Jeremy Shoham, "Impact Evaluation of Different Cash-based Intervention Modalities on Child and Maternal Nutritional Status in Sindh Province, Pakistan, at 6 mo and at 1 y: A Cluster Randomised Controlled Trial," *PLoS Medicine* 14, no. 5 (2017): e1002305.
35. The authors state that this effect is statistically significant, but the associated hypothesis test is misleading. The confidence interval they provide identifies only the plausible range of values for the "grand mean" and says nothing about the plausible range of actual treatment effects. A more appropriate statistical test would instead use a prediction interval, but the study doesn't provide this. In line with discussions of meta-analyses in other chapters, I will here avoid interpreting misleading statistical tests, whether they

work for or against my argument. For further reading on this issue, see Joanna IntHout, John P. A. Ioannidis, Maroeska M. Rovers, and Jelle J. Goeman, "Plea for Routinely Presenting Prediction Intervals in Meta-analysis," *BMJ Open* 6, no. 7 (2016): e010247.
36. Emily C. Keats, Jai K. Das, Rehana A. Salam, Zohra S. Lassi, Aamer Imdad, Robert E. Black, and Zulfiqar A. Bhutta, "Effective Interventions to Address Maternal and Child Malnutrition: An Update of the Evidence," *The Lancet Child & Adolescent Health* 5, no. 5 (2021): 367–384.
37. UNICEF, *The State of the World's Children 2019*.
38. United Nations, *World Social Report 2023: Leaving No One Behind in an Ageing World* (New York: United Nations, 2023).
39. United Nations, *World Social Report 2023*.
40. United Nations, *World Social Report 2023*, Fig. 4.1, 81.
41. United Nations, *World Social Report 2023*.
42. Robert T. Jensen and Kaspar Richter, "The Health Implications of Social Security Failure: Evidence from the Russian Pension Crisis," *Journal of Public Economics* 88, nos. 1–2 (2004): 209–236.
43. Stephen E. Snyder and William N. Evans, "The Effect of Income on Mortality: Evidence from the Social Security Notch," *Review of Economics and Statistics* 88, no. 3 (2006): 482–495.
44. Tania Barham and Jacob Rowberry, "Living Longer: The Effect of the Mexican Conditional Cash Transfer Program on Elderly Mortality," *Journal of Development Economics* 105 (2013): 226–236.
45. Kevin Feeney, "Cash Transfers and Adult Mortality: Evidence from Pension Policies" (PhD diss., University of California, Berkeley, 2017).
46. Jef L. Leroy, Paola Gadsden, Teresa González de Cossío, and Paul Gertler, "Cash and In-kind Transfers Lead to Excess Weight Gain in a Population of Women with a High Prevalence of Overweight in Rural Mexico," *Journal of Nutrition* 143, no. 3 (2013): 378–383.
47. Ian Forde, T. Chandola, S. Garcia, M. G. Marmot, and O. Attanasio, "The Impact of Cash Transfers to Poor Women in Colombia on BMI and Obesity: Prospective Cohort Study," *International Journal of Obesity* 36, no. 9 (2012): 1209–1214.
48. Emmanuel Skoufias, Benjamin Davis, and Sergio De La Vega, "Targeting the Poor in Mexico: An Evaluation of the Selection of Households into PROGRESA," *World Development* 29, no. 10 (2001): 1769–1784.

Chapter 8 · Transformative Change

1. Bill Gates, "Why I Would Raise Chickens," *Gates Notes,* June 7, 2016, , https://www.gatesnotes.com/Why-I-Would-Raise-Chickens#:~:text=In%20fact%2C%20if%20I%20were,they'll%20grow%20faster.
2. Christopher Blattman, "Bill Gates Wants to Give the Poor Chickens. What They Need Is Cash," *Vox,* March 14, 2017, https://www.vox.com/the-big-idea/2017/3/14/14914996/bill-gates-chickens-cash-africa-poor-development.
3. Blattman, "Bill Gates Wants to Give the Poor Chickens."
4. Blattman, "Bill Gates Wants to Give the Poor Chickens."
5. Blattman, "Bill Gates Wants to Give the Poor Chickens."

6. Lant Pritchett, "Getting Kinky with Chickens," blogpost, Center for Global Development, March 28, 2017, https://www.cgdev.org/blog/getting-kinky-chickens.
7. Pritchett, "Getting Kinky with Chickens."
8. Pritchett, "Getting Kinky with Chickens."
9. David Calnitsky, "Structural and Individualistic Theories of Poverty," *Sociology Compass* 12, no. 12 (2018): e12640.
10. Blattman, "Bill Gates Wants to Give the Poor Chickens."
11. Johannes Haushofer and Ernst Fehr, "On the Psychology of Poverty," *Science* 344, no. 6186 (2014): 862–867.
12. Anandi Mani, Sendhil Mullainathan, Eldar Shafir, and Jiaying Zhao, "Poverty Impedes Cognitive Function," *Science* 341, no. 6149 (2013): 976–980.
13. Gary S. Becker, "Human Capital and Poverty Alleviation," World Bank Human Resources Development and Operations Policy Working Paper 52 (Washington, DC: World Bank, 1995), http://go.worldbank.org/FYLM8NJRU0; Edward Royce, *Poverty and Power: A Structural Perspective on American Inequality* (Lanham, MD: Rowman and Littlefield, 2009).
14. For additional discussion and examples, see Calnitsky, "Structural and Individualistic Theories of Poverty."
15. For a discussion of Raúl Prebisch and Hans Singer's research, see Anton Jäger and Daniel Zamora Vargas, *Welfare for Markets: A Global History of Basic Income* (Chicago: University of Chicago Press, 2023), ch. 5.
16. For a discussion of institutions and how they relate to social structure, see Geoffrey M. Hodgson, "What Are Institutions?" *Journal of Economic Issues* 40, no. 1 (2006): 1–25.
17. Daron Acemoglu and James A. Robinson, *Why Nations Fail: The Origins of Power, Prosperity, and Poverty* (New York: Currency, 2012).
18. Details and references are provided in Mark Koyama and Jared Rubin, *How the World Became Rich: The Historical Origins of Economic Growth* (Cambridge: Polity Press, 2022), ch. 6.
19. Elizabeth Oltmans Ananat, "The Wrong Side(s) of the Tracks: The Causal Effects of Racial Segregation on Urban Poverty and Inequality," *American Economic Journal: Applied Economics* 3, no. 2 (2011): 34–66.
20. David Brady, "Theories of the Causes of Poverty," *Annual Review of Sociology* 45 (2019): 155–175.
21. Calnitsky, "Structural and Individualistic Theories of Poverty," 2.
22. Daron Acemoglu, Simon Johnson, and James A. Robinson, "Institutions as a Fundamental Cause of Long-run Growth," in *The Handbook of Economic Growth,* ed. Philippe Aghion and Steven N. Durlauf (Amsterdam: Elsevier, 2005), 385–472.
23. Acemoglu, Johnson, and Robinson, "Institutions as a Fundamental Cause of Long-run Growth," 406.
24. The estimate of 35 percent is the raw or unadjusted difference in incomes taken from Abhijit Banerjee, Esther Duflo, and Garima Sharma, "Long-term Effects of the Targeting the Ultra Poor Program," *American Economic Review: Insights* 3, no. 4 (2021): 471–486.
25. For a similar argument that also uses the Targeting the Ultra Poor program as a benchmark, see Lant Pritchett, "Alleviating Global Poverty: Labor Mobility, Direct Assistance, and Economic Growth," Working Paper No. 479, Center for Global Development, May 18, 2018.

26. Daron Acemoglu, Simon Johnson, and James A. Robinson, "The Colonial Origins of Comparative Development: An Empirical Investigation," *American Economic Review* 91, no. 5 (2001): 1369–1401.
27. Koyama and Rubin, *How the World Became Rich.*
28. Koyama and Rubin, *How the World Became Rich,* 219.
29. Michael A. Clemens, Claudio E. Montenegro, and Lant Pritchett, "The Place Premium: Bounding the Price Equivalent of Migration Barriers," *Review of Economics and Statistics* 101, no. 2 (2019): 201–213.
30. Francesca Bastagli, Jessica Hagen-Zanker, and Georgina Sturge, *Cash Transfers: What Does the Evidence Say?* technical report, Overseas Development Institute, July 2016.
31. Bastagli et al., *Cash Transfers: What Does the Evidence Say?* 22.
32. Martina Ulrichs and Keetie Roelen, "Equal Opportunities for All?—A Critical Analysis of Mexico's Oportunidades," IDS Working Paper 2012, no. 413 Institute of Development Studies, December 2012, 8.
33. Ulrichs and Roelen, "Equal Opportunities for All?" 17.
34. Jäger and Vargas, *Welfare for Markets,* ch. 5.
35. Jäger and Vargas, *Welfare for Markets,* 153.
36. Margaret Wokuri, Besigye campaign communications officer, quoted in Josh Kron, "Longtime Uganda President Takes Large Lead in Election," *New York Times,* February 20, 2011, 9.
37. For more detailed discussion and references, see Christopher Blattman, Mathilde Emeriau, and Nathan Fiala, "Do Anti-poverty Programs Sway Voters? Experimental Evidence from Uganda," *Review of Economics and Statistics* 100, no. 5 (2018): 891–905.
38. Blattman, Emeriau, and Fiala, "Do Anti-poverty Programs Sway Voters?"
39. Kosuke Imai, Gary King, and Carlos Velasco Rivera, "Do Nonpartisan Programmatic Policies Have Partisan Electoral Effects? Evidence from Two Large-scale Experiments," *Journal of Politics* 82, no. 2 (2020): 714–730.
40. Victor Araújo, "Do Anti-poverty Policies Sway Voters? Evidence from a Meta-analysis of Conditional Cash Transfers," *Research & Politics* 8, no. 1 (2021): 1–9.
41. Blattman, Emeriau, and Fiala, "Do Anti-poverty Programs Sway Voters?" 904.
42. Dennis Egger, Johannes Haushofer, Edward Miguel, Paul Niehaus, and Michael Walker, "General Equilibrium Effects of Cash Transfers: Experimental Evidence from Kenya," *Econometrica* 90, no. 6 (2022): 2603–2643.
43. For a similar result in the context of a more developed country, see Damon Jones and Ioana Marinescu, "The Labor Market Impacts of Universal and Permanent Cash Transfers: Evidence from the Alaska Permanent Fund," *American Economic Journal: Economic Policy* 14, no. 2 (2022): 315–340.
44. Natalie Bau, "Can Policy Change Culture? Government Pension Plans and Traditional Kinship Practices," *American Economic Review* 111, no. 6 (2021): 1880–1917.

Chapter 9 · Paternalism Revisited

1. Unless noted otherwise, details of this story are from personal correspondence with Anthony Kalulu.
2. Anthony Kalulu, "From a Life in Extreme Poverty, He Is Inspired to Help Others," Stories of Change, ATD Quart Monde, February 13, 2018, https://storiesofchange

.atd-fourthworld.org/from-a-life-in-extreme-poverty-he-is-inspired-to-help-others-763ba3e0d1f8.
3. Kalulu, "From a Life in Extreme Poverty."
4. Anthony Kalulu, "My Intended Solution," Dear Humanity, n.d., https://dear-humanity.org/my-intended-solution, accessed September 21, 2023.
5. Anthony Kalulu, "Effective Altruism Is Worse Than Traditional Philanthropy in the Way It Excludes the Extreme Poor in the Global South," Dear Humanity, December 3, 2022, http://dear-humanity.org/effective-altruism-worse-for-poor, accessed September 21, 2023.
6. The philanthropic drive toward giving more effectively is most visible in the ever-growing "effective altruism" movement, but these ideas have also been increasingly adopted by foreign aid agencies. For example, see Daniel Handel, "We're Finally Figuring Out If Foreign Aid Is Any Better Than Handing Out Cash," *Vox*, September 5, 2023, https://www.vox.com/future-perfect/23854173/foreign-aid-cash-benchmarking-evidence-usaid.
7. Kalulu, "Effective Altruism Is Worse than Traditional Philanthropy."
8. See Chapter 6 for discussion of the issues associated with resource pooling.
9. Justin Sandefur, Nancy Birdsall, and Mujobu Moyo, "The Political Paradox of Cash Transfers," blogpost, Center for Global Development, September 16, 2015, https://www.cgdev.org/blog/political-paradox-cash-transfers.
10. Stuti Khemani, James Habyarimana, and Irfan Nooruddin, "What Do Poor People Think about Direct Cash Transfers?" commentary, Brookings Institution, April 8, 2019, https://www.brookings.edu/articles/what-do-poor-people-think-about-direct-cash-transfers.
11. Survey on social, economic, and political issues in Mongolia, Politbarometer 22, March 2023, Sant Maral Foundation, https://www.santmaral.org/publications. (The 80 percent figure cited here is derived from question E4, by adding the nationwide responses for the second and fourth options.)
12. Sirin Kale, "'Being an MP Was Bad for My Brain, Body and Soul': Rory Stewart on Politics, Privilege and Podcast Stardom," *The Guardian*, August 29, 2022.
13. MacKay refers to this definition as "welfare state paternalism." See Douglas MacKay, "Basic Income, Cash Transfers, and Welfare State Paternalism," *Journal of Political Philosophy* 27, no. 4 (2019): 422–447, 431.
14. Nicolas Cornell, "A Third Theory of Paternalism," *Michigan Law Review* 113, no. 8 (2015): 1295–1336.
15. For the full quote and reference, see MacKay, "Basic Income, Cash Transfers," 423.
16. It's worth noting that there are potentially situations where in-kind programs wouldn't be considered paternalistic. For example, if policymakers simply believe people have a right to food, then the direct provision of food wouldn't express any negative judgment about people's decision-making abilities. For additional discussion, see MacKay, "Basic Income, Cash Transfers."
17. Ariel Fiszbein and Norbert Schady, *Conditional Cash Transfers: Reducing Present and Future Poverty* (Washington, DC: World Bank, 2009), ch. 2.
18. For a detailed discussion of the paternalism of conditional programs, see Douglas MacKay, "Parenting the Parents: The Ethics of Parent-targeted Paternalism in the Context of Anti-poverty Policies," in *Philosophy and Child Poverty: Reflections on the*

Ethics and Politics of Poor Children and Their Families, ed. Nicolás Brando and Gottfried Schweiger (Cham, Switzerland: Springer, 2019), 321–340.

19. Fotis Georgiadis, "GiveDirectly: Paul Niehaus's Big Idea That Might Change the World," *Authority Magazine,* March 1, 2022, accessed October 6, 2023, https://medium.com/authority-magazine/givedirectly-paul-niehauss-big-idea-that-might-change-the-world-aecadb90e83c.

20. Jordan Kyle, "Local Corruption and Popular Support for Fuel Subsidy Reform in Indonesia," *Comparative Political Studies* 51, no. 11 (2018): 1472–1503.

21. Reetika Khera, "Cash vs. In-kind Transfers: Indian Data Meets Theory," *Food Policy* 46 (2014): 116–128.

22. Khera, "Cash vs. In-kind Transfers," 121.

23. For a full discussion of these factors, see MacKay, "Basic Income, Cash Transfers."

24. The budgeting process would later include assemblies organized around thematic areas of interest (for example, transportation, education, and economic development) that would run parallel to the regional process. For detailed discussion, see Rebecca Abers, Robin King, Daniely Votto, and Igor Brandao, "Porto Alegre: Participatory Budgeting and the Challenge of Sustaining Transformative Change," case study, World Resources Institute, June 13, 2018.

25. Amartya Sen, *Development as Freedom* (New York: Anchor Books, 1999), ch. 6.

26. Rutger Claassen, *Capabilities in a Just Society: A Theory of Navigational Agency* (Cambridge: Cambridge University Press, 2018).

27. Michael Hillebrecht, Stefan Klonner, Noraogo A. Pacere, and Aurélia Souares, "Community-based versus Statistical Targeting of Anti-poverty Programs: Evidence from Burkina Faso," *Journal of African Economies* 29, no. 3 (2020): 271–305.

28. Harold Alderman, "Do Local Officials Know Something We Don't? Decentralization of Targeted Transfers in Albania," *Journal of Public Economics* 83, no. 3 (2002): 375–404.

29. These results have been echoed by similar studies, confirming that decentralization has an important instrumental role in alleviating poverty. For an example of a similar finding, see Vivi Alatas, Abhijit Banerjee, Rema Hanna, Benjamin A. Olken, and Julia Tobias, "Targeting the Poor: Evidence from a Field Experiment in Indonesia," *American Economic Review* 102, no. 4 (2012): 1206–1240.

30. Elinor Ostrom, *Governing the Commons: The Evolution of Institutions for Collective Action* (Cambridge: Cambridge University Press, 1990).

31. Yuen Yuen Ang, *How China Escaped the Poverty Trap* (Ithaca, NY: Cornell University Press, 2016).

32. A. Sen, *Development as Freedom,* 157–158.

33. Dennis Chirawurah, James Fishkin, Niagia Santuah, Alice Siu, Ayaga Bawah, and Gordana Kranjac-Berisavljevic, "Deliberation for Development: Ghana's First Deliberative Poll," *Journal of Deliberative Democracy* 15, no. 1 (2019), article 3.

34. For detailed discussion, see Chirawurah et al., "Deliberation for Development."

35. Abers et al., "Porto Alegre."

36. Peter Evans, "Bringing Deliberation into the Developmental State," in *Deliberation and Development: Rethinking the Role of Voice and Collective Action in Unequal Societies,* ed. Patrick Heller and Vijayendra Rao (Washington, DC: World Bank, 2015), 51–66.

37. David A. Crocker, *Ethics of Global Development: Agency, Capability, and Deliberative Democracy* (Cambridge: Cambridge University Press, 2008), ch. 10.

38. For more detailed discussion and references, see Andre Bächtiger, Marco R. Steenbergen, and Simon Niemeyer, "Deliberative Democracy: An Introduction," in *The Oxford Handbook of Deliberative Democracy*, ed. André Bächtiger, John S. Dryzek, Jane Mansbridge, and Mark E. Warren (Oxford: Oxford University Press, 2018), 1–32.
39. Cass R. Sunstein, "The Law of Group Polarization," *Journal of Political Philosophy* 10, no. 2 (2002): 175–195.
40. Bächtiger et al., "Deliberative Democracy."
41. *Participedia*, https://participedia.net, accessed November 12, 2023.
42. Lindsay Mayka and Jared Abbott, "Varieties of Participatory Institutions and Interest Intermediation," *World Development* 171 (2023): 106369.
43. Susan Wong and Scott Guggenheim, "Community-driven Development: Myths and Realities," Policy Research Working Paper 8435, World Bank, May 2018.
44. John S. Dryzek, André Bächtiger, et al., "The Crisis of Democracy and the Science of Deliberation," *Science* 363, no. 6432 (2019): 1144–1146, 1145.
45. Mayka and Abbott, "Varieties of Participatory Institutions."
46. Stefania Ravazzi, "When a Government Attempts to Institutionalize and Regulate Deliberative Democracy: The How and Why from a Process-tracing Perspective," *Critical Policy Studies* 11, no. 1 (2017): 79–100.
47. Paromita Sanyal and Vijayendra Rao, *Oral Democracy: Deliberation in Indian Village Assemblies* (Cambridge: Cambridge University Press, 2018).
48. For further discussion, see Samuel Hickey, "Conceptualising the Politics of Social Protection in Africa," Working Paper 4, Brooks World Poverty Institute, University of Manchester, October 2007.
49. Wong and Guggenheim, "Community-driven Development."
50. Boaventura de Sousa Santos, "Participatory Budgeting in Porto Alegre: Toward a Redistributive Democracy," *Politics & Society* 26, no. 4 (1998): 461–510.
51. Dryzek et al., "The Crisis of Democracy and the Science of Deliberation," 1145.
52. Crocker, *Ethics of Global Development*, ch. 10.
53. Wong and Guggenheim, "Community-driven Development," 17.
54. Wong and Guggenheim, "Community-driven Development," 18.
55. Bächtiger et al., "Deliberative Democracy."
56. Kim Strandberg, Staffan Himmelroos, and Kimmo Grönlund, "Do Discussions in Likeminded Groups Necessarily Lead to More Extreme Opinions? Deliberative Democracy and Group Polarization," *International Political Science Review* 40, no. 1 (2019): 41–57.
57. Scott A. Fritzen, "Can the Design of Community-driven Development Reduce the Risk of Elite Capture? Evidence from Indonesia," *World Development* 35, no. 8 (2007): 1359–1375.
58. Robert Chambers, *Rural Development: Putting the Last First* (New York: Routledge, 1983).

Chapter 10 · Deliberative Democracy

1. All quotes are taken from Nurith Aizenman, "It's Not a Come-on from a Cult. It's a New Kind of Poll!" *NPR Goats and Soda*, May 18, 2015, https://www.npr.org/sections/goatsandsoda/2015/05/18/406462789/its-not-a-come-on-from-a-satanic-cult-its-a-new-kind-of-poll.

2. Justin Sandefur, Nancy Birdsall, James Fishkin, and Mujobu Moyo, "Democratic Deliberation and the Resource Curse: A Nationwide Experiment in Tanzania," *World Politics* 74, no. 4 (2022): 564–609.
3. Aizenman, "It's Not a Come-on from a Cult."
4. Justin Sandefur, Nancy Birdsall, and Mujobu Moyo, "The Political Paradox of Cash Transfers," blogpost, Center for Global Development, September 16, 2015, https://www.cgdev.org/blog/political-paradox-cash-transfers.
5. Justin Sandefur, Nancy Birdsall, and Mujobu Moyo, "Tanzania Poll Results: Can Deliberative Democracy Cure the Resource Curse?" blogpost, Center for Global Development, September 8, 2015, https://www.cgdev.org/blog/tanzania-poll-results-can-deliberative-democracy-cure-resource-curse.
6. Sandefur et al., "Democratic Deliberation and the Resource Curse."
7. For detailed discussion of these results, see Sandefur et al., "Democratic Deliberation and the Resource Curse."
8. Bruce Ackerman and James Fishkin, *Deliberation Day* (New Haven, CT: Yale University Press, 2004).
9. The subsequent discussion of these values draws heavily on James Fishkin, *When the People Speak: Deliberative Democracy and Public Consultation* (Oxford: Oxford University Press, 2009), ch. 2.
10. Fishkin, *When the People Speak*, 46–47.
11. Fishkin, *When the People Speak*, ch. 2.
12. Scott Guggenheim, Tatag Wiranto, Yogana Prasta, and Susan Wong, "Indonesia's Kecamatan Development Program: A Large-scale Use of Community Development to Reduce Poverty," Working Paper 30779, World Bank, May 1, 2004.
13. Scott Guggenheim, "Origins of Community-driven Development: Indonesia and the Kecamatan Development Program," Development Reflections, World Bank, April 2021.
14. Benjamin A. Olken, "Direct Democracy and Local Public Goods: Evidence from a Field Experiment in Indonesia," *American Political Science Review* 104, no. 2 (2010): 243–267.
15. Olken, "Direct Democracy and Local Public Goods."
16. For a full listing, see Guggenheim et al., "Indonesia's Kecamatan Development Program."
17. In 2006, it was renamed the National Program for Community Empowerment.
18. Guggenheim, "Origins of Community-driven Development."
19. John Voss, "Impact Evaluation of the Second Phase of the Kecamatan Development Program in Indonesia," Working Paper 45590, World Bank, June 1, 2008.
20. Katherine Casey, "Radical Decentralization: Does Community-driven Development Work?" *Annual Review of Economics* 10 (2018): 139–163.
21. Katherine Casey, Rachel Glennerster, Edward Miguel, and Maarten J. Voors, "Long-run Effects of Aid: Forecasts and Evidence from Sierra Leone," *The Economic Journal* 133, no. 652 (2023): 1348–1370.
22. Eric Mvukiyehe and Peter van der Windt, "Assessing the Longer Term Impact of Community-driven Development Programs: Evidence from a Field Experiment in the Democratic Republic of Congo," Policy Research Working Paper 9140, World Bank, January 2020.
23. Audrey Sacks and Benjamin Olken, "Indonesia: Long-term Impact Evaluation of Generasi," report AUS0000289, World Bank, May 2018.

24. Howard White, Radhika Menon, and Hugh Waddington, "Community-driven Development: Does It Build Social Cohesion or Infrastructure? A Mixed Method Evidence Synthesis," Working Paper 30, International Initiative for Impact Evaluation, March 2018.
25. "Marginalized Groups in PNPM-Rural," AKATIGA Center for Social Analysis, Bandung, Indonesia, June 2010.
26. Julien Labonne and Robert S. Chase, "Who Is at the Wheel When Communities Drive Development? Evidence from the Philippines," *World Development* 37, no. 1 (2009): 219-231.
27. This discussion of the different variants of microcosmic deliberation draws on OECD, "Innovative Citizen Participation and New Democratic Institutions: Catching the Deliberative Wave" (Paris: OECD, 2020). For additional discussion, see Fishkin, *When the People Speak*, ch. 2.
28. For a more comprehensive discussion, see OECD, "Innovative Citizen Participation."
29. For a complete listing of projects, see Deliberative Democracy Lab, Stanford University, https://deliberation.stanford.edu, accessed January 18, 2024.
30. James Fishkin, *Democracy When the People Are Thinking: Revitalizing Our Politics through Public Deliberation* (Oxford: Oxford University Press, 2018)
31. Fishkin, *Democracy When the People Are Thinking.*
32. For additional discussion, see Fishkin, *Democracy When the People Are Thinking.*
33. For discussion and references, see Fishkin, *Democracy When the People Are Thinking.*
34. More detailed discussion is provided in Graham Smith and Maija Setälä, "Mini-publics and Deliberative Democracy," in *The Oxford Handbook of Deliberative Democracy*, ed. Andre Bächtiger et al. (Oxford: Oxford University Press, 2018), 300-314.
35. "British Colombia Citizens' Assembly on Electoral Reform," case, Participedia, n.d., https://participedia.net/case/1, accessed January 18, 2024.

Conclusion

1. Stephanie Wykstra, "Microcredit Was a Hugely Hyped Solution to Global Poverty. What Happened?" *Vox*, January 15, 2019, https://www.vox.com/future-perfect/2019/1/15/18182167/microcredit-microfinance-poverty-grameen-bank-yunus.
2. "Of Property and Poverty," *The Economist*, August 24, 2006.
3. Howard W. French, "The Not-so-great Professor: Jeffrey Sachs' Incredible Failure to Eradicate Poverty in Africa," *Pacific Standard*, September 17, 2013, https://psmag.com/social-justice/smart-guy-jeffrey-sachs-nina-munk-idealist-poverty-failure-africa-65348/.
4. Chris Hughes, "The Most Effective Intervention in the Fight for Economic Justice Is Cash in the Hands of the People Who Need It Most," *Quartz*, February 27, 2018, https://qz.com/1216511/the-most-effective-intervention-in-the-fight-for-economic-justice-is-cash-in-the-hands-of-the-people-who-need-it-most.
5. Cecilia W. Dugger, "To Help Poor Be Pupils, Not Wage Earners, Brazil Pays Parents," *New York Times*, January 3, 2004.
6. Dylan Matthews, "The Rise and Rise of GiveDirectly," *Vox*, August 31, 2022, https://www.vox.com/future-perfect/2022/8/31/23329242/givedirectly-cash-transfers-rory-stewart.
7. Amartya Sen, *Development as Freedom* (New York: Anchor Books, 1999), 11.

8. Sirin Kale, "'Being an MP Was Bad for My Brain, Body and Soul': Rory Stewart on Politics, Privilege and Podcast Stardom," *The Guardian,* August 29, 2022.
9. Kale, "Being an MP Was Bad."
10. Karthik Muralidharan, Paul Niehaus, and Sandip Sukhtankar, "We Need a Choice-based Approach in the Public Distribution System," *Hindustan Times,* October 3, 2018, https://www.hindustantimes.com/columns/we-need-a-choice-based-approach-to-the-public-distribution-system/story-RY7jEYDmXfsxOMEsZguxmJ.html.
11. For a complete listing of projects, see Deliberative Democracy Lab, Stanford University, https://deliberation.stanford.edu, accessed January 18, 2024.

Acknowledgments

IF THERE'S EVER a good time to start writing a book, it's probably not at the tail end of a pandemic, with two small kids, spotty childcare, and a sick family member. I never would have done it without the enthusiastic support of my wife, Katy. Well beyond encouraging me to take up this project, Katy patiently dealt with me stressing about finding writing time and was always supportive when I needed to work nights or weekends. She also gave me constant feedback—about my arguments, my ideas for book and chapter titles, my questions about navigating the publication process, and more. Nothing good comes easily, but this project would have been impossible without such a caring and supportive partner. Of course, every day along the way was also made better by my two exceedingly energetic and happy kids, Thea and Beau.

Drake University provided generous financial support and a highly collegial environment for writing this book. First and foremost, I couldn't have researched and written it if I didn't have a year-long sabbatical to devote exclusively to the project. I'm especially grateful to my department colleagues for encouraging me to take that sabbatical and picking up the slack while I was away. I'm also extremely grateful to Kailey Inman, who provided excellent research assistance at every stage of the project, from digging up case studies to proofreading chapter drafts. Finally, I want to extend a special thanks to Carl Vieregger for taking a special interest in the book and providing extensive comments on nearly every chapter. Carl is a gifted copy editor and his feedback significantly improved the quality of my writing.

Many, many people made valuable contributions to individual chapters of the book. Anthony Kalulu and Francis Kamuhanda graciously agreed to have their stories featured in the book and patiently answered my questions about the details of their lives. I would encourage readers to learn more about their projects—Uganda Community Farms and Sure Prospects—and to consider donating to them. I also want to thank Jean Drèze, Raj Shekar, and Aninjit Pakhale for entertaining my questions about the Jharkhand protests featured in the opening chapter of the book. Jean Drèze's work has long been an inspiration to me and I'm especially honored to have his contribution. Further, I'm deeply grateful to Scott Guggenheim and Vic Bottini, who gave detailed and thoughtful responses to all my questions on the Kecamatan Development Program.

The list goes on. I'd like to thank Rutger Claassen for thoughtfully reviewing Chapter 2 and Joshua Merfeld for providing detailed comments on Chapter 3. Tara Patricia Cookson and Maria Floro graciously commented on Chapter 5, and Brian Vander Naald gave me extremely helpful feedback on Chapter 6. James Manley and Ethan Sager were both a great help with Chapter 7—James generously answering my questions on his work and Ethan diligently reviewing the entire chapter. Regarding Chapter 9, I'm indebted to Douglas MacKay for his detailed feedback on the arguments there, especially those related to his work on paternalism. Lastly, I'd like to thank Alice Siu for enthusiastically answering my questions about deliberative polling, providing information critical to the development of Chapter 10.

I initially expected the publication process for the book to be pretty arduous, but Grigory Tovbis and the rest of the team at Harvard University Press made everything remarkably pleasant. I'm especially thankful for Grigory's attention to detail and thoughtful guidance, which helped make the book much more accessible, interesting, and rigorous. I also want to thank Eric Maisel for expertly coaching me in the preparation of a book proposal, helping me navigate the submission process, and encouraging me to submit my proposal to HUP. I'm further grateful to Enrica Chiappero-Martinetti, Marion Ouma, Smriti Tiwari, Seth Gitter, Mari Kangasniemi, and two anonymous readers for agreeing to serve as peer reviewers for either my proposal or the full manuscript.

This book is dedicated to my father-in-law, Rick Swalwell. Rick was diagnosed with pancreatic cancer about the same time I started writing the book and he passed away only a few short months later. I often had Rick in mind while I was writing this book, in part because he was a great example of the kind of person I wanted to reach—curious, open-minded, and compassionate. Rick was also an extremely principled person who was much more interested in doing what was right than what was popular at the moment. I've done my best to channel that spirit in this book. Rick's puns may have been a little questionable at times, but he was an unquestionably down-to-earth person, and I hope this book brings some of his humility to the discourse on global poverty.

Finally, all proceeds from this book will be donated to JustGive Participatory Philanthropy. I started JustGive in 2024 with the goal of advancing a different kind of philanthropy, one based on many of the ideas discussed in this book. My view is that much of current philanthropy is based on a top-down approach to decision-making that tends to exclude the very people who are impacted by those decisions. JustGive, by contrast, uses democratic decision-making to identify causes that people in need view as valuable and impactful. The basic idea is that people in need not only know their lives best, but also have a right to be heard in any decisions that affect their lives. While JustGive is very much a long-term project, my hope is that the proceeds from this book will help keep it moving in the right direction.

Index

adverse selection, 106, 112
age-based allowances, 6, 8, 64
age-based societies, extent benefits of cash transfers reaching children in, 92–93
agency: alleviation of poverty and, 198, 199–200, 201; basic capabilities for, 34; capability approach and, 31–32; microcosmic deliberation and, 184; radical decentralization and, 167; view of poverty and, 37
agency neglect, targeting and, 72
agent, defined, 31
agent-oriented view of poverty, 198
aging, demographic transition and population, 131–132. *See also* old age
Albania, Ndihma Ekonomike program, 43, 168
Astek program (Indonesia), 93, 154–155
asymmetric information, 106–107, 112
autonomy, paternalistic programs disrespecting people's, 165
autonomy objection, radical decentralization and, 171, 173–174
average treatment effect, 56–57

Baby's First Years Study, 38–40
Bangladesh: asset-transfer program for women in, 89–90; Targeting the Ultra Poor program, 144, 146
Bantuan Langsung Tunai (Indonesia), 13, 72–74
bargaining power within household, 83, 84, 85; effect of cash transfers on women's, 89–90, 95, 96–97

barriers to entry, 105–106, 110
basic needs, measuring poverty and defining, 24
basic services, 106
behavior, utility function and, 81–83. *See also* household behavior
bias, 54–56
Blair, Cherie, 126–127
Blattman, Christopher, 156; asset-based view of poverty, 140–141; cash transfer program in Ethiopia and, 50–51; criticism of Gates's program, 137–138; use of randomized trials to evaluate poverty programs, 138, 139–140; Youth Opportunities Program and, 47–49, 151–153
blood market, 99–101, 215n4
Bolivida program (Bolivia), 94
Bolsa Família (Brazil), 6, 12
Bono de Desarrollo Humano (Human Development Bonus) (Ecuador), 49, 90
Brazil: Bolsa Família program, 6, 12; decision-making experiment in, 165–167, 170–171, 200
briefing materials, for deliberative polling, 194, 201
Burkina Faso, community-based targeting scheme in, 168

Canada: Citizen's Assembly on Electoral Reform, 174–175, 195; negative income taxes in, 11
capability: defined, 29; targeting and, 72

| 233

capability approach, 15, 27–33, 198;
agency and, 31–32, 34, 167; choice and,
34–35; conversion factors and, 30–31;
criticism of, 33–37; each person as an
end and, 32–33; focus on functioning,
28–29, 32–33; liberalism and, 36–37;
life dimensions and, 33–34; means-
ends distinction and, 30–31, 35, 37;
operationalizing, 35–36; poverty as
injustice and, 33; value pluralism and,
31–32

capacity problem, deliberative decision-
making and, 171, 174

Care Dependency Grant (South Africa),
125

cash-plus programs, 9

cash transfer, defined, 5

cash transfer programs: aging population
and, 133–136; alternatives to, 17–18,
178–180; children and, 92–98; choice
and, 34–35, 164; corruption and,
163–164; costs for women, 87–89;
critique of, 14–17; effect on cultural
traditions, 154–155; electoral effects,
151–153; history of, 9–14; individualist
orientation of, 146–151, 159–160;
limitations of, 1–2, 3–4, 198–199;
missing markets and, 113–117;
missing-women problem and, 80–81;
overstating impacts of, 54–57,
197–198; as palliative, 151–156;
paternalism of, 17, 160–165, 199;
people with disabilities and, 124–126;
theory of change, 146–149; as top-
down approach, 199–200; typology
of, 5–9. *See also* conditional cash
transfer programs; *individual programs*

cash transfer program studies, 38–57;
average treatment effect, 56–57;
long-term effects of cash, 47–52,
53–54; selective outcome reporting
and, 55–56; short-term effects of cash,
41–47, 53; site-selection bias and,
54–55; summary of evidence, 53

categorical targeting, 61–62, 64–65,
66–67, 117

centralized poverty-alleviation programs,
160. *See also* in-kind transfers

Chad, cash transfer program in, 58–61, 66

chickens, poverty alleviation and gift of,
137–138

child anthropometric indicators, effects
of cash transfers on, 46, 51–52, 75, 129,
130, 131, 147

Child Grant Programme (Lesotho),
125–126

child labor, effects of cash transfers on,
52, 94, 146

children, cash transfers and, 92–98;
cultural factors in extent benefits
allocated to, 92–93; household
decision-maker characteristics and,
94–98; local market functioning and,
93–94; long-term effects, 48, 51–52;
malnutrition, income, and, 129–131;
share of household resources and,
26; targeting through women, 88–89,
94–97

children, deworming initiatives for,
127–128

children with disabilities, school
attendance and, 118–121, 123, 125, 126

child tax credits, Baby's First Years Study
as evidence for, 39

China, 13, 78

choice, cash transfers and, 34–35, 164

Citizen's Assembly on Electoral Reform
(British Columbia), 174–175, 195

citizens' jury, 190, 191

civil liberties, 21, 27, 34, 101

clientelism, 151, 170

climate change, as market failure,
107–108

cognitive functioning, living in poverty
and, 141

cohort effect, population aging and, 132

collective consent, deliberation and
securing, 180–181

collective investments, community
preferences for, 159–160

collective model of household behavior,
84, 213n13

INDEX | 235

Colombia, Familias en Acción (Families in Action), 116–117, 135
common-pool resources, rivalrous nature of, 104, 105
community-based targeting, 63–64, 67, 69, 168
community-driven development, 186
conceptual problems in measuring poverty using income, 26–27
conditional cash transfer programs, 5–9, 40–41, 162; Juntos program, 86–89
confidence intervals, 208n15, 209n17, 218n35
consensus conferences, 190, 191
consent: collective, 180–181; mass, 181, 195; to program or policy, 161–162
constructive value of decentralization, 169–170
consumer theory, example of, 82–83
consumption: effects of cash transfers on, 50–51; measuring living standards and, 25–26; nonmarket goods and, 27
consumption bundle, indifference curve and, 82–83
context, capability approach and, 31–33
contextual factors, cash transfers and, 147–148
contributory pensions, 133–134, 154
conversion factors: capability approach and, 30–31; malnutrition and, 121, 129–131; old age and, 121, 131–136; people / children with disabilities and, 118, 121–126
conversion failure: aging and, 132–133; child development and, 129; people with disabilities and, 124–126
cooperation, cash transfers and, 116–117
cooperative models of household behavior, 83–84
correlations, 40
corruption, cash transfer programs considered less prone to, 163–164
cost-of-living differences within countries, global poverty measures and, 24–25

Covid-19 pandemic, use of cash transfers during, 14
credit, poverty and access to, 140, 146
cultural factors in extent benefits of cash transfers reaching children, 92–93
cultural traditions, effects of cash transfers on, 154–155

decentralization, alleviating poverty and, 223n29
decentralization, radical, 17, 160, 165–170; perils of, 170–176
decision-making, 17. *See also* deliberative democracy; deliberative polling; microcosmic deliberation
decision-making abilities, paternalistic view of people's, 161, 162–163
deliberation: defined, 180; in democratic trilemma, 180–181; mobilized, 182, 183. *See also* microcosmic deliberation; participatory budgeting
Deliberation Day, 180–182
deliberative democracy, 177–196; democratic trilemma, 180–186; designing deliberations, 191–196; experiment in Tanzania, 177–180; limitations of, 200; as response to top-down or technocratic approaches, 199–200. *See also* microcosmic deliberation
deliberative polling, 18, 178–180, 183, 200–201; briefing materials, 194, 201; designing, 191–196; facilitating, 194, 201; geographic scope of use, 192, 196; linking referendum to, 195; mass consent sacrificed in, 195; mitigating power imbalances in, 194–195; sampling participants, 193–194; secret ballots, 194–195; setting agenda for, 192–193
democratic experiments in public decision-making: in Brazil, 165–167, 170–171; in Ghana, 169–170
Democratic Republic of Congo, Tuungane program, 188

democratic trilemma, 180–186; deliberation, equality, and participation, 180–181; options in, 182–184
demographic targeting, 64, 68, 211n16, 211n17
demographic transition, population aging and, 131–132
Deng Xiaoping, 144–145
dependency theory, 142
developing world / countries: rise of cash transfer programs in, 12–13; universal income programs in, 13–14; use of term, 18. *See also individual countries*
development, redefinition of, 149–150
Devi Rupak program (India), 4, 81
Direct Benefit Transfer for Food Subsidy (DBT) (India), 2–4, 200
direct cash assistance, 5
direct value of decentralization, 166–167
disability: aging and, 132; as conversion factor, 121–126; measuring, 122; medical *vs.* social models of, 121–122; self-reports of, 217n15. *See also* children with disabilities; people with disabilities
disability grants, neglect of social side of disability and, 124–125
diversity neglect, targeting and, 72
domestic violence, impact of cash transfer aimed at women and, 90
durable assets, effects of cash transfers on, 48

earned income tax credits, 6, 8–9, 11
economic development: cash transfers and, 153–154; role of political institutions in, 142
economic stimulus, as spillover effect of cash transfer programs, 76
Ecuador, Bono de Desarrollo Humano program, 49, 90
education: effects of cash transfers on, 44–45, 48, 49, 51–52, 148–149; missing markets and, 111–112. *See also under* school
effective altruism movement, 222n6

effectiveness: choosing implementation details of cash programs and, 163; evaluation of anti-poverty programs and, 158–159; marginalization of local actors and, 162–163
effectiveness motivation, 161–162, 165
efficiency, Pareto, 215n8
efficient outcomes, household behavior models and, 83–84
eligibility for programs: full means test, 62, 69, 70–71. *See also* proxy means test
elite capture: community-based targeting and, 64; decentralization, political equality, and, 185; deliberative decision-making and, 172, 175; deliberative polling and, 200–201; kecamatan model and, 188–190
ends of well-being, 30, 37, 44, 53
England, poor relief in, 9–10
environmental conversion factors, 31, 32
equal citizens, paternalistic programs disrespecting status as, 165
equality: decentralization and commitment to, 185–186; deliberative polling and, 196; democratic trilemma and, 180, 181; mass democracy and, 182–183; microcosmic deliberation and, 183
"Equality of What?" (Sen), 27–28
equivalence scales, 206n22
ethical individualism, 35
Ethiopia, long-term effects of cash transfer program in, 50–51
Europe, social insurance and social pensions in, 10–11
European colonial powers, 143, 144
EuroPolis deliberative poll, 175
excludable goods, 103, 104, 105, 106
exclusion errors, 211n16; demographic targeting and, 64; targeting problem and, 67–72, 77
extended proxy means test, 211n19
externalities, market failures and, 105

facilitation: of deliberative polling, 194, 201; of microcosmic deliberation, 191

Familias en Acción (Families in Action) (Colombia), 116–117, 135
female mortality, excess, 78, 79–80
Finland, Social Insurance Institution, 14
first-order outcomes, of theory of change, 146
Fishkin, James, 177–178, 180, 181–182, 191, 194
food security / expenditures, effects of cash transfers on, 43–44, 47, 56–57, 74–76
free-rider problem, 105, 114–116, 159
full means test, 62; exclusion errors and, 69, 70–71
functionings: agency and, 31–32; capability approach and, 28–29, 32–33; value pluralism and, 31
functionings-capabilities distinction, targeting and, 72
future, investments in children and attitudes about the, 95–97

Gates, Bill, 1, 137–138, 141
Generasi program (Indonesia), 188
geographic scope, deliberative polling and, 192, 196
geographic targeting, 64–65, 66, 68, 211n16, 211n17
Germany, Mein Grundeinkommen, 14
Ghana, democratic experiment in Tamale, 169–170, 184, 192
GiveDirectly, 1, 14, 76, 153–154
global development community, 197; top-down approach to poverty, 158–159
global poverty, World Bank measurement of, 22, 23–27
GoBifo project (Sierra Leone), 188
goods, typology of, 103, 104
government: cash transfers and role of, 163–164; infrastructure and, 110; missing markets and, 108–109; public preferences about spending and, 178–180; structural reforms and, 163–164
group dynamics, deliberative decision-making and, 172

group polarization, deliberative polls and, 195, 200–201
guaranteed minimum income, 5, 6, 8, 197
Guatemala, experiment about income and poverty in Peña Blanca, 19–21

Hamisi, Hamisi, 177, 178–179, 180
hard conditions, 7
HARKing (hypothesizing after the results are known), 55
health: aging and, 132–133, 135; effects of cash transfer programs on, 45–47, 48, 135; inequality in investment in girl's, 79; outdoor air pollution and, 109
healthcare: asymmetric information about quality of, 112; cash transfers and access to, 147; effects of cash transfers on use of health services, 46; people with disabilities and access to, 123–124
health insurance markets, asymmetric information and, 106–107
hidden actions / attributes, missing markets and, 106–107
history of cash transfer programs, 9–14
household behavior: collective model of, 84; cooperative models of, 83–84; noncooperative models of, 83–85; unitary model of, 83, 85; utility function and, 81–83
household decision-makers, characteristics of, 94–98
household level, estimating living standards at, 25–26
households: allocation of resources within, 16, 26, 199; effects of cash transfers on expenditures, 43; reaching individuals by targeting, 70
households, inequality within, 78–98; cash transfers and children, 92–98; missing-women problem, 78–81; mothers, cash transfers, and, 86–92; theory of household behavior, 81–86
human capital, income poverty and, 141

Human Development Fund (Mongolia), 13
Human Development Index, 36
Hunger Safety Net Program (Kenya), 93
husbands, women's time preferences and effect of cash transfers on children and, 96–97

import substitution industrialization, 149–150
inclusion errors, 64, 67, 211n16
income: child development and, 38–40; conceptual problems in measuring poverty using, 26–27; effects of cash transfers on, 50–51, 52; measuring living standards and, 25–26; poverty defined as lack of, 19, 22–27, 198; targeting on basis of, 71–72; well-being and, 21
income effects, as first-order outcome, 146
income-pooling hypothesis, 85
incumbent support hypothesis, 152
India: basic income program pilot in, 13–14; climate change impact in, 107–108; Devi Rupak, 4, 81; Direct Benefit Transfer for Food Subsidy, 2–4, 200; diversion of education stipends from children with disabilities, 125; male-biased sex ratios in, 79–80; National Rural Employment Guarantee Scheme, 5–6, 7–8, 13, 66, 69–70; policy reforms and growth accelerations in, 139; preference for collective investment in, 159; preferences for cash or in-kind transfers in, 164
indifference curve, in consumer theory, 82–83
individual / household assessment targeting, 61–64, 66–67
individualism, capability approach and, 35
individualist orientation of cash transfer programs, 146–151, 159–160
individualist view of poverty, 16, 25–26, 140–141, 143, 155

Indonesia: Astek program, 93, 154–155; Bantuan Langsung Tunai, 13, 72–74, 164; Generasi program, 188; Kecamatan Development Program, 186–190, 200; Program Keluarga Harpan, 13; Urban Poverty Project, 175
indoor poor relief, 10
inefficient behavior, household behavior and, 83–86
inequality objection, radical decentralization and, 172, 174
influencing incentives, self-targeting and, 65–66
information, learning crisis and parents' lack of, 111. *See also* asymmetric information
infrastructure, 3, 106, 110, 114–116
Ingrasci, Zach, 19–21
injustice, views of poverty and, 33, 198
in-kind transfers, 3; corruption and, 163–164; paternalism and, 160, 161, 162, 222n16
institutional design, deliberative decision-making and, 175–176
institutions, poverty reduction and, 144–145
instrumental value of decentralization, 167
international poverty line, 22
internet networks, lack of in parts of Africa, 110
intimate partner violence, impact of cash transfers on, 90
investments: collective, 159–160; radical decentralization and local decision-making about, 166–170
Iran, universal basic income in, 13

job guarantee programs, 5–6, 7–8, 66
Juntos program (Peru), 86–89
justice, as opposite of poverty, 33

Kalahi-CIDSS program (Philippines), 189
Kalulu, Anthony, 157–159, 162

Kecamatan Development Program (KDP) (Indonesia) / kecamatan model, 186-190, 200

Kenya: basic income program in, 14; blood market and, 99-101; GiveDirectly program, 76, 153-154; Hunger Safety Net Program, 93; school-based deworming program in, 127

kin-based societies, extent benefits of cash transfers reaching children in, 92-93

Korea, poverty and partitioning of, 143-144

labeled conditional programs, 7
labor supply, effects of cash transfers on, 42-43, 133, 147
learning crisis, global, 111-112
Lesotho, Child Grant Programme, 125-126
liberal, capability approach termed, 36
life dimensions, capability approach and selecting to prioritize, 33-34
Living on One Dollar (documentary), 19-20, 26
living standards: measuring poverty and estimating, 25; people with disabilities and lower, 123
local markets, impact of cash transfers on children and functioning of, 93-94
local values and knowledge, decentralization and, 167-169
long-term effects of cash, studies on, 47-52, 53-54
Low-Income Allowance (Uzbekistan), 71

MacKay, Douglas, 161-162, 164-165
macro-level effects of cash transfers, 147
Malawi: Schooling, Income, and Health Risk, 50; Social Action Fund, 75; Social Cash Transfer, 94
male-biased sex ratios, 78-79
malnutrition among women and children, 121, 129-131

marginal costs and benefits, goods and, 102-105
marginal social costs and benefits, markets and, 102-103, 104
market efficiency, 102-103
market failures, 99-117; blood market, 99-101; climate change and, 107-108; as justification for cash transfers, 113; missing markets, 102-107; overcoming missing markets, 112-117; repugnant markets, 101-102; ubiquity of missing markets, 107-112
markets, 100, 158
marriage markets, gender imbalances in, 80-81
marriage problem, radical decentralization and, 171, 172-173
mass consent, 181, 195
mass democracy, 182-183
matrilocal societies, cash transfers and, 93, 154-155
McNamara, Robert, 23, 150
means-ends distinction, 30-31, 35, 37, 71-72
means of well-being, 30, 37
means testing: full, 62, 69, 70-71. *See also* proxy means test
measuring poverty, 22-27, 36
medical model of disability, 121-122
Mein Grundeinkommen (Germany), 14
mental health, cash transfers and, 9, 48, 147
meso-level effects of cash transfers, 147
methodological individualism, 35
mévente, cash transfer program in Chad and, 58-61
Mexico: 70 y Más, 134-135; Oportunidades (Progresa), 6, 12, 90, 134, 135, 148-149, 155, 162; Programa de Apoyo, 135; structural adjustment loan, 150
microcosmic deliberation, 17-18, 180, 182, 186-191; developing poverty-alleviation strategies and, 183-184, 185-186; elite capture and, 188-190; Kecamatan Development Program,

microcosmic deliberation (*continued*)
  186–190; nonrandom selection of
  participants, 185–186; quality of
  decision-making and, 185; random
  selection of participants, 185–186;
  variations on, 190–191. *See also*
  deliberative polling
microcredit, 197
microeconomics, theory of household
  behavior, 81–82
migration, economic returns on, 145–146
Millennium Villages Project, 197, 200
Minimum Livelihood Guarantee Scheme
  (Di Bao) (China), 13
missing markets: asymmetric information
  and, 106–107; cash transfers and,
  113–117; defined, 102; education and,
  111–112; governments and, 108–109
missing-women problem, 78–81
mobilized deliberation, 182, 183
monadic acquisition of personal traits, 140
monetary poverty lines, 22–23
monetary view of poverty, 15
Mongolia: Human Development Fund,
  13; preference for collective investment
  in, 159
moral hazard, 107, 112
Morocco, Tayssir program, 95
mortality rates, pension programs and,
  133–136
motivated reasoning, deliberative
  decision-making and, 171
Multidimensional Poverty Index, 36

Namibia, basic income program in, 13
national development: Korean
  partitioning and, 143–144; poverty
  and, 138–140; redefined, 149–150
National Rural Employment Guarantee
  Scheme (India), 5–6, 7–8, 13, 66, 69–70
natural experiments, 143–146
navigational agency, 167
Ndihma Ekonomike program (Albania),
  43, 168
negative income taxes, 5, 6, 8, 9, 11
negative spillover effects, 72–77

noncontributory pensions, 5, 133–136
noncooperative models of household
  behavior, 83–85, 94–95
non-excludable goods, 103–105; air
  quality and, 109; cash transfers
  and, 113; climate change and,
  107–108; infrastructure and, 110; water
  resources, 109–110
nonmarket goods, consumption and use
  of, 27
nonrandom selection of participants for
  microcosmic deliberation, 185–186, 187
non-rival goods, 103, 104–105
Nussbaum, Martha, 27–28, 33–34

odds ratio, 208n15
old age, cash transfers and vulnerabilities
  of, 121, 131–136
Old Age Grant (South Africa), 70
Operation Barga (India), 79–80
Oportunidades (Progresa) (Mexico), 6,
  12, 90, 134, 135, 148–149, 155, 162
outdoor poor relief, 10
Overseas Development Institute (ODI)
  systematic review of literature on cash
  transfers, 41–47

Pakistan, 107–108, 112
Pantawid (Philippines), 74–75
Paraguay, Tekoporã program, 43–44
Pareto efficiency, 215n8
participants for microcosmic
  deliberation: number of, 191; selection
  of, 185–186, 190
participation: in capability approach,
  33–34; democratic trilemma and, 180,
  181; mass democracy and, 182–183;
  mobilized deliberation and, 183
participational agency, 167
participatory budgeting, 166–167, 170–171,
  173, 200. *See also* decentralization,
  radical
participatory distortion, 183
Participedia, 172–173
paternalism: cash transfers and, 17, 160–165,
  199; defined, 161–162; deliberative

INDEX | 241

decision-making and, 175–176; in-kind transfers and, 160, 161, 162, 222n16; local actors and, 162–163
paternalistic policies, morality of, 164–165
patrilineality, 79–80
patrilocality, 79, 80, 154, 155
pension programs: contributory, 133–134, 154; cultural implications of, 154–155; effect on cash transfers benefiting children, 93, 94; noncontributory, 5, 133–136
people with disabilities: access to education and healthcare, 123–124; cash transfers and, 124–126; income and standard of living, 26; risk of poverty for, 122–123
Permanent Fund Dividend (Alaska), 5
personal conversion factors, 30, 32
personal traits, causes of poverty and, 140
Peru, Juntos program, 86–89
p-hacking, 56
Philippines: Kalahi-CIDSS, 189; Pantawid, 74–75
philosophical liberalism, capability approach and, 36–37
planning cells, 190–191
political liberties, 34, 101
poor relief, 9–10
population partitioning, poverty and, 142–143
poverty: aging and, 132; causes of, 140–146; defining, 15, 19, 22; disability and, 122–123; identifying people in, 15; individualist view of, 16, 25–26, 140–141, 143, 155; injustice and, 33, 198; as lack of capabilities, 27–33; as lack of income, 15, 22–27; local conceptions of, 168; market-oriented reform and increases in, 150–151; measuring, 22–27, 36; natural experiments on, 143–146; population partitioning and, 142–143; structuralist view of, 16–17, 138–140, 142–143, 155, 156; temporary vs. chronic, 21

poverty alleviation: classification of programs, 160; decentralization and, 223n29; focus on individuals and households, 138, 140; focus on structural issues, 138–140; local values and, 167–168; microcosmic deliberation and, 183–184, 185–186; radical decentralization and, 166–170; use of randomized trials to evaluate programs for, 138. See also cash transfer programs
poverty lines, setting, 22–24
poverty maps / mapping, 22–23, 64–65
prediction intervals, 208n15, 209n17, 218n35
pricelessness of non-excludable goods, 103–104
prices: cash transfer programs and, 60, 74–75; missing markets and, 102–103; purchasing power parity conversion and, 24; of water, 109–110
principle of each person as an end, 32–33
Pritchett, Lant, 138–140, 143, 145, 156
private and public goods, distinction between, 84
productivity, 141, 147
Programa de Apoyo (Mexico), 135
Program Keluarga Harpan (Indonesia), 13
Progresa (Oportunidades, Prospera) (Mexico), 6, 12, 90, 134, 135, 148–149, 155, 162
proportionality condition, household behavior models and, 85
proxy means test, 62–63, 211n16, 211n17; Bantuan Langsung Tunai and, 73; demographic targeting and, 64; effectiveness criterion and, 163; exclusion errors and, 68–69; extended, 211n19
public goods: cash transfer programs and, 114–116; household behavior and underprovision of, 84–85; marginal benefits of, 104–105
public goods game, 115–117
public works projects, spillover effects of, 75–76

purchasing power parity (PPP) conversion rates and measuring poverty, 24

quality of public discussions, 174–175, 185
questionnaires, deliberative polling and confidential, 195, 201

radical decentralization, 17, 160, 165–170; perils of, 170–176
referendum, deliberative polling linked to, 195
relational acquisition of personal traits, 140
repugnant markets, 101–102
resource allocation within households, 16, 26, 199
resource pooling, free-rider problem and, 114–116
rights, markets and, 101
rival goods, 103, 104
Russia, mortality and contributory pension system in, 133

sampling procedure, deliberative polling, 193–194
savings, effects of cash transfers on, 41–42, 44, 95
school attendance: children with disabilities and, 118–121, 125, 126; effects of cash transfers on, 44–45, 146–147
school enrollment, effects of cash transfers on, 45, 48, 146–147
Schooling, Income, and Health Risk program (Malawi), 50
scientific evidence of effectiveness, cash program implementation details and, 158, 162–163
second-order outcomes, of theory of change, 146–147
secret ballots, for deliberative polling, 194–195
selective outcome reporting, 55–56
self-targeting, 61, 62, 65–67, 69–70

semi-decentralized poverty-alleviation programs, 160. *See also* cash transfer programs
Sen, Amartya: on benefits of democratic approaches to fighting poverty, 166, 169; "Equality of What?," 27–28; on income and poverty, 22; on individuals shaping own destiny, 198; on lack of famine in democracies, 168–169; on missing-women problem, 78; on public participation, 33
Senior Citizen Grant (SCG) (Uganda), 92–93, 117
70 y Más (Mexico), 134–135
sex ratios, male-biased, 78–79
shadow conditions, Juntos program and, 87–89
short-term effects of cash payments, studies on, 41–47, 53
Sierra Leone, GoBifo project, 188
site-selection bias, 54–55
Social Action Fund (Malawi), 75
Social Assistance Act (South Africa), 126
Social Cash Transfer (SCT) scheme (Malawi), 94
social cohesion, cash transfers and, 74, 76, 116, 117, 147
social conflict, cash transfers and increased, 58–61, 73–74, 117, 147
social conversion factors, 30–31, 32
social insurance, 5, 10–11, 12, 14
social model of disability, 121–122
social pensions, 6, 11
Social Security system (United States), 133–134
sociodemographic characteristics, proxy means testing and, 62–63
soft conditions, 7
sons, preference for, 78–81
South Africa: Care Dependency Grant, 125; child support grant, 12–13; Disability Grant, 125; Old Age Grant, 70; Social Assistance Act, 126
specification searching, 55–56
status quo, cash transfer programs and perpetuation of, 151–153

Stewart, Rory, 1, 40, 160, 197, 199–200
stigma: aging and, 132–133; children with disabilities and, 118, 120; poor relief and, 10
structural adjustment loans, 150
structuralist view of poverty, 16–17, 138–140, 142–143, 155, 156
structural reforms, community preference for, 163–164
Sure Prospects (Uganda), 120–121

Tanzania: access to transportation, 107; cash transfers and time preferences experiment, 96–97; collective investment in, 159; deliberative democracy experiment, 177–180, 183, 184, 192, 200
targeted cash transfer programs, 6, 8–9, 15
targeting, 61–67; cash transfers, social cohesion, and, 117; categorical, 61–62, 64–65, 66–67; community-based, 63–64, 67; demographic targeting, 64; effectiveness criterion and, 163; errors and harmful effects by, 198–199; geographic, 64–65, 66; individual / household assessment, 61–64, 66–67; negative spillover effects, 72–77; self-targeting, 61, 62, 65–67
targeting problem, 67–72; agency neglect and, 72; diversity neglect and, 72; exclusion errors and, 77; mévente and, 58–61
Targeting the Ultra Poor program (Bangladesh), 144, 146
taxes: earned income tax credit, 6, 8–9, 11; negative income, 5, 6, 11
Tayssir program (Morocco), 95
Tekoporã program (Paraguay), 43–44
Temple, Chris, 19–21
temporary public works, 6, 8
theory of change, 146–149
third-order outcomes, of theory of change, 147
time preferences, investments in children and, 95–97

tragedy of the commons, 105
transaction costs, asymmetric information and, 107
transformative change, structuralist view of poverty and, 155, 156
transportation costs, market access and, 107
Tuungane program (Democratic Republic of Congo), 188

Uganda: cash transfer program for women, 138; Community Farm, 157–158; education and children with disabilities in, 118–121; Senior Citizen Grant, 92–93, 117; 2011 presidential election, 151–152; use of deliberative polling in, 192; Youth Opportunities Program, 47–49, 151–153
unconditional cash transfers, 5–8; paternalism and, 162–163. *See also* cash transfer programs
unitary model of household behavior, 83, 85, 213n13
United States: Alaskan Permanent Fund Dividend, 5, 11; Earned Income Tax Credit, 6, 11; full means testing in, 62; Mayors for a Guaranteed Income, 14; negative income taxes in, 11; poverty and partitioning of Native Americans in, 142–143; Social Security system, 133–134
universal basic income, 1, 5–6, 7, 13–14, 61, 204n18
universal eligibility, self-targeting and, 62
universality, defined, 204n16
Urban Poverty Project (Indonesia), 175
Uruguay, cash transfer program, 91
utility function, 81–85
Uzbekistan, Low-Income Allowance, 71

value pluralism, capability approach and, 30, 31–32
Virtual Agora Project (Pittsburgh), 175

water, as nonmarket good, 109–110
well-being: focus on functionings or capabilities, 29–33; means and ends of, 30, 37; money / income and, 16, 21; poverty defined as lack of, 22
women: affluence and malnutrition and, 129–131; cash transfer programs directed at, 86–92, 94–97; excluded in kecamatan meetings, 188–189; share of household resources and, 26

work, effect of cash transfers on, 42, 48–49, 91, 147, 208n11
World Bank, 1, 111, 173, 187; concept and measures of poverty, 22, 23–27, 150
World Economic Forum meeting in Davos, 126–128
World Health Organization (WHO), 100, 122, 124

Youth Opportunities Program (Uganda), 47–49, 151–153